Andres Kuusk

Financial contagion: a meta-analysis based approach

D1744229

Andres Kuusk

Financial contagion: a meta-analysis based approach

LAP LAMBERT Academic Publishing

Impressum / Imprint

Bibliografische Information der Deutschen Nationalbibliothek: Die Deutsche Nationalbibliothek verzeichnet diese Publikation in der Deutschen Nationalbibliografie; detaillierte bibliografische Daten sind im Internet über http://dnb.d-nb.de abrufbar.

Alle in diesem Buch genannten Marken und Produktnamen unterliegen warenzeichen-, marken- oder patentrechtlichem Schutz bzw. sind Warenzeichen oder eingetragene Warenzeichen der jeweiligen Inhaber. Die Wiedergabe von Marken, Produktnamen, Gebrauchsnamen, Handelsnamen, Warenbezeichnungen u.s.w. in diesem Werk berechtigt auch ohne besondere Kennzeichnung nicht zu der Annahme, dass solche Namen im Sinne der Warenzeichen- und Markenschutzgesetzgebung als frei zu betrachten wären und daher von jedermann benutzt werden dürften.

Bibliographic information published by the Deutsche Nationalbibliothek: The Deutsche Nationalbibliothek lists this publication in the Deutsche Nationalbibliografie; detailed bibliographic data are available in the Internet at http://dnb.d-nb.de.

Any brand names and product names mentioned in this book are subject to trademark, brand or patent protection and are trademarks or registered trademarks of their respective holders. The use of brand names, product names, common names, trade names, product descriptions etc. even without a particular marking in this work is in no way to be construed to mean that such names may be regarded as unrestricted in respect of trademark and brand protection legislation and could thus be used by anyone.

Coverbild / Cover image: www.ingimage.com

Verlag / Publisher:
LAP LAMBERT Academic Publishing
ist ein Imprint der / is a trademark of
OmniScriptum GmbH & Co. KG
Heinrich-Böcking-Str. 6-8, 66121 Saarbrücken, Deutschland / Germany
Email: info@lap-publishing.com

Herstellung: siehe letzte Seite /
Printed at: see last page
ISBN: 978-3-659-55719-4

Zugl. / Approved by: Tartu, University of Tartu, 2012

TABLE OF CONTENTS

THE LIST OF AUTHOR'S PUBLICATIONS AND CONFERENCE PRESENTATIONS

I Articles in international journals

1. **Kuusk, A., Paas, T.; Viikmaa, K. (2011).** Financial contagion of the 2008 crisis: is there evidence of financial contagion from the US to the Baltic States. *Eastern Journal of European Studies*, 2(2), pp. 61-76.
2. **Kuusk, A; Paas, T. (2011).** Contagion of financial crises: what does the empirical evidence show. Baltic Journal of Management, 7(1), pp. 25-48.
3. **Kuusk, A., Paas, T. (2010).** The role of meta-analysis in examining results of empirical studies about financial contagion. Mäeltsemees, S; Reiljan, J. (Eds.). *Discussions on Estonian Economic Policy*, pp. 176-194, Berlin, Tallinn: Berliner Wissenschafts-Verlag, Mattimar.
4. **Paas, T.; Schlitte, F.; Kuusk, A. (2006).** Modeling Regional Income Convergence in EU-25. Global Economic Modelling Network (ECOMOD) Conference - Regional and Urban Modelling; Brussels, Belgium, 1-2 June 2006, pp. 1-20.
5. **Kuusk, A., Paas, T. (2012).** A meta-analysis based approach for examining financial contagion with special emphasis on CEE economies. Accepted for publication in *Eastern European Economics*, 50(6), scheduled in November 2012.

II Other research articles and conference presentations

1. **Kuusk, A.; Paas, T. (2010).** Contagion of financial crises with special emphasis on CEE economies: a meta-analysis. University of Tartu, Faculty of Economics and Business Administration, Working Paper Series (1 - 46). Tartu University Press.
2. **Paas, T.; Kuusk, A. (2010).** Meta-analüüsi roll finantskriiside ülekandumise uurimisel. In: XVIII majanduspoliitika teaduskonverents "Majanduspoliitika Euroopa Liidu riikides - aasta 2010"; Tartu and Värska 1.-3.07.2010: (Eds.) Mäeltsemees, S; Reiljan, J.. Berlin, Tallinn: Berliner Wissenchafts-Verlag, Mattimar, 2010, (Eesti majanduspoliitilised väitlused; 18), pp. 550 - 554.

3. Paas, T.; Kuusk, A.; Schlitte, F.; Võrk, A. (2007). Econometric analysis of income convergence in selected EU countries and their NUTS 3 level regions. University of Tartu, Faculty of Economics and Business Administration, Working Paper Series, 60, pp. 1 - 56.

4. **Paas, T.; Kuusk, A.; Schlitte, F. (2006).** Regional Income Convergence During the Pre-Enlargement Period of the European Union. In: Reports-papers of the XIV scientific and educational conference: 14th scientific conference on economic policy, Tartu-Värska, Estonia; 29June-1 July 2006. Berlin, Tallinn: Berliner Wissenchafts-Verlaq, Mattimar, 2006, pp. 85-97.

5. **Paas, T.; Kuusk, A.; Võrk, A.; Schlitte, F. (2006)** Regional income convergence or divergence during the EU pre-enlargement period? - International Workshop on: Spatial Econometrics and Statistics, 25-27 May 2006, Rome, Italy; CD-ROM.

INTRODUCTION

List of papers

The main findings of the dissertation are based on the following four original publications, which will be referred in the text using their respective numbers:

Study 1: Paas, T., **Kuusk, A.** (2011). Contagion of financial crises: what does the empirical evidence show? *Baltic Journal of Management*, Vol. 7(1), pp. 25-48[1].

Study 2: **Kuusk, A.**, Paas, T. and Viikmaa, K. (2011). Financial contagion of the 2008 crisis: is there evidence of financial contagion from the US to the Baltic States. *Eastern Journal of European Studies*, 2(2), pp. 61-76[2].

Study 3: **Kuusk, A.**, Paas, T. (2012). A meta-analysis based approach for examining financial contagion with special emphasis on CEE economies. Accepted for publication in *Eastern European Economics*, 50(6), scheduled in November 2012[3].

Study 4: **Kuusk, A.**, Paas, T. (2010). The role of meta-analysis in examining results of empirical studies about financial contagion. Mäeltsemees, S; Reiljan, J. (Eds.). *Discussions on Estonian Economic Policy*, pp. 176-194, Berlin, Tallinn: Berliner Wissenschafts-Verlag, Mattimar[4].

As the dissertation, although being based on the articles, is practically in the form of a monograph, this means it is possible for the publications to be amended and brought up-to-date. In addition, there were some reduplicative paragraphs and small shortcomings in some of the publications that have been fixed in the monograph. Therefore, the dissertation can be thought of as an improved version of the publications. In all of these publications the contribution of the author of the dissertation has been the greatest in all parts of the publications. A more detailed

---

[1] Full text of the article in Appendix 7.1.
[2] Full text of the article in Appendix 7.2.
[3] Full text of the article in Appendix 7.3.
[4] Full text of the article in Appendix 7.4.

overview of the contribution of the individual authors in these papers will be given later in the introduction section.

Background and motivation for the research

Managing and preventing financial crises have long been important challenges for policy makers. Several crises in the 1980s, 1990s and in the present century were transmitted rapidly to other countries that were sometimes quite different in size and economic structure compared to the country of origin, and often even located on the other side of the globe. Researchers in the field of economics have borrowed an expression from epidemiology to describe this phenomenon as *financial contagion,* although when and by whom the term was first coined is probably not known. It is important to make clear that it is not yet contagion – as defined in the dissertation – if a crisis spills over from one country to another. Transmissions of crises may be caused by strong stable fundamental linkages between countries – financial, real or political – and these transmissions are not considered to be incidences of contagion. However, if there are breaks in the international transmition mechanisms of the crises, that is what financial contagion is all about.

The issue of contagion has been one of the most debated topics in international finance since the Asian crisis (1997) and the phenomenon is by no means only a thing of the past. It has been argued (e.g. by Didier, Mauro and Schmukler 2008) that the factors underlying the channels that generated contagion during the crises in the 1990s seem potentially to be at least as strong today as they were one and half decades ago. Considering the events of 2008, when yet another financial crisis snowballed around the world, the phenomenon of financial contagion is perhaps more important than ever before to examine, interpret and understand.

In the globally integrated world there is no doubt that crises that occur in one country spill over into one or more other countries. However, only some and not all of these propagations of crises can be considered contagious. There are several reasons why distinguishing between contagion and simple fundamentals-based spillovers (interdependence between countries) is necessary. The importance of this distinction and of contagion studies generally is clearest in relation to the merits of international diversification. The rationale being that theoretically,

6

international diversification should significantly reduce portfolio risk, but in the case of financial contagion when cross-country correlations increase during crises, much of the rationale is undermined. So, if the contagion hypothesis holds, it can be assumed that the irrational behaviour of financial agents (at the collective rather than individual level, where the same behaviour may be rational) plays an important role, and that the benefit of a internationally diversified portfolio is substantially diminished.

At the government level it is important to know what can be done to prevent crises from spilling over into a country, and whether and how the susceptibility to financial contagion can be decreased. In the case of strong financial contagion it is advisable for countries to keep some finances in reserves during the good times, even if there seems no particular reason to expect the economic outlook to worsen. As there is no good way to defend your economy against the propagation of crises, countries should at least have some tools at their disposal to deal with the consequences.

In spite of significant theoretical and empirical interest on the topic, the financial contagion puzzle is still open to discussion and it seems that every new analysis undermines the rationale of those developed earlier. Therefore, an assessment of previous empirical findings is clearly called for. However, aggregates of previous empirical results have so far been limited to qualitative analysis and no quantitative summaries have yet been conducted. It is one of the main motivations of the thesis to fill this void and by doing so, complete the tasks left undone by previous qualitative analyses. This will be accomplished using a meta-analysis approach.

Meta-analysis methods and techniques are widely used in the behavioural sciences and medicine, but are quite uncommon among economic scientists. In the field of financial contagion, no meta-analysis has been conducted before, despite the fact that considering the multi-dimensionality of the research problem, this seems to be the best way to get something useful from results that seem hopelessly mixed at first glance. The application of a meta-analysis not only helps to identify a clear quantitative conclusion from this seemingly un-navigable jungle, it also allows us to detect moderating variables, which determine the contagiousness of the crises.

Another motivation is to identify how susceptible Eastern European countries, as small open economies with a post-socialist path dependence, are to financial contagion. The case of countries in Central and Eastern

Europe (CEE) is particularly interesting in view of their entry into the third stage of the European Economic and Monetary Union. The Maastricht criteria require that candidate countries should not have devalued their currency in the two years prior to adopting the euro, and should also have avoided sharp movements of certain other financial variables such as inflation and long-term interest rates. In the context of financial turmoil, these criteria are not likely to be met. In this field, the research task of the thesis is to examine whether recent instabilities in the stock markets in these countries have been due to financial contagion or poor policies and fundamentals. Additionally, the thesis investigates whether CEE economies exhibit above or below average susceptibility to financial contagion.

There are two main reasons why CEE countries may differ from the average in terms of their openness to contagion. On the one hand, the economic openness that is taken almost to extremes in some of CEE countries and was one of the main reasons for their noticeable success in the transition period, may have now performed a disservice to these countries, as one can expect such a level of openness could make a country more vulnerable to financial contagion. This hypothesis is supported by the findings of Didier *et al* (2012)[5]. On the other hand, there has been less speculative financing in the stock markets of CEE economies compared to many other countries, which decreases the likelihood of bubbles occurring, and should offer some protection against financial contagion. It would be an interesting finding to discover which of these two aspects is dominant.

Yet another motivation relates to the inclusion of the present crisis, which took off in the US in 2007 and became serious in global terms in 2008. The contagiousness of this crisis has been so far investigated only shallowly in the literature. As the 2008 crisis[6] spilled over practically across the entire world, one can expect that the crisis was very contagious, but without confirming evidence, this level of propagation could also be associated with a strong interdependence between countries. The present thesis will attempt to provide some answers in regard to this question.

---

[5] Findings of Didier *et al* (2012) show that financial openness may increase susceptibility to contagion in crisis period while there is no such evidence for trade openness.

[6] In the literature the recent global financial crisis is called sometimes as crisis of 2007 and sometimes as crisis of 2008. It is true that the crisis started in the US already in 2007 but it become serious globally in 2008, therefore the crisis is named the US 2008 crisis in the dissertation.

The aim and research tasks of the dissertation

The aim of the study is to find out whether the propagation of financial crises in numerous past crisis episodes has been amplified by financial contagion or is based solely on stable fundamental linkages between countries. The reasons for this distinction can be summarised as follows. If crises are transmitted through stable fundamental linkages, then only countries with weak economic fundamentals will be affected and good fundamentals can offer protection. On the other hand, if there is something other than fundamentals driving the transmission of the crisis – be it speculative attacks, financial panic, herd behaviour or some other form of irrational behaviour by the financial agents – then even countries with good fundamentals can be seriously affected. From here, depending on the results, the abovementioned inferences can be drawn about country-level economic policies and international investment strategies.

To be absolutely clear it is worth mentioning that the thesis does not test whether crises are propagated from country to country – it is assumed that they do. The question is whether the transmission is contagious, and this necessitates identifying whether a structural break occurs in the linear transmission mechanism of financial shocks during periods of crisis.

To achieve the aim, the following research tasks were identified:

1. Provide a theoretical overview of theories explaining propagation of shocks and crises;

2. Explore theoretical frameworks of financial contagion including definitions, transmission channels and testing methodologies;

3. Qualitatively analyse previous empirical findings on the subject;

4. Work out suitable measure that affords quantitative aggregation of results of individual studies and conduct meta-analysis of empirical literature using values of this measure as input;

5. Analyse contagiousness of the last worldwide crisis that took off in the US in 2007.

Research methodology and data

The methodology for fulfilling the research task is as follows. First, the theoretical background of financial contagion is explored to achieve a good basis or framework for subsequent analysis. Secondly, the qualitative analysis of empirical literature is conducted with the aim of obtaining some preliminary and general results. Next, a meta-analysis of empirical study results is conducted to obtain more tangible and reliable results. Finally, as the US 2008 crisis is left out of the meta-analysis (because of no data points), a separate analysis is conducted based on this crisis using two alternative frameworks. Firstly, correlation coefficients based method is used to test whether correlations of returns in stock indeces have been significantly higher during the crisis period relative to the non-crisis period. Secondly, volatility spillovers in stock markets are investigated using a generalized conditional autoregressive heteroskedasticity model. During all these steps, particular attention is paid to CEE economies as destination countries.

The data for the meta-analysis comes from previous empirical analyses. When searching for appropriate studies, the Thomson Reuters (formerly ISI) Web of Knowledge database and the Contagion of Financial Crises Website from the World Bank Group are used. From the Web of Knowledge database, studies corresponding to the keywords *financial contagion* are used. As in the empirical section, contagion is defined as an increase in cross-country asset price correlations during times of crisis relative to asset price correlations during non-crisis times, only studies that report on the correlations of both pre-crisis and post-crisis asset prices between countries are included. These restrictions reduce the data set to 716 data points, of which 394 are independent (independent means that these data points come from different sources or differ in some important characteristics like investigated crisis, destination country or financial index). The data set has been drawn from 28 constructs (17 studies by 12 authors).

To investigate the contagiousness of the US 2008 crisis, daily stock returns from between 3 March 2008 and 9 March 2009 are used with the bankruptcy of Lehman Brothers on 15 September 2008 as the starting point of the crisis. Stock returns data for the Baltic countries are collected from the official web pages of the Tallinn, Riga and Vilnius stock exchanges and the historic data for S&P 500 comes from google.com/finance.

Contribution of individual authors in the studies of the dissertation

All four studies the dissertation is based on, and which are given in the list of papers above, are co-authored and the author of this dissertation performed the central part in all studies. The respective contributions of the author of the dissertation and the co-authors in the studies will now be described.

In Study 1, the general research framework, the theoretical part of the study and the qualitative analysis were prepared and put into practice by the author. Additionally, the conclusions and discussion of the findings were mainly the responsibility of the author. In Study 1, the co-author primarily assisted in highlighting the main findings and important policy implications. In Study 2, the dissertation author was responsible for the study framework, the theoretical background of the analysis, the data gathering process, the empirical data analysis and the discussion of the findings. The co-authors helped in formulating the aim, contribution, policy implications and limitations of the study and also in editing the text. In Study 3, the author contributed by designing the theoretical approach, collecting data via a comprehensive literature review, conducting empirical data analysis and elaborating the discussion. A co-author assisted mainly with suggestions regarding the interpretation and implications of the empirical results, but also with ideas regarding the introduction and discussion sections. In Study 4, the co-author again primarily contributed to the introduction and discussion, while the author of the thesis was responsible for the general research framework, data collection, and theoretical and empirical analysis. Note that Study 3 is an updated version of Study 4. Table 1 provides an overview of how the author contributed to each study and how this then formed the basis of the corresponding sub-chapters of the thesis.

Table 1. Contribution of the author to the studies and the chapters in the thesis corresponding to the respective studies

Studies	Contribution of the author	Corresponding

		sub-chapters in the thesis
Study 1	Development of theoretical framework Working with the literature Qualitative and quantitative analysis Discussion of the findings	1.1 2.1 – 2.6 2.8
Study 2	Development of theoretical framework Data gathering process Data analysis Discussion of the findings	3.2 4.2
Study 3	Development of research framework Data gathering process Data processing and analysis Discussion of the findings	3.1 4.1
Study 4	Development of research framework Data gathering process Data processing and analysis Discussion of the findings	3.1 4.1.1

Source: compiled by the author.

Research contribution

The present thesis contributes to the literature on contagion of financial crises in many novel ways. First, a meta-analysis is conducted, which has not been used before in this field. To this end, the thesis offers a conceptual feature to facilitate a meta-analytic test of the significance in the increase of correlation coefficients. The thesis proposes the use of the difference between post- and pre-crisis correlations of asset returns between a crisis and destination country as a common measure in all relevant studies, and to use the same differences as individual effect sizes in the subsequent meta-analysis. It is argued in the thesis that the given individual effect sizes can be handled in two alternative ways in meta-analytic computations – as treatment effects or as correlations – and is shown through practical analysis that the results differ only slightly. Secondly, the analysis of a new and until recently practically uninvestigated crisis (the US 2008 crisis) is added. At the time that the abovementioned four articles were written, there were no publications investigating the contagiousness of the US 2008 crisis; therefore, it was impossible to include this crisis in the meta-analysis, and a separate article analysing the US 2008 crisis had to be written by the author. By now, a few publications analysing the contagiousness of the US 2008 crisis have emerged, and therefore, the first of these articles is a little out-dated. This is one of the main reasons why it was decided to present the thesis in the form of a monograph as this allows the author to include these recent additions in the thesis, so the thesis can be considered an updated version of the four published articles.

In addition to these main contributions, the thesis also gives the most comprehensive qualitative summary of previous empirical research findings from among all publications so far. Previous literature reviews mainly focus on the questions of which definition of financial contagion is investigated and which testing methodology is used; practically no one bothers to try to summarise the results (findings regarding the existence of financial contagion) of empirical analyses. Because of the multidimensionality of the research problem of financial contagion, this ignorance is fully understandable. However, the thesis still accepts the challenge and tries to find and compare the frequencies of different results.

The findings of the research provide economic policy makers a good basis for decision-making in the context of global crises. Supplied with this kind of knowledge, decision-makers at the government level have an important tool at their disposal in order to prevent or mitigate the negative effects of financial contagion. Developing an understanding of the way financial crises spread from country to country and what can be done to prevent this happening are therefore the straightforward contributions of this thesis in the field of economic policy making.

Structure of the thesis

The thesis consists of four chapters. The first chapter begins with an overview of alternative definitions, interpretations and main transmission channels of financial contagion (sub-chapter 1.1). The chapter then offers a brief introduction to theories that explain why shocks and crises spill over to other countries and how to differentiate which transmission channels are in accordance with financial contagion and which are not (sub-chapter 1.2). Sub-chapter 1.1 is based on Study 1 (see list of papers) while sub-chapter 1.2 is an addition written specially for the thesis (for an overview of how the sub-chapters are based on each study, see Table 1).

The second chapter presents a review of previous empirical studies. It starts by introducing theoretical aspects that may influence the results of empirical studies. Next, the previous empirical studies are divided into four groups on the basis of their testing methodologies, and an overview of all empirical findings is given separately for these groups. The chapter concludes with a summarising qualitative analysis of the findings of the empirical literature. This chapter is based on Study 1 with the exception of the sub-chapter 2.7, which updates the thesis with the very latest information.

The third chapter of the thesis introduces the data and testing methodologies used in the empirical part of the study. The first part of the chapter is dedicated to the framework and main components and tools of the meta-analysis. It begins by introducing the meta-analysis, its methodology and the steps involved. Next, special aspects are introduced that are specific to the analysis of the present thesis. In addition, the data used in the meta-sample is introduced. The first half of the third chapter (sub-chapter 3.1) is based on Studies 3 and 4. In the second part of the chapter, the methods used in analysing the contagiousness of the US financial crisis in 2008 is explained. Both the cross-market correlation coefficients based method and the MA (1) - GARCH (1, 1) – M model from the ARCH-GARCH framework are presented and data used in these analyses is introduced. The second half of chapter three (sub-chapter 3.2) is based on Study 2 with slight improvement in the testing method regarding to the correlation coefficients based analysis.

In the fourth chapter of the thesis, the results of the empirical investigation are presented. As in the third chapter, the main findings obtained using the meta-analysis are brought out first and then the results of the separate analysis of the US crisis in 2008 are given. The chapter ends with a comparison of the results of the two alternative methodologies. Sub-chapter 4.1.1 is based on Studies 3 and 4, while sub-chapter 4.1.2 on Study 3 alone. The analyses in these papers have been updated for the thesis by adding financial markets as a potential moderator to the analysis. Sub-chapter 4.2 is based on Study 2, but the data set is slightly modified (two-day rolling average changes in logarithmic stock prices are used instead of changes in logarithmic two-day moving average stock prices), and an alternative length of the rolling average period (weekly average in addition to two-day average) is added for robustness purposes. Therefore, the results of the sub-chapter differ a little from those in the respective article, but the general conclusion does not change much.

The thesis ends with a conclusion that summarises the main findings of the research. Based on these findings, the section suggests some policy recommendations, which would help in mitigating the negative effects of financial contagion. The concluding section also points out some limitations in the thesis and suggests potential future research in the field of financial contagion.

As mentioned at the beginning of the introduction, the dissertation is primarily based on the four published papers listed above. In addition to the findings of these publications, the theoretical framework of the study, the overview of the research methodology and the main generalized empirical results are presented in this volume. Some minor shortcomings in these papers are also corrected and some sections are updated in the thesis. As financial contagion is extremely topical, new findings develop quickly and theoretical ideas emerge rapidly. That is why the thesis is in the form of a monograph, so as to take into account up-to-date information, and present the thesis as an improved version of the initial publications.

Acknowledgements

During the years it took to write the doctoral dissertation, I received support from many people who have encouraged and supported me in different ways. Words cannot possibly express the extent of my gratitude to all of them, but I will nevertheless try my best.

First of all, I am grateful to my supervisor, Professor Tiiu Paas not only for her guidance, comments and suggestions but also for her patience throughout these prolonged years of study. She is also a great motivator being able to keep me going even in the darkest of times.

The dissertation has been improved considerably due to insightful comments and constructive criticism from Senior Research Fellow Kadri Männasoo and Docent Priit Sander in the pre-defence. I would also like to thank Professor Armin Rohde for finding the time to contribute to the defence of the thesis.

Next I would like to thank all the current and former members of the chair of economic modelling. This list includes in addition to Professor Tiiu Paas also Kärt Rõigas, Helen Poltimäe, Juta Sikk, Anne Kuigo, Kaia Philips, Otto Karma, Andres Võrk, Jaan Masso and Toomas Raus. These people have been alongside me all these long years.

I am very grateful to Kertu Lääts for her physical and moral support in the final years of this long journey. Her positiveness and helpfulness gave me lot of motivation and even more so her promise to meet me on the tennis court if I manage to successfully defend my thesis.

Finally, many thanks to my family for their support and patience and even more to my long-time girlfriend Karmen, who in addition to tremendous moral support, also managed to co-author an article with me.

1. THEORETICAL FRAMEWORK FOR FINANCIAL CONTAGION

1.1. Definitions and relevance of financial contagion

Financial contagion has become an increasingly popular research field in recent decades. Several crises in the last twenty or thirty years were transmitted rapidly to other countries, some seemingly exhibiting no similarity, no geographical proximity nor strong fundamental links with the country of origin. Borrowing the phrase from epidemiology this phenomenon has been called *financial contagion* in the economic literature. Until the 1980s, the issue of financial contagion had practically not been explored at all. The reason for this is that financial contagion, as it is currently defined, was not seen as a plausible reason for countries falling victim of financial crises. Even in the 1980s, when many countries one after another, especially in South America, had to face severe devaluations and banking crises, the possibility of financial contagion was largely ignored and the blame was apportioned to poor domestic policies and high real interest rates in the US. Only in the 1990s did the picture change drastically due to the contagious nature of the Mexican (1994) and Asian (1997) crises, among others. According to Rigobon (2002), the issue of *contagion* has been one of the most debated topics in international finance since the Asian crisis, and even crises from the previous decade started to be looked at in a different light. The last decade of the twentieth century is considered especially contagious given the speed and virulence of the propagation of crises at that time, but as argued by Didier, Mauro and Schmukler (2008), the factors underlying the channels that generated contagion during the crises of the 1990s seem to be potentially at least as strong today as they were back then. Events in recent years have seen yet another financial crisis 'snowball' around the world, and as such, the need to understand this kind of contagion is increasingly important, particularly for policy makers looking to avoid or manage the spread of possible future crises. This crisis is a typical example emphasizing the importance of improvements in the activities of financial institutions and their management. When seeking to improve the activities of financial institutions, the possible transmission channels of crises, the role of

17

monitoring and data quality as well as the systematic analysis of the lessons learnt from previous crises and their contagion should be taken into account. The results of such analyses offer additional information to help improve national policies and the institutional environment and thereby enhance risk management.

One of the main interests in contagion studies is associated with the merits of international diversification. The rationale being that theoretically international diversification should significantly reduce portfolio risk, but when cross-country correlations increase during crises much of this rationale is undermined. In addition, issues such as appropriate financial architecture and investment opportunities and risks for local markets can be answered by studies of financial contagion.

In spite of significant theoretical and empirical interest in the topic, there is still no consensus among researchers either on the theoretical or empirical procedure for identifying financial contagion. The economic literature offers conceptually different definitions of financial contagion. Using the Contagion of Financial Crises Website summary (the World Bank Group 2009), three main definitions of financial contagion can be distinguished:

1) Definition 1. The broadest definition considers contagion as the cross-country transmission of shocks or as general cross-country spillover effects. Unlike other definitions this one includes fundamental linkages as a channel of financial contagion, and therefore, is sometimes called *fundamentals-based contagion* (Calvo and Reinhart 1996) or recently *interdependence* (Forbes and Rigobon 2001, 2002) in the literature.

2) Definition 2. Contagion is the transmission of shocks to other countries or cross-country correlations, beyond any fundamental linkages between countries and beyond common shocks. For example Masson (1999) defines contagion to mean only those transmissions of crises that cannot be identified with observed changes in macroeconomic fundamentals. Going for a somewhat different testing methodology, Eichengreen et al (1996) argue that there is contagion if the probability of a crisis in a given country increases conditional on the occurrence of a crisis elsewhere, after controlling for the standard set of macroeconomic fundamentals. This definition is sometimes referred as *excess co-movement* (e.g.

Edwards, 2000) – a correlation that remains even after controlling for fundamentals and common shocks. Herding behaviour is usually argued to be responsible for that more-than-expected co-movement.

3) Definition 3. According to the most restrictive approach, contagion occurs when there exist not only the transmissions of shocks to other countries but these transmissions also have to be different (in practice this means linkages through which shocks transmit are stronger) during times of crisis compared to tranquil times. This definition is sometimes referred to as *shift-contagion* (term coined by Forbes and Rigobon 2001 and 2002) or *pure contagion* (Masson, 1999), and it excludes a constant high degree of co-movement in a crisis period. In the latter case, markets are just interdependent. This definition is used in the empirical analysis of the thesis.

In addition to the abovementioned approaches, there also exist some other definitions of this phenomenon that are less often used. For example, according to Sola et al (2002) there is contagion if the probability of having a crisis at home country equals one if there is crisis in another market; on the other hand, Bae et al (2003) consider coincidence of extreme return shocks across countries as evidence of financial contagion.

In the theoretical part of the dissertation (first two chapters) alternative definitions of financial contagion are considered, as the objective is to have a comprehensive view of the subject. In the empirical part, however, a choice has to be made, and therefore, only the third, most restrictive definition (shift-contagion) is used.

1.2. Theoretical framework of mechanisms for the transmission of shocks and crises

1.2.1. Introduction

The current understanding of the phenomenon of financial contagion is closely related to its transmission channels, but the authors of papers considering financial crises have not yet achieved consensus on the channels through which contagion spreads. Several trade issues, the macro environment, common lender, market psychology and so on have all been considered as determinants of the degree of contagion. Different opinions are well summarised by the World Bank Group (2009): "Some claim that contagion is explained by real links, while others provide a financial explanation. At the same time, other studies argue that herding behaviour is the key element to understand the recent contagious episodes. Although one can show that these factors are present in the cross-country transmission of crises, an even more difficult problem is to determine the relative importance of each component." This summary accords with the statement pointed out by Dornbusch et al (2000a) who argue that the exact causes and channels of contagion are both unknown as are the precise policy interventions that can most effectively reduce it.

Starting from the influential studies by Forbes and Rigobon (2001 and 2002), which can be considered as the cornerstone in the field of financial contagion, a distinction has been made between *contagion* and *interdependence* according to transmission channels (see also Rigobon 2002 and Kleimeier et al 2008). If crises are transmitted through stable fundamental linkages, then only countries with weak economic fundamentals will be affected and good fundamentals can offer protection. On the other hand, if irrational behaviour by agents (in the form of speculative attacks, financial panic and/or herd behaviour) is the transmission force, then even countries with good fundamentals can be seriously affected. In the former case we have only interdependence and not contagion between countries, while in the latter case we have true contagion. Considering this distinction, the first definition presented above (sub-chapter 1.1) may only be interdependence and not contagion.

There are a lot of theories that explain how shocks and crises are propagated internationally. It is important to understand these theories to be able to determine whether or not the propagation of crisis can be considered contagion. These theories can be classified into two groups according to whether they assume that transmission channels do or do not change during times of crisis: crisis-contingent theories and non-crisis-contingent theories[7]. This kind of distinction was first made by Forbes and Rigobon (2001) and helps to distinguish shift-contagion (the third definition) from the broader definitions. Non-crisis contingent theories are in accordance

---

[7] Dornbusch et al (2000b) use different classification with similar idea: fundamentals-based (real and financial linkages) and financial agents' behavior based transmissions of shocks.

with interdependence or the broader definitions of contagion. Financial contagion is non-existent according to these theories, and crises spill over into countries because of strong but unchangeable linkages. Crisis-contingent theories, on the other hand, are in accordance with financial contagion even in its most restrictive definition.

1.2.2. Non-crisis contingent theories

Non-crisis-contingent theories are those that assume transmission mechanisms are the same during a crisis as during more stable periods, and therefore, cross-market linkages do not increase after a shock. Large cross-market correlations after a shock are a continuation of linkages that exist before the crisis. Because of the nature of the majority of propagation channels brought out by this group of theories, they are sometimes called real links based or fundamentals-based contagion in the literature, but of course, if we are distinguishing between contagion and interdependence, these kinds of transmissions are not contagion at all. Non-crisis contingent theories can be divided into four broad channels according to Forbes and Rigobon (2001): trade, policy coordination, country re-evaluation and random aggregate shocks. A similar classification is given by Costinot et al (2000), only policy coordination is replaced by financial links and country re-evaluation is called "learning". Instead of four, Dornbusch et al (2000b) present three non-crisis contingent theories. In their classification, compared to that of Costinot et al (2000), financial links remain in place as also do random aggregate shocks, but these are called common shocks. They also agree with Costinot et al (2000) and Forbes and Rigobon (2001) that trade linkages should be one channel here, but Dornbusch et al (2000b) combine them with competitive devaluations. A brief overview of all these channels is given below.

Trade spillovers come from the fact that when a country faces a significant depreciation of its currency, other countries, as trading partners or competitors in the same foreign markets, can suffer from decreased competitiveness of export and domestic sales within the country. If the loss in competitiveness is severe enough, it could also increase the expectation of an exchange rate devaluation in these countries, which in turn increases the probability of currency attacks, especially when currencies are not freely floating (Dornbusch et al 2000b, Forbes and Rigobon 2001).

Dornbusch et al (2000b) make a distinction between trade links and competitive devaluations within this concept. According to their approach the transmission of shocks through trade links means that any major trade partner in a country where a financial crisis has caused significant currency depreciation could experience problems because investors foresee a decline in its exports to the crisis country, and therefore, some deterioration in its trade account. When talking about competitive devaluations as a transmission channel these authors point to the fact that devaluation in the first crisis country increases its competitiveness in third markets, which puts pressure on the currencies of the main trading partners. This pressure can be especially high when those currencies are not floating freely.

Eichengreen and Rose (1999), Forbes (2001, 2004) and Glick and Rose (1999) who investigated the 1992–1993 European Exchange Rate Mechanism (ERM) crisis, the 1994 Mexican crisis, the 1997 Asian crisis, and the 1999 Brazilian crisis respectively, have argued that trade links are the primary channel through which the crises were transmitted to other countries. Eichengreen et al (1996) and Valdes (1997) have also found some empirical evidence to support this theory. On the other hand, Didier, Mauro and Schmukler (2008) argue that although the trade channel seems to have played a role to different degrees in the crises of the 1990s, it does not explain the contagion observed in the context of the 1998 Russian crisis, where the trade links among the affected countries were quite limited. Thus, the experience of the Russian crisis suggests that trade is unlikely to be the only channel of contagion, and other channels are also necessary to account for these observations (For models of contagion based on trade linkage and macroeconomic similarities see Eichengreen et al 1996, Goldstein 1998 and Gerlach and Smets 1995).

The second transmission mechanism in this group – referred to as *country re-evaluation* by Forbes and Rigobon (2001), *wake-up call* by Goldstein (1998), *learning* by Costinot et al (2000) and *demonstration effects* by Didier et al (2012) – conveys the idea that investors may apply the lessons learned after a shock to one country to other countries with similar macroeconomic structures and policies.

Goldstein (1998) argues that a crisis in one country constitutes a "wake-up call" for other economies. This happens when the fundamentals of these other economies are bad, but investors do not realize this until problems in the crisis country arise. According to Goldstein (1998), these wake-up calls were one of the main reasons for the spreading of the Asian crisis. He argues that after the crisis hit Thailand, many international investors reassessed the creditworthiness of Asian borrowers and in doing so found that many Asian economies had similar weaknesses to those in Thailand (weak financial sector, large external deficit, appreciating real exchange rates and so on). This, of course, was fatal to the outlook for these countries and the crisis spread. This idea is supported by empirical analysis conducted by Goldstein and Hawkins (1998), who found that a weighted average of fourteen important (according to the literature) fundamentals, which places Thailand (the first economy to get into trouble) as the most vulnerable, indicates Indonesia (the economy subsequently worst affected) as the second-most vulnerable. Fundamental-based rankings correspond much more closely to the observed impact on economies than do rankings of the economies on the basis of their bilateral relationship with Thailand. In the case of the US crisis in 2008, the economic vulnerabilities that were likely to make investors revaluate the creditworthiness of a country were low levels of bank capital, high bank exposure to the real estate sector and high corporate leverage (Didier et al (2012)).

It is important to note that these wake-up calls are also considered an example of *multiple equilibria* (explained below as part of crisis-contingent theory) by some authors (e.g. Masson 1999, 2004). His reasoning being that although in reality there has always been only one (bad) equilibrium, the practical progress of events rather favours the multiple equilibria story. For example, in the case of the Thai crisis, an optimistic view of East Asian economies prevailed for a long time, the change in this view was rapid and the resulting crisis was so sudden and severe that it supports a multiple equilibria hypothesis. Masson claims that shifts in sentiment towards investing in Asia were not all related to learning about these countries' true fundamentals.

The third non-crisis-contingent theory *policy coordination* occurs as one country responds to another country's economic shock with similar policies to the ones employed by the crisis country. Forbes and Rigobon (2001) offer the example of when a trade agreement might include a clause in which lax monetary policy in one country forces other members to raise trade barriers.

The fourth non-crisis-contingent theory has many names in the literature. As mentioned above, Forbes and Rigobon (2001) call it *random aggregate shocks* or *global shocks*, Dornbusch et al (2000b) use the term *common shocks*, Costinot et al (2000) call it *common external factors,* and finally, Masson (2004) suggests the term *monsoonal effects.* What is meant by all of these terms is that major economic shifts could simultaneously affect the fundamentals of several economies and lead to co-movement in asset prices or capital flows. Often used examples of common shocks are the rise in international interest rates, a slowdown in world aggregate demand and others.

There are *financial links* between countries when these countries are connected through an international financial system. According to Costinot et al (2000), these links can induce the propagation of shocks when investors are induced to rebalance their portfolios after the initial shock because of risk management or liquidity problems. Defined as such, this channel is close to *endogenous liquidity,* which will be discussed later in the sub-chapter dedicated to crisis-contingent theories.

Dornbusch et al (2000b) define financial links as the shock transmission channel somewhat differently apportioning to it a more fundamental basis and distinguishing it from behavioural aspects. They argue that in the presence of heavy economic integration, which typically involves both trade and financial links, if one country is hit by a crisis, it limits the ability of others to engage in foreign direct investments and extend credit.

Two examples given by the World Bank Group (2009) are as follows. Firstly, financial links can be distinguished when leveraged institutions face margin calls. When the value of their collateral falls due to a negative shock in one country, leveraged companies need to increase their reserves. Therefore, they sell part of their valuable holdings on the countries that are still unaffected by the initial shock. This mechanism propagates the shock to other economies. Secondly, financial links can be distinguished if open-end mutual funds foresee future redemptions after there is a shock in one country. Mutual funds need to raise cash and, consequently, they sell assets in third countries. These examples show that the World Bank Group definition of a financial linkages based transmission is rather similar to that of Costinot et al (2000) given above, and hardly distinguishable from the endogenous liquidity problems based transmission (see next sub-chapter).

Therefore, although Dornbusch et al (2000b) consider financial links as one of the fundamentals, it is not easy to delimit these links outside behavioural aspects. That is probably the reason why Forbes and Rigobon (2001) have not used this channel at all in their classification.

According to Didier, Mauro and Schmukler (2008), financial links appear to have been the main transmission channel of the Mexican 1994 crisis. Also, Baig and Goldfajn (1999), Caramazza et al (2004), Kaminsky and Reinhart (2000) and Van Rijckeghem and Weder (2001) have argued that the financial links was the main channel of transmission for shocks across countries during the 1990s (For those models see Calvo 2005, Calvo and Mendoza 2000 and Kaminsky and Reinhart 2000).

Didier et al (2012) distinguish between direct and indirect financial linkages. According to their approach direct financial linkages arise due to direct financial exposures between the crisis-hit country and other countries, while indirect financial linkages involve the actions of international investors that lead to co-movement across the various countries where they hold assets either because of margin calls, changes in risk aversion or herding behaviour. Thus, direct financial linkages are in accordance with non-crisis contingent theories and indirect financial linkages with crisis-contingent theories.

Hernandez and Valdez (2001) investigate the relative importance of alternative fundamental links during the Thai, Russian and Brazilian crises. Results differ according to whether the crises are measured on the basis of changes in sovereign bond spreads or stock market returns. In the former case, financial links seem to be clearly the dominant transmission channel. In the latter case, both trade links and neighbourhood effects appear to be relevant contagion channels during the Thai and Brazilian crises, while financial competition remains the only relevant channel in the case of the Russian crisis.

Rigobon (2003) presents two main implications of non-crisis-contingent theories. Firstly, stock market indices tend to be integrated with one another, and secondly, transmission channels of shocks are similar in tranquil and crisis periods. The first of these implications implies that crises do propagate from one country to others, and the second suggests that this propagation can only be considered contagious if using broader definitions of financial contagion.

1.2.3. Crisis contingent theories

Crisis-contingent theories assume that transmission mechanisms change during a crisis, and therefore, cross-market linkages increase after a shock. These theories explain what is behind the changes in transmission mechanisms, which means they refer to cases where the transmission is not justified either by real linkages between markets or economic and financial fundamentals. Forbes and Rigobon (2001) present three basic mechanisms that according to these theories are behind the international transmission of shocks and crises: multiple equilibria, endogenous liquidity shocks and political economy. Costinot et al (2000) also mention three channels, but herding behaviour is suggested instead of political contagion. Some main characteristics of all these channels are introduced as follows.

Multiple equilibria as a propagation channel is based on investor psychology and occurs when a crisis in one country coordinates investor expectations for another economy, mostly negatively (Masson 1999). Investors, after a shock in one country, shift in a coordinated fashion from good to bad equilibrium for another country and in doing so cause a crisis there. It is important to note that the shift from good to bad equilibrium takes place without any change in a country's fundamentals and is driven solely by a change in investor beliefs that are self-fulfilling.

One reason why this kind of thing can easily happen is given by Masson (1999, 2004) and Dornbusch et al (2000b) – namely when a crisis in one country is used as a sunspot for other countries. A crisis in one country affects investor expectations in the second, which induces a coordination of investor expectations on the bad equilibrium for this country.

Another explanation for shifting from good to bad equilibrium is given by Mullainathan (2002). His approach is based on narratives that associate the crises and the imperfect memory of financial agents. When a crisis hits it triggers investors' memories of past crises, which are usually related to negative emotions. Therefore, investors assign a higher probability of a bad equilibrium and reconsider their investments. The resulting switch to bad equilibrium thus occurs because of the correlated memories of the investors, not the correlated fundamentals of the countries.

An important implication highlighted by Jeanne (1997) is that multiple equilibria are only possible in a certain range for macroeconomic fundamentals. If this hypothesis holds, contagion cannot completely be separated from fundamentals, and policymakers should try to avoid that critical range.

Jeanne and Masson (2000) have pointed out that incomplete and asymmetric information are not necessary criteria for multiple equilibria to occur. The switch to bad equilibrium may simply happen if investors are sufficiently forward-looking.

Forbes and Rigobon (2001) summarise that in the multiple equilibria based models the shift from a good to bad equilibrium and the transmission of the initial shock is therefore driven by a change in investor expectations or beliefs and not by any real linkages. Multiple equilibria based theories are able to explain why speculative attacks occur in economies that appear to be fundamentally sound. After the crisis in the first victim economy, investors change their expectations, and therefore, transmit the shock through a propagation mechanism that does not exist during stable periods.

A second category of crisis-contingent theories is *endogenous liquidity*. This theory refers to a situation where a crisis in one country reduces the liquidity of market participants. Forbes and Rigobon (2001) argue that in this kind of situation investors are more or less forced to recompose their portfolio and sell assets in other countries in order to continue operating in the market, satisfy margin calls or meet regulatory requirements. If the liquidity shock is large enough, a crisis in one country could increase the degree of credit rationing and force investors to sell their holdings of assets in countries not affected by the initial crisis. This kind of model was developed by Valdes (1997), who shows that the probability of the repayment of one country is negatively affected by the degree of illiquidity in other countries.

Calvo (2005, preliminary version as a working paper 1999) and Kodres and Pritsker (2002) introduce liquidity problems in the conditions where asymmetrical information is present. The logic is that when informed investors are hit by liquidity shocks, and therefore, are forced to sell their holdings, the uninformed investors are unaware whether the reason for these jumping out is liquidity problems or some bad signal that these (presumably) informed investors received. At least some of uninformed agents expect the latter and behave respectively. The distinction between this kind of model and the herding behaviour based model (see later in the sub-chapter) is quite thin.

Forbes and Rigobon (2001) draw parallels between models presented by Valdes and Calvo (introduced above) summarising that in both of these models, the liquidity shock leads to an increased correlation in asset prices. This transmission mechanism does not occur during stable periods and only occurs after the initial shock (which makes this branch of theories crisis-contingent).

An often pointed out (e.g. Kaminsky and Reinhart 1998) implication of liquidity constraints based models is that countries where asset returns have a higher correlation with the asset returns of the crisis country are also more vulnerable to the propagation of the crisis. Another implication is given by Calvo and Mendoza (2000), who argue that the more country assets are traded on financial markets the more vulnerable the country is to contagion.

Multiple equilibria and endogenous liquidity are both based on investor behaviour, and it is not easy in practice to determine which of these two has been the main transmission channel. This is, for example, the case in the explanation by Calvo and Mendoza (2000) and Agenor and Aizenman (1997), who argue that in response to a negative shock, investors often withdraw their money from the assets markets of the region without confirming whether the market they have invested in has been affected or not by that shock. It is difficult to say in these cases whether the retreat was due to some weaknesses that the crisis elsewhere has highlighted or because of liquidity problems (or even herd behaviour).

The third transmission mechanism that can be categorized as crisis-contingent, *political contagion,* can be defined as a mechanism of contagion that is intrinsically political (Drazen 1999), meaning that contagion arises due to decisions made by policy makers with solely political (not economical) objectives. An example of this kind of political contagion can easily arise if a group of countries have fixed exchange rates. If one of these countries decides to abandon its peg, this reduces the political costs to other countries of abandoning their respective pegs, which in turn makes it more likely that these countries also abandon their pegs. Therefore, exchange rate crises are likely to spread because of political contagion. This kind of progress of events, according to many authors (Goldstein 1998, Drazen 1999), was evident in the ERM crisis of 1992–1993. Dornbusch et al (2000b) argue that if investors do expect this kind of "game" of competitive devaluations after a currency crisis in one country, it is most natural for them to sell their holdings of securities in other countries, which results in still greater depreciation relative to what could have been attained in a cooperative equilibrium.

If one compares the explanation in terms of political links with those focusing on trade links (see previous sub-chapter), it can be seen that the distinction between the two in practice is rather difficult. What happens is more or less the same – after the devaluation of the currency in one country, other countries also devalue their currencies. What is different is why these successive devaluations occur. The theory of the trade links based propagation of shocks says the reason for this is that the first devaluation worsens the competitiveness of other countries and devaluation or abandoning their peg can improve their competiveness and their currencies are more susceptible to speculative attacks, while according to the theory of political contagion the same thing happens because the political costs of abandoning the peg is lower if another country has already done that. Finding out the true reason may of course not be an easy task in practice.

Herding behaviour needs special attention as this phenomenon is present in the majority of episodes of the propagation of shocks based on investor or other financial agent behaviour. Many authors have found that fundamental links (and commons shocks) do not fully explain the relationship and changes in relationships among countries. That being the case, herding behaviour is suggested as one reason for spillover effects and contagion between countries. Herding behaviour refers to the situation where instead of incurring expenses for obtaining missing information, under-informed investors observe the actions of supposedly better informed investors and try to follow them as they think these actions are based on superior information. The typical conditions for herding behaviour to arise are when information about countries' fundamentals is incomplete, asymmetrical and too expensive for less informed investors and there are no serious restrictions for investors choosing their actions[8]. If some investors take their holdings out of a country, it may seem to others that this action was due to certain information and they may also retreat from the market. But it is possible that those supposedly well informed investors did not act on the basis of information about the countries' fundamentals,

---

[8] For a good overview of financial crises based on the asymmetric information approach see Mishkin (1991), for a more general overview of information asymmetry see Rotschild and Stiglitz (1976).

but were just making adjustments to their portfolio after having experienced losses in a country hit by the crisis. This kind of herding behaviour based model was first presented by Calvo (1996).

Forbes and Rigobon (2001) have not included herding as a crisis-contingent channel in their classification, but it has an important role to play in both multiple equilibria and liquidity problems theories. When discussing multiple equilibria as a channel for the transmission of shocks and crises, these authors claim that the shift from a good to bad equilibrium is driven by a change in investor expectations or beliefs, but for many of the agents (probably even the majority of them) these changes in beliefs do not stem from the sunspots but from the behaviour of other, presumably better informed investors. Similar mimicking behaviour may occur when some investors are forced to sell their holdings because of liquidity problems. It is not easy for other investors to know whether these sales are due to liquidity issues or some signals with a negative undertone. To ensure against the latter, it seems rational to follow the herd.

In the case of herding behaviour, individual investors may act rationally but the whole market does not, and therefore, even countries with sound fundamentals are not protected against the transmission of crises. According to Alvarez-Plata and Schrooten (2003), the pull effect caused by investors all behaving in the same way makes economic fundamentals unimportant and leads to the rapid withdrawal of capital from the economies concerned or possibly even from entire regions. Claessens et al (2001) argue that as spreads directly reflect the risk perception of financial markets, pure contagion may be solely the result of the behaviour of investors or other financial agents.

Evidence of herding or some other form of investor behaviour based transmission of crises has been found by many authors. Eichengreen, Rose and Wyplosz (1996) highlight that the countries that came under speculative attack during the ERM crisis had heterogeneous macroeconomic fundamentals, and only in some cases could the attack be justified by the fundamentals. Pindyck and Rotemberg (1990 and 1993) find that after taking into account common fundamentals there is still residual co-movement across stocks with very different industry and idiosyncratic fundamentals. These results point to the important role played during the crisis by irrationally behaving investors and speculators. Also, Moussalli (2007), Alvarez-Plata and Schrooten (2003) and Woo (2000) have argued that herding is the main channel for spillover effects between countries. Findings from a recent study by Boschi and Goenka (2012) show that financial crises can be transmitted across seemingly unrelated countries through the risk attitudes of international investors. Thus, the authors argue, to understand financial crises it is not sufficient to look at the countries in question, but also at the portfolios of international investors. Here what is important is not the magnitude of absolute losses but the losses of investors relative to their portfolios.

Common to all crisis-contingent theories is the fact that the crisis causes a structural shift, a break in linkages between countries. As the transmission mechanism changes, the propagation of shocks and crises that occur in correspondence to these theories can be considered as financial contagion.

One key word that characterizes most crisis-contingent theories is irrationality. There is something irrational in the behaviour of financial agents (it does not mean that investors individually act irrationally, but rather that their collective behaviour is not rational) that fosters or even causes the propagation of shocks. This irrationality based propagation makes lot of sense, as financial contagion does not affect all countries in a similar fashion, not even those with similar levels of development or economic conditions (Ramirez and Martinez 2011).

According to crisis-contingent theories only countries behind an iron curtain are protected against financial contagion. Sound fundamentals offer no protection because they are overruled by the self-fulfilling expectations of investors.

Note that these channels (both crisis-contingent and non-crisis-contingent) are called both transmission channels of shocks and transmission channels of contagion in the literature. Some (mostly earlier) papers use these two more or less as synonyms. But if we adopt the most restrictive (third) definition of financial contagion, only transmission mechanisms in accordance with crisis-contingent theories can be called channels of contagion. Shocks and crises propagate through other channels also, of course, but this kind of transmission is not considered contagious.

As can be seen from the previous overview, the distinctions between the different theories are sometimes quite thin and even in the case of some crisis-contingent and non-crisis-contingent theories. Here the author of the thesis suggests thinking in terms of non-crisis-contingent theories as those that describe the propagation of crises via fundamental linkages and crisis-contingent theories as those that explain such propagations through investor behaviour.

To summarise the findings of the chapter, it can be concluded that the economic literature provides heterogeneous views on financial contagion and its transmission channels, and therefore, it is understandable that the results of empirical studies may also vary depending on the theoretical and empirical frameworks for considering the concept of financial contagion as well as several other factors. The next chapter focuses on the qualitative analysis of empirical evidence of financial contagion, first of all taking into account the variability of the methodological approaches used in empirical studies.

2. QUALITATIVE OVERVIEW OF PREVIOUS EMPIRICAL FINDINGS

2.1. Some main reasons explaining the variability of empirical evidence

Drawing finite conclusions on financial contagion based on the results of previous empirical findings is not easy. Empirical analyses differ in terms of the conceptual definition of contagion adopted, the crises under analysis, destination countries and the financial market under investigation, but all of these aspects may affect the results of the empirical studies. In addition, as pointed out by Billio and Pellizon (2003), Dungey and Zhumabekova (2001) and Serwa and Bohl (2005), the problems of omitted variables, feedback dependencies between stock markets, different time zones and the arbitrary selection of crisis periods can all affect the results of financial contagion tests. This diversity of results is well illustrated in the research by Daniel Serwa (2005), who used four different testing methodologies and different samples for robustness purposes only to achieve mixed results. According to his findings, contagion is a rather rare phenomenon, but patterns of capital and information flow to stock markets still change during turbulent periods.

There is also no consensus on the issue of whether the contagiousness of crises increases or decreases over time. A lot of discussion has focused on the theme of whether recent crises have been more contagious than those before the 1990s. While some authors (Haile and Pozo 2008) argue that currency crises prior to the 1990s did not appear to spread across countries with the virulence and speed observed recently, others (Bordo and Murshid 2000a and b) have found no evidence to confirm this.

Finally, there are also other problems measuring contagion (see for instance Cheung et al (2009). Rigobon (2002 and 2003) points out that financial contagion has been associated with high frequency events: it has been measured on stock market returns, interest rates, exchange rates or linear combinations of them. Rigobon argues that this data is plagued with simultaneous equations, omitted variables, conditional and unconditional heteroskedasticity, serial correlations, non-linearity and non-normality problems. Unfortunately, no such procedure has yet been found that can handle all these problems at the same time without representing some important restrictions (see Forbes and Rigobon (2001) and Rigobon (2002)).

Following in the footsteps of some earlier papers (for example Dornbusch et al, 2000a), recent empirical analyses are divided into the following categories according to the testing methodology adopted: tests based on cross-market correlation coefficients, tests based on the conditional probabilities of financial crisis and tests measuring changes in volatility. Furthermore, there are some more seldom used tests discussed under the heading "other tests". An overview of papers investigating financial contagion and the results of previous empirical studies is presented in Appendices 1–4. In compiling this overview, the focus is primarily on empirical evidence found in the papers (contagion or not), but also the particularities of the data sets (variability of countries, time periods, crises under investigation) and financial markets (stocks, bonds, exchange rates etc). A short introduction to the methodology is given at the beginning of the each of the following sub-chapters. That is as far as this thesis extends in terms of introducing specific mathematical models for each methodological framework, as this is outside the scope of the study. The two most popular of these methodologies – those based on correlation coefficients and volatility changes – are also used in the thesis, and therefore, a detailed overview of these models is given in chapter 3. To obtain an in-depth overview of these models see for example Wolf (1999) or Serwa (2005).

2.2. Tests based on cross-market correlation coefficients

Tests based on cross-market correlation coefficients are the most common and widely used approach to testing for contagion. These tests measure the correlation in returns between two markets during a stable period and then test for a significant increase in this correlation coefficient after a shock. A significant increase in the correlation coefficient after a crisis is considered evidence of contagion. These tests are mainly consistent with the third definition of financial contagion. An overview of contagion studies that implement correlation coefficient based tests is presented in Appendix 1.

The majority of studies that estimate correlations among markets and do not adjust for the presence of heteroskedasticity have found evidence for contagion. For instance, in one of the pioneering studies of financial contagion, King and Wadhwani (1990) found that correlations between the US, UK and Japan increased significantly after the US 1987 crisis. Lee and Kim (1993) came to the same conclusion using a sample of 12 major markets. Baig and Goldfajn (1999) found evidence of contagion between emerging markets during the 1997-98 East Asian crises.

Several authors have found that the Mexican crisis in 1994 was contagious. Evidence for contagion has been found by Calvo and Reinhart (1996) and Frankel and Schmukler (1998) using the sample of Asian and Latin American emerging markets; by Valdes (1997) using the sample of Latin America and by Agenor, Aizenman and Hoffmaister (1998) using the sample of Argentina.

However, Forbes and Rigobon (2001 and 2002) and Rigobon (2002 and 2003) argue that simple correlations are biased due to the presence of heteroskedasticity, endogeneity and omitted variables. Therefore, they argue, an increase in correlations among markets in different countries may not be evidence of contagion but only interdependence. Forbes and Rigobon (2002) show that in the presence of heteroskedasticity of asset price movements, an increase in correlation could be just a continuation of strong transmission mechanisms, which also exist in tranquil times. Given that volatility usually increases during a crisis, the heteroskedasticity is actually likely and expected. If there is historically high cross correlation among markets, then a rapid and extensive change in one market will also lead to significant changes in the other markets, and according to Forbes and Rigobon (2002), these changes should not be counted as evidence of contagion. Forbes and Rigobon (2002) also show that an increase in correlations of asset prices may result when changes in economic fundamentals, risk perception and preferences are correlated without any additional contagion being present.

A deeper, mathematical, explanation to why it is necessary to distinguish contagion from interdependence is amongst others given by Forbes and Rigobon (2002), Rigobon (2002), Boyer et al (1999), Loretan and English (2000) and Corsetti et al (2005), and goes along the following lines. When two random variables X and Y are positively correlated, their correlation coefficient may be an increasing function of the variance of each of them. In particular, this is always the case if X and Y are normally distributed or if one variable is a linear function of the other variable. Pericoli and Sbracia (2003) conclude that in general, correlation coefficients in specific subsamples tend to be biased in the presence of heteroskedasticity and endogeneity or if some variables are omitted. Therefore, they argue, when comparing correlation coefficients over a specific subsample, one needs to correct the bias in the coefficients generated by the different variances in that subsample. For instance, during the crisis periods, economic variables generally show an increase in volatility. Hence, empirical tests that do not correct for the bias typically tend to favour the hypothesis of excessive transmission.

Unfortunately, to adjust for the effects of heteroskedasticity some restrictive assumptions have to be made; nevertheless, this may be the lesser evil. Forbes and Rigobon (2002, first version of the paper 1999) show that correlation coefficients across multi-country returns are not significantly higher during crisis periods (1987 US stock market crash, the 1994 Mexican peso crisis, and the 1997 East Asian crisis) if the problems of endogenous variables, omitted variables and changes in the variance of residuals are properly corrected for. Their revolutionary result of *no contagion, only interdependence* means that large cross-market linkages after a shock are simply a continuation of strong transmission mechanisms that exist in more stable periods, and has been the object of heated discussion and controversy since. Forbes and Rigobon (2000) find no clear evidence of contagion in stock and bond markets during the Latin American crises in the 1990s. Similarly, Arias, Hausman and Rigobon (1998) find only limited evidence for contagion. Boyer et al (1999) and Loretan and English (2000) use a slightly refined methodology (by calculating corrected correlation coefficients under the assumption of normally distributed variables) and also find no evidence for contagion.

Gelos and Sahay (2001) apply a simplified version of this methodology and find no contagion from the Czech Republic, Asia and Russia to CEE stock markets. However, they find significant changes in the relationship between exchange markets in the crisis-origin country (Russia and Czech Republic) and other markets during the crisis periods. Serwa (2005) uses the extension of the models presented by Forbes and Rigobon (2002) and Corsetti, Pericoli, and Sbracia (2005) to investigate 7 crises using the sample of a selection of CEE and Western European countries and found that contagion occurred hardly ever or not frequently during the investigated crises.

However, some authors have found evidence of financial contagion even after controlling for heteroskedasticity. For example, Favero and Giavazzi (1999) find that, after controlling for normal interdependence in the context of an ERM crisis there was still evidence of contagion in interest rates residuals. Hon, Strauss and Yong (2004) show that even after correcting for inter-sample heteroskedasticity and intra-sample GARCH effects the terrorist attack in the United States on 11 September 2001 resulted in contagion. Baig and Goldfajn (1999) find clear evidence for contagion with regards to sovereign spreads (however, evidence with regards to exchange rates, stock markets and interest rates co-movements is mixed at best). Kleimeier et al (2008) use a time-alignment-of-data approach and also find evidence of contagion[9]. The same result is found by Kallberg and Pasquariello (2008), who investigate excess co-movement in US stock indices using adjustments proposed by Forbes and Rigobon (2002). Sander and Kleimeier (2003) extend the measurement methodology by directly investigating changing causality patterns by using the Granger-causality methodology and find that Asian crisis episodes were contagious.

Corsetti et al (2005) show that the finding of *no contagion only interdependence* obtained by Forbes and Rigobon (2002) is due to some arbitrary assumptions that concerned the variance of the market-specific noise in the country where the crisis originated. These assumptions cause the tests to be biased towards the null hypothesis of interdependence and against the hypothesis of contagion. And indeed, Corsetti et al (2005) find evidence for contagion from Hong Kong to the stock markets in Singapore, the Philippines, France, Italy and the UK. In addition, Serwa (2005) shows

---

[9] Kleimeier et al (2008) make an important step forward investigating synchronized data. Whether this kind of data needs to be time-aligned or not may be one of the main discussion objects in the future research.

that the adjusted correlation coefficients of Forbes and Rigobon (2002) (and its extension by Corsetti, Pericoli, and Sbracia 2005), that may have different values in stable and crisis periods, may in some situations be biased. Kleimeier et al (2008) have gone even so far as to claim that it is a well known fact that the *no contagion only interdependence* result of Forbes and Rigobon (2002) is due to the poor size properties of their methodology.

Bordo and Murshid (2000b) examine the contagiousness of financial crises over the past 120 years and find some evidence that correlations among markets were higher during crisis periods. However, as the volatility in correlation coefficients is quite high in turbulent periods, they (using the same reasoning as given by Forbes and Rigobon, 2002) find no solid evidence that contagion has been increasing over time.

Recently, Choe et al (2012) have come out with the interesting revelation that heteroskedasticity is not only an econometric factor that can cause a statistical bias in correlation coefficient based contagion tests, but also an important risk factor that can induce the intertemporal risk-return adjustment among risk-averse investors. These authors show that there is a significant relationship between cross-market co-movement and volatility, and that the time-varying component of cross-market co-movements is attributed to the intertemporal risk-return adjustment among risk-averse investors in responding to changing volatility. Thus, they cast doubt on the entire family of constant correlation tests claiming that these tests are not capable of incorporating the time-varying aspect of cross-market co-movements into the test for contagion. Instead, these authors propose a time-varying conditional correlation test for contagion and define financial contagion as a structural break in the dynamics of the conditional correlation process during a crisis, while a temporal change in the correlation dynamics is defined as a reflection of time-varying cross-market co-movements induced by the intertemporal risk-return adjustment. Using this methodology and the dynamic conditional correlation multivariate GARCH model as an estimation tool, Choe et al (2012) find that out of the countries reporting contagion evidence under the constant correlation test, none of the countries exhibits contagion evidence from the 1997 Asian crisis. As this revelation is still very new and there has not been enough time for proper criticism, this approach is not followed in the present dissertation.

In sum, the overview of the previous empirical studies applying tests based on cross-market correlation analysis confirms the opinion that empirical evidence of financial contagion is sensitive to data sets and testing methods. When the correlations are not adjusted for the presence of heteroskedasticity, evidence for contagion is found in the majority of studies and periods, but when heteroskedasticity is taken into account the results of the studies are more mixed.

2.3. Tests based on the conditional probabilities of crisis

Rather than using raw correlations some authors study conditional correlation or probabilities to test financial contagion. The overview of the main studies that investigate the presence of financial contagion using conditional probability based tests is presented in Appendix 2.

The most commonly used methodology, introduced by Eichengreen, Rose and Wyplosz (1996) and Sachs, Tornell and Velasco (1996), examines whether the likelihood of crisis is higher in a given country when there are crises in some other country (countries) by estimating the probability of a crisis conditional on information about the occurrence of crisis elsewhere. This approach has some clear advantages: first, it permits statistical tests of the existence of contagion, and second, these tests can also try to investigate the channels through which contagion may occur (Dornbusch et al 2000b). However, these tests do not allow testing whether there have been structural breaks in the transmission mechanisms of crises, and therefore, one cannot straightforwardly distinguish crisis-contingent and non-crisis-contingent propagation channels.

Using a probit model and a sample of 20 industrial economies from 1959 through 1993, Eichengreen et al (1996) show that the probability of a domestic currency crisis increases with a speculative attack elsewhere. Using a similar methodology, De Gregorio and Valdes (1999) found that the 1994 Mexican crisis was less contagious than the 1982 debt crisis and the Asian crisis. They also concluded that debt composition and exchange rate flexibility limit the extent of contagion, whereas capital controls do not appear to curb it. Caramazza et al (2000 and 2004) on the other hand have found that the contagious nature of the Mexican, Asian and Russian crises does not differ much.

Haile and Bozo (2008) use quarterly data (1960–1998) for a set of 37 advanced and emerging-market economies and find that countries face currency crises because of both unsustainable macroeconomic fundamentals and contagion. Other important findings of their work are that contagion is regional and it operates through the trade channel. Glick and Rose (1999) apply a similar approach to five episodes of currency crises and 161 countries and find that trade linkages are important in propagating a crisis. They argue that contagion tends to be rather regional than global because trade tends to be more intra-regional than inter-regional (see also Diwan and Hoekman 1999). Kaminsky and Reinhart (2000) find some evidence for contagion, but similarly to Haile and Bozo (2008) and Glick and Rose (1999) conclude it has been a primarily regional phenomenon (see also Calvo and Reinhart 1996, Kaminsky and Schmukler 2003).

Alba et al (1998) argue that the effects of competitive devaluations alone could not have explained the large depreciation of other regional currencies after the Thai devaluation, which hints at some evidence for contagion. For transition economies, Gelos and Sahay (2001) find that correlations in exchange market pressures can be explained by direct trade links, but not by measures of other fundamentals. According to their study shock propagation mechanisms were weak during the Asian and Czech crises, but strong during the Russian crisis. Forbes (1999 and 2004) finds that country-specific effects and trade are all important transmission mechanisms during the Asian and Russian crises. Using closed-end country fund data, Frankel and Schmukler (1998) test whether adverse shocks from the Mexican crisis were transmitted directly to other Latin American and East Asian countries or through New York. They find that the Mexican crisis was spread through Wall Street to East Asian countries, but was directly transmitted to other Latin American countries. Lomakin and Paiz (1999) use a probit analysis and find that after adjustment for heteroskedasticity, the strength of cross-country linkages are significantly reduced.

An approach analogous to the conditional probability approach is taken by Hartmann et al (2001) who derive non-parametric estimates for the expected number of market crashes given that at least one market crashes. Using G-5 countries as a sample they find only very weak evidence for contagion and suggest it may be advisable to differentiate between the various types of countries (as destination) in future research.

To summarise the findings obtained using conditional probability based tests, it can be said that results once again are mixed. One has to keep in mind that these tests usually do not investigate the shift-contagion (the most restrictive definition of contagion), which makes it more likely to find supporting evidence for contagion.

2.4. Tests measuring changes in volatility

Tests measuring changes in volatility examine whether conditional variances of financial variables are related to each other among countries during the crisis period. This means using an ARCH or GARCH framework to estimate changes in the variance-covariance matrix (Hamao et al 1990; Edwards 1998) or the co-integrating vector across countries (Chou et al 1994; Longin and Solnik 1995). Some of the authors have additionally to conditional variances (volatility contagion) investigated relationships in conditional means (mean contagion), which can also be done using the ARCH and GARCH model test equations. The overview of the main contagion studies that measure changes in volatility is presented in Appendix 3.

Using this procedure Chou et al (1994) and Hamao et al (1990) find evidence of contagion after the 1987 US stock market crisis. Using an augmented GARCH model, Edwards (1998) focuses on the 1994 Mexican crisis and finds that there was strong evidence for contagion from Mexico to Argentina, but not from Mexico to Chile. Park and Song (1998) apply a GARCH model and find that the effects of the crisis in Indonesia and Thailand were transmitted to the Korean foreign exchange market, while the Korean crisis was not contagious to the two Southeast Asian countries. Longin and Solnik (1995) find that the correlation of monthly excess returns for seven major countries over the period 1960–90 rises in periods of high volatility. In a subsequent paper the same authors (Longin and Solnik 2001) investigate five major stock markets (US, UK, Germany, France, Japan) over the period 1959–1996 and also find evidence for contagion. Supporting evidence for the contagion hypothesis is also found by Hon, Strauss and Yong (2004) who investigate the 2001 terrorist attack and use stock markets from 25 countries as the sample.

Rigobon (2000, 2002 and 2003) has investigated variance-covariance matrices several times. He has focused on the crises in the 1990s and used data for all bonds, stocks and Brady bonds, but clear evidence of contagion was not found in any of his three studies. Baur (2003) introduces a test that concentrates on the transmission mechanism of shocks directly and differentiates between mean contagion and volatility contagion in an asymmetrical manner. Empirical results for 11 Asian stock markets show that there was mean and volatility contagion in the Asian crisis.

It is important to note that authors using these testing approaches usually have not controlled for fundamentals, and therefore, the tests do not make it possible to distinguish between pure (shift-contagion) and fundamentals-based contagion (interdependence) (Dornbusch et al (2000b). As it is easier to come to a conclusion that supports financial contagion in the case of less restrictive definitions, it is not surprising that such findings dominate. Subsequent studies that use more refined models have come to the no contagion conclusion much more frequently than older ones.

2.5. Other tests

There are also many more tests that are used less often (see Appendix 4). One of the most popular is a methodology called the Markov switching framework. Sola et al (2002) use this approach and find some support for financial contagion from Thailand to South Korea during the 1997 Asian crisis. However, in the case of South Korea and Brazil, contagion hypothesis is rejected. Serwa (2005) introduces the concept of causality using the same framework and finds no evidence for contagion between the Japanese (Nikkei 225) and Hong Kong (HSI) markets during the Asian crisis.

Abeysinghe (2001) applies a full trade model for crisis-affected East Asian countries and finds that, although transmission through trade played an important role, the immediate economic contractions are largely a result of direct shocks that are attributable to pure contagion[10] (see Dornbusch et al 2000b). Serwa (2005) employs a threshold vector autoregressive model to investigate the 1997 Asian crisis and finds evidence for financial contagion according to both the following definitions: financial crisis spilling over from one market to other markets (practically the same as definition 1 above) and a break in the interdependency structure between countries (definition 3 above or shift-contagion).

Gravelle et al (2003) developed a methodology to detect shift-contagion in pairs of asset returns using a bootstrap procedure. Their findings suggest that shift-contagion occurs among the currency markets in developed countries (for the period 1985–2001) but not bond markets in emerging-market countries (1991–2001). Kali and Reyes (2005) use quite original methods that they call a network approach. Their main finding is that the network effect of the crisis epicentre country was substantially higher for the 1994 Mexican crisis, the 1997 Asian crisis and the 1998 Russian crisis than for the Venezuelan and Argentine crises. That was the reason, they argue, why these first three crises were highly contagious while the other two were not.

Craig, Dravid and Richardson (1995) and Iwatsubo and Inagaki (2006) propose alternative (to the mainstream) measures for identifying financial contagion between non-synchronous trading markets[11]. Craig, Dravid and Richardson (1995) find that Japanese Nikkei index-based futures traded in the US provide complete information about contemporaneous overnight Japanese returns. The finding that information is rationally incorporated into prices even across international markets casts doubts on irrational financial agents based models. Iwatsubo and Inagaki (2006) investigate the bilateral contagion effects between US and Asian stock markets and find that there exist significant bilateral contagion effects in returns and return volatility between US and Asian markets, and the intensity of contagion was significantly greater during the Asian financial crisis than after the crisis.

Villar Frexedas and Vaya (2005) and Kelejian et al (2006) have used spatial econometric tools to investigate the financial contagion phenomenon. Both papers detect that contagion seems to have a clearly regional component.

Tornell (1999) does not actually test for the presence of contagion, but rather how the crisis, if it occurs, spreads across emerging markets. His

---

[10] The authors consider the most restrictive definition of contagion as *pure contagion*.

[11] In the models used by Craig, Dravid and Richardson (1995), given informationally efficient market investors' perceptions about the given stock market (Japan in their case) that are reflected in the returns of this stock market index, futures traded in some other market with different trading hours (US) influence one-to-one returns in the given (Japanese) stock market when it opens. A similar idea is used in the models of Iwatsubo and Inagaki (2006). Most of the other models suggest that this kind of information is ignored by the investors and observed price movements in the other (US) market make them react accordingly.

findings suggest that crises do not spread to countries with strong fundamentals, which of course does not support the contagion hypothesis (at least in terms of the more restrictive definitions of contagion).

In summary, the results of empirical studies investigating financial crises and applying different test methods are highly heterogeneous, and do not provide a clear and synthesized picture of financial contagion. Thus, the application of additional methodological approaches that make it possible to systematically analyse and adequately summarise the consequences of previous financial crises is necessary when examining the phenomenon of financial contagion.

2.6. Findings for CEE countries

The literature investigating financial contagion in the case of transition economies is rather vague focusing mainly on only three CEE economies (Hungary, Poland and the Czech Republic). Wang and Moore (2008) investigate the co-movement between a set of three major CEE emerging markets (Poland, Hungary and the Czech Republic) and the aggregate eurozone market using the dynamic conditional correlation technique[12]. Between these two collectives, the authors find significant dynamic correlations and a higher level of linkages in the aftermath of the crises. The authors' findings include a revelation that the increase in stock market co-movements cannot be explained by the macroeconomic convergence process or by monetary convergence with the eurozone, so contagion may well have been a driving force.

Gelos and Sahay (2001) find that correlations in foreign exchange market pressures can be explained by direct trade links, but not by other measured fundamentals. They find no financial contagion spillovers from either the Czech Republic or Asia to CEE stock markets, but shocks to the Russian stock market Granger caused movements in the Czech, Hungarian and Polish stock markets.

Serwa (2005) uses an extension of the models presented by Forbes and Rigobon (2002) and Corsetti et al (2005) to investigate seven financial crises on a sample of selected CEE and Western European countries. His findings show that financial contagion infrequently or rarely occurred over the course of the investigated financial crises. Jokipii and Lucey (2006) investigate co-movements in the banking sector for Poland, Hungary and the Czech Republic over a period of approximately ten years. They find that financial contagion spreads from the Czech Republic to Hungary. Schotman and Zalewska (2006) analyze the impact of Asian and Russian crises on CEE stock markets and find that the Hungarian market was the most and the Czech market the least affected. Lucey and Voronkova (2008)

---

[12] The dynamic conditional correlation measures the contemporaneous conditional correlation between the two series.

examine contagion from Russia to Hungary, the Czech Republic and Poland during the Russian crisis and find contagion supporting evidence in the case of short-term links. In addition to the papers testing contagion, some others have investigated links between CEE and selected major markets. These papers include Scheicher (2001), Gilmore and McManus (2002), Voronkova (2004), Syriopoulos (2004 and 2007) and Syllignakis and Kouretas (2010) and typically some albeit modest links were found.

An important theoretical statement according to the susceptibility to financial contagion in CEE transition economies has been made by Weller and Morzuch (2000), who argue that during historic times as well as more recent times of global financial turmoil, default risk has been lower in CEE transition countries than in other developing economies. The authors posit an explanation that there is apparently less speculative financing and a reduced chance of asset market bubbles in CEE transition countries, and consequently, a diminished vulnerability to short-term capital flows. Given that default and maturity risks would generally be lower in CEE transition countries than in other emerging economies during past periods of global financial turmoil, it is suspected by Weller and Morzuch (2000) that interest rate risk and exchange rate risk are also less likely to materialize. Thus, they conclude, as long as no appreciable problems afflict the financial sector or the real sector in CEE transition countries, international investors tend to be less inclined to withdraw their funds from these markets. Of course one has to keep in mind that this reasoning is more than ten years old now, and given the shifty political and economic situation in CEE economies, it is also subject to change.

2.7. Studies investigating contagiousness in the US 2008 crisis

Next, studies investigating contagiousness in the US 2008 crisis will be examined. A separate section is dedicated to the US 2008 financial crisis as studies investigating this crisis were not available at the time the dissertation articles were written. Therefore, this section is completely new and is not covered in the publications listed in the list of papers and given in the attachments.

The very first papers investigating the contagiousness of the US 2008 crisis were already published as preliminary versions in 2008, and therefore, only took into account the beginning of the crisis when the crisis had not yet peaked. Idier (2011) and Fry et al (2010) use the Markov switching framework to investigate the US 2008 crisis[13], while Dungey et al (2010) construct a latent factor model based on that by Kodres and Pritsker (2002) that takes into account several crises over a ten-year period.

---

[13] Fry et al (2010) also investigate the Hong Kong 1997 crisis, while Idier (2011) examines altogether seven crisis episodes.

All these authors find evidence of financial contagion during the US 2008 crisis.

Longstaff (2010) investigates the pricing of the subprime asset-packed collateralized debt obligations and their contagion effects on other markets. Using a VAR framework, the author finds clear evidence of shift-contagion. The relevance of alternative propagation channels from the crisis are also investigated in the study. The findings show that contagion spread mainly via liquidity and financing channels, but not via the correlated information channel.

Horta et al (2010) use copula theory, which has become popular in recent years, to investigate contagion from US to European stock markets in the NYSE Euronext group. Their time frame also ends in the middle of the crisis (April 2008), and the starting point of the crisis is chosen as 1 August 2007. Their findings show that co-movements between analysed stock markets have become more pronounced after the bursting of the mortgage bubble, which confirms the shift-contagion hypothesis. Additionally, not only did the strength of the links between markets become stronger during the crisis, but also their nature was significantly changed and the connections with the US market became more heterogeneous. One more interesting finding reveals that the crisis affected all countries in the sample with similar strength.

Chiang and Wang (2011) study how the stock markets in G7 countries were influenced by the subprime mortgage crisis that began in 2007. They investigate volatility contagion instead of contagion in returns by using a time-varying logarithmic conditional autoregressive range model with a lognormal distribution and find that volatility contagion did occur from the US to the French, UK, Italian and Japanese markets during the subprime mortgage crisis period.

Aloui et al (2011) employ a multivariate copula approach to investigate extreme co-movement between the US and four emerging markets, namely Brazil, Russia, India and China. They find evidence of extreme co-movement for all market pairs in a bearish market, but the same applies for bullish markets as well, so no strong evidence of shift-contagion was found. Interestingly, they did find that dependency from the US is stronger for commodity-price dependent markets (Brazil and Russia) than for finished-product export-oriented markets (India and China).

Xue et al (2012) investigate the contagiousness of the US 2008 crisis for Asian markets. Their findings suggest that financial contagion might not play a crucial role in transmitting the crisis from the US to Asia. This seemingly surprising finding comes, in their opinion, from the relatively conservative banking philosophy in Asian countries. The losses in banks in developed Asia-Pacific regions were relatively small compared to European countries such as the UK or Germany, because Asian banks were less aggressive in their investments. The authors suggest that the US crisis propagated to Asia via trade channels.

Similar findings appear in the study by Burdekin and Siklos (2012). Their dynamic conditional correlations based methodology suggests decreasing co-movement between the US and Asia-Pacific markets and rising co-movement among all Asia-Pacific markets over time, accelerating after the onset of the global financial crisis in 2007.

Grammatikos and Vermeulen (2012) use daily data on stock market indexes for the US and 15 euro area countries to test for the presence of the transmission of the 2007–2010 financial and sovereign debt crises. They consider both a financials sector index and a non-financials market index (i.e. total market index excluding financials) and find strong evidence of crisis transmission from US non-financials to European non-financials, whereas the increase in the dependence of European financials on US financials is rather limited. Results also show that following the collapse of Lehman Brothers, financials become much more dependent on changes in Greek CDS[14] spreads compared to the pre-Lehman sub-period. However, the increase is modest for non-financials.

Didier et al (2012) examined the relative importance of three transmission channels, namely trade links, financial links and demonstration effects, in determining co-movement between US stock market returns and local stock market returns across 83 countries during the US 2008 crisis. Their findings showed that the main factors driving co-movement were financial, which, of course, was not a big surprise given the nature of the crisis and the fact that the focus was on financial markets. The authors also found evidence of demonstration effects in the first stage of the crisis, when countries with vulnerable banking and corporate sectors exhibited a higher co-movement with the US stock market. Despite a collapse in trade across countries, evidence for trade linkages as the driving factor for co-movement with the US across countries was not found. One additional interesting finding was that it showed that financial openness makes countries significantly more vulnerable to the propagation of crises.

Syllignakis and Kouretas (2010) analyse three crisis episodes: the Asian crisis in 1997, the Russian default in 1998 and recent financial crisis that took off in the US in 2007 and became global in 2008. Therefore, this paper is one of the very few that put together the US 2008 crisis and CEE economies as destination countries in financial contagion analysis. The authors use the framework of the multivariate dynamic conditional correlation GARCH model and find substantial evidence of the existence of contagion effects due to herding behaviour during the period of 2007–2009, and in particular in the second half of 2008. The authors suggest that herding behaviour may be attributed to the increased participation of foreign investors in the CEE stock markets, as well as to the increased

[14] Credit Default Swap.

financial liberalization, particularly after the accession of CEE countries to the European Union in 2004. Additionally, their rolling regression analysis of the conditional correlations with the conditional volatility provided further evidence of the presence of contagion effects around the peak of the financial crisis in October 2008. Other financial crisis episodes investigated were not found to be contagious.

Summing up the findings of the sub-chapter one might conclude that most of the studies analysing the US 2008 crisis have found the crisis to be contagious with the only exception being the propagation of the crisis to the Pacific-Asian economies, which was not contagious. As the testing methods used are quite different, the finding can be considered rather robust. However, there are still some contradictions with some papers claiming that the crisis affected all countries with a similar strength, while others propose that Asia-Pacific countries were significantly better protected compared to European countries.

2.8. Summary of qualitative analysis

So far qualitative literature reviews in the field of financial contagion (e.g. Dornbusch et al 2000a, Cheung et al 2009, Pericoli and Sbracia 2003, and others) have been clearly biased towards the methodology used instead of the results obtained. Of course, it is the main findings of the individual studies that are brought out in these overviews, but practically no effort has been made to summarise the findings of different studies with the only exception being the conclusion that earlier works that used correlation coefficients based tests and did not adjust for the presence of heteroskedasticity almost unanimously found evidence of financial contagion. Given the multidimensionality of the research problem, this kind of approach is understandable, as it is not clear whether the findings from different analyses are comparable – quite different aspects may be investigated under the single heading *financial contagion*. Therefore, the following attempt to summarise the empirical findings by simple counting is actually something that has not been done previously.

Appendices 1–4 summarise the empirical results in the field of financial contagion presenting information about the analysis methodology, data, markets observed as well as the results concerning evidence of contagion (Yes, No, Mixed). As it can be seen from the tables in Appendices 1–4 and from the preceding literature review, the results obtained in studies of financial contagion are highly heterogeneous. One should keep in mind that in many cases the chosen result in favour of *Yes*, *No* or *Mixed* in the Appendices is not clear-cut. For example, in correlation coefficients based tests, there are mostly different results in the studies – some correlations have increased significantly during crises, some have not changed much and some have even decreased. Also, note that not all the papers presented in this overview actually test for the presence of financial contagion. So in some cases the results presented in the fourth column of the table (whether evidence for contagion has been found or not) may be somewhat disputable (see also different definitions of financial contagion). So simply summing up the results for a single *Yes* or *No* conclusion may not be the perfect way to conclude contagion analysis. The following briefly summarises the main results from four previously defined groups of studies, which are separated according to financial contagion testing methodologies.

Appendix 1 summarises the results obtained by studies using correlation coefficients based methodologies. Clearly, results supporting the contagion hypothesis dominate here being twice as frequent as the no-contagion result. However, the *Yes* results are undermined by later papers because the testing methodologies applied are questionable. As pointed out earlier, it has been suggested that not adjusting for the presence of heteroskedasticity may affect the results and the findings tend to be biased towards the existence of contagion. When papers with heteroskedasticity adjusted post-crises correlations are taken into account, *Yes* and *No* results are found to be quite balanced.

Moving on to the Appendix 2, and papers using conditional probability based tests, it is clear that results supporting the contagion hypothesis dominate. From 11 studies, seven have found clear evidence of contagion and three more have found support for the contagion hypothesis. Still, one has to keep in mind that these papers do not investigate the most restrictive definition of financial contagion (shift-contagion), which makes finding supporting evidence more likely.

Appendix 3 summarises the results from studies that investigate volatility changes to test for contagion. Again the majority of the studies using this methodology have found evidence of contagion with only a few studies resulting in the opposite or mixed results. But, of course, this may be attributable to the fact that these studies usually only test for the two broader definitions of financial contagion and most of them do not even control for fundamentals.

Appendix 4 summarises the results from studies that use other methodologies than those presented in Appendices 1–3. From these studies the Markov switching framework has been used the most. Both results supporting and contradicting the contagion hypothesis have been found using this methodology. From studies using other methodologies both results have also been found many times with slightly stronger support for the existence of contagion.

It is beyond the aim of this study to estimate the quality of each model or methodology, so no attempt is made in the thesis to prefer one or another and a neutral view is taken (with the exception of the unadjusted correlation coefficients based method, which has been proven to be inferior). As pointed out earlier, there are so many problematic aspects in financial contagion analysis that no methodology so far has been able to take into account all of them without making some restricting assumptions. Improvements in previous models will probably continue and it is hard to imagine when a model that everybody accepts as correct will emerge. The author's suggestion in this respect is rather to put more emphasis on finding singular numerical values that are interpretable and comparable across relevant studies (and therefore can be aggregated), than trying to find a statistical significance measure of a certain parameter of contagion. The author strongly believes that a much better picture of financial contagion can be achieved if all the authors of the individual studies work towards increasing the volume of input for future meta-analyses.

There are so many dimensions in financial contagion studies that drawing definitive conclusions based on a qualitative literature review is probably too much to ask. If we forget for a moment all these heterogeneities, it can be concluded that results supporting the financial contagion hypothesis are clearly dominant. However, a lot of times the supporting findings have been found by studies not adjusting for the presence of heteroskedasticity. If one wants to specify the definition of contagion clearly separating it from interdependence and to take into account heteroskedasticity problems, a completely different picture emerges and the debate over the existence of financial contagion is pretty much open.

3. DATA AND METHODOLOGY FOR ANALYSING FINANCIAL CONTAGION

3.1. The main steps in implementing a meta-analysis and the data sources

As seen from the previous chapter despite of a lot of investigation the financial contagion puzzle is pretty much unsolved. It is still not clear whether crises spread from one country to others because of fundamental links between countries or is there also something that can be considered financial contagion, behind these transmissions. As qualitative analysis was not able to provide answers turning attention to the quantitative approach seems like logical continuation. This is done in the thesis by using the approach of meta-analysis.

Given the multiple dimensions of the financial contagion research problem it is surprising that no meta-analysis has been conducted so far on the subject. It is well known in behavioural sciences that this kind of research problems cannot usually be solved satisfactorily by qualitative literature review, even more so by individual studies. Therefore, the thesis has taken the pioneering role here.

De Dominicis et al (2006) have given as the purpose of meta-analysis to review and quantitatively summarise the literature using statistical approach. This very general aim is in the heart of every meta-analysis but there are different approaches and methodologies used under that label and the unique definition of meta-analysis is still not worked out.

The term meta-analysis was first coined by Gene Glass in 1976, although some procedures later known as meta-analytic (for example the concept of effect size) were already present in Karl Pearson's study in 1904. By Glass's definition meta-analysis "...refers to the statistical analysis of a large collection of results from individual studies for the purpose of integrating the findings. It connotes a rigorous alternative to the casual, narrative discussions of research studies which typify our attempt to make sense of the rapidly expanding research literature." (Glass 1976: 3). By Schultze (2004) meta-analysis is a method for systematic literature reviews on a certain substantive question of interest, more specifically on his words: „meta-analysis is a systematic process of quantitatively combining empirical reports to arrive at a summary and an evaluation of a research findings".

Basu (2003: 3) defines meta-analysis as „synthesis of available literature about a topic. Ideally, synthesis of randomized trials to arrive at a single summary estimate is used". By James Neill's (2006) version meta-analysis is a statistical technique for amalgamating, summarising, and reviewing previous quantitative research. The simplest definition the author of the dissertation has seen was given by Hunter and Schmidt (1990) who defined meta-analysis as analysis of analyses.

To summarise various definitions, it follows that meta-analysis is a research method that amalgamates, quantitatively synthesizes and summarises data from previous empirical analyses on a subject. To achieve these tasks the meta-analytic procedure can be shortly summarised as follows. Every meta-analysis uses an established singular measure that is common to all studies to be analysed. This measure is called the 'effect size' – an important concept in all meta-analyses. Synthesizing and summarising is carried out by aggregating all individual effects and after the characteristics of the study have been considered, the resulting overall outcomes can be presented as the 'meta-effect size'.

Many advantages that a meta-analysis has over a traditional literature review have been pointed out, from which some of the most important are:

- Quantitative estimation and statistical testing of overall effect sizes
- Generalization to the population of the studies
- Finding moderator variables to explain heterogeneity in the distribution.

The main difference between a meta-analysis and a traditional literature review is that a meta-analysis uses summary statistics from individual studies as data points. By accumulating results across studies, it is possible to obtain a more accurate representation of the population relationship than any of the individual studies can provide.

The main disadvantage of a meta-analysis is the fact that the number of studies included in the analysis is mostly smaller than in a qualitative analysis because not all studies provide numerical results that are comparable across studies. This is also the case in the present analysis, where the meta-analysis is based on a much smaller number of studies than the qualitative analysis of previous empirical findings presented in the previous chapter. However, this is not a problem inherent in meta-analytic tools and techniques, but rather to do with individual studies that do not provide findings that are useful as inputs in a meta-analysis.

In order to implement the meta-analysis here, six steps were put in place in the thesis. The first step was to calculate relevant individual effect sizes and control for their independence. The next was to calculate weights for all individual effect sizes. In the third step, the meta-effect sizes were computed based on previously calculated effect size weights. The confidence intervals for the meta-effect sizes were then determined along with the statistical significance of the meta-effect sizes. Penultimately, homogeneity was tested before finally concluding and interpreting the results.

Before the first of these steps, data from all of the studies to be analysed must be collected. When searching for appropriate studies to use in the meta-analysis, the Thomson Reuters (formerly ISI) Web of Knowledge database and the Contagion of Financial Crisis Website from the World Bank Group were used. From the Thomson Reuters Web of Knowledge database, studies corresponding to the keywords *financial contagion* were used. The Contagion of Financial Crisis Website also included some working papers that had not yet been published, but none of these were included in the meta-analysis so the meta-sample was only based on publications and not working papers. The potential publication bias that may occur if only published articles are included in the meta-analysis will be discussed in more detail later in the thesis.

For the purposes of the meta-analysis, financial contagion is defined in the dissertation as an increase in cross-country asset[15] price correlations during a crisis relative to asset price correlations during non-crisis times. This is the most common definition of financial contagion in empirical analyses in the 21st century, also known as shift-contagion as introduced by Forbes and Rigobon (2001 and 2002) and according to which financial contagion is interpreted as the change in transmission mechanisms that takes place during a period of turmoil (see definition 3 in the first chapter). As noted in chapter one, this definition excludes scenarios characterized by a constant high degree of co-movement, where markets are instead deemed as interdependent. This very restrictive definition is adopted not only for the meta-analysis but for the quantitative analysis in this dissertation. In addition to its straightforward testing framework, the chosen definition is preferred because its ability to shed light on the following three main issues: international diversification, evaluation of the role and potential effectiveness of international institutions and bail-out funds and

---

[15] Typically, the assets used are stocks, bonds, interest rates and exchange rates.

51

propagation mechanisms (Forbes and Rigobon 2001, Billio and Caporin 2010).

Given the chosen definition, the only studies included in the analysis are those that report on the asset price correlations between countries for both pre-crisis and post-crisis periods (or the difference between them). These restrictions reduce the data set for the meta-analysis to 716 data points, of which 394 are independent (independent means that these data points come from different sources or differ in some important characteristics like the crisis under observation, destination country or financial market). The data points have been drawn from 28 constructs and 17 studies (by 12 authors). In the event that post-crisis correlations are reported for both the long and short-term period, independency problems are avoided by opting to include only the short-term data, although the problem of independence is discussed in greater detail later on in the thesis. As can be seen, the number of studies included in the analysis is much smaller than was the case in the empirical literature review, where the respective number was more than 75. The fact that the meta-analysis is based on a much smaller number of studies than the qualitative literature review, of course, makes it disputable whether the results obtained using the meta-analysis can be more reliable, but one has to keep in mind that all data points in the meta-sample are standardized so they correspond to the same definition and testing methodology of financial contagion. Thus, the meta-analysis makes it possible to deal with the multidimensionality of a research task, which caused problems in the qualitative literature review. In addition, as the sample size in the meta-analysis is not the number of studies but the number of individual effect sizes, then the sample size is actually much larger than in a traditional literature review (more than 700 instead of more than 70). Of course, some information is lost as the findings from the studies that do not use correlation coefficients cannot be used; therefore, the focus of the meta-analysis is much narrower than that of the qualitative empirical literature review, being related only with the most restrictive definition of contagion (shift-contagion). One additional positive aspect of the current meta-analysis is that being aware of this kind of analysis in the field of financial contagion, and its potential for being implemented again in the future, may influence future authors so they report quantitative values that can be used as comparable individual effect sizes in future meta-analyses.

To conduct the first step, appropriate individual effect sizes have to be found. The effect size statistic produces a statistical standardization of the study findings so that the resulting numerical values are interpretable in a consistent fashion across all the variables and measures involved (Lipsey and Wilson 2001). An effect size statistic must be defined so that it is capable of representing the quantitative findings of the studies in a standardized way that affords meaningful numerical comparison between studies. The "correct" individual effect sizes for the research problem of financial contagion had not previously been worked out in the meta-analysis literature, so the author had to make some choices. It is proposed in the thesis to use the difference between pre- and post-crisis correlations of asset prices as an effect size in any given study or construct[16]. If individual effect sizes are defined as such the abovementioned requirements are achieved. Mathematically, the individual effect sizes used in the analysis are computed as:

$$ES_i = r_{post_i} - r_{pre_i} \tag{1}$$

where ES_i is the individual effect size for study (construct) i and r_{pre_i} and r_{post_i} are pre- and post-crisis correlations respectively for study (construct) i.

After establishing individual effect sizes they have to be aggregated into one meta-effect size. Here the traditional meta-analysis approach is used assuming that the best estimate for the population effect size is the weighted average of the individual effect sizes.

The weights have to be determined for every individual effect size so that an overall value could be found. Hedges (1982) (Hedges and Olkin 1985) has demonstrated, that the optimal weights are based on the standard error of the effect size. For Hedges (1982), as a larger standard error corresponds to a less precise effect size value, the actual respective weights of the individual effect sizes should be computed as the inverse of the squared standard error value, known in the meta-analysis lexicon as the inverse variance weight. This same approach is used in the present thesis.

Computing weights depends on which type of individual effect sizes we are dealing with. There are no rules given in the literature for which is the

---

[16] It can not be right to use the results of statistical significance testing as individual effect sizes. It is easy to show that the same quantitative finding (for example value of correlation coefficient) can be statistically significant in one study and insignificant in another.

correct type of effect sizes if the individual effect sizes that are going to be summarised are changes in correlation coefficients over time. More precisely, it is not intuitively clear whether these differences should be dealt with as pre-post contrasts or associations between variables. On the one hand, even if one is not interested in the correlation coefficients themselves but their changes over two points in time, it is not quite clear why these two approaches should differ so much (in terms of the properties of the effect sizes) that one could not use the same computational procedures. As such, it could be concluded that these individual effect sizes should be taken to signify correlations. On the other hand, there are data points for both before and after crises and we are interested in the difference between them – the change to be precise. The situation is analogous to that when the treatment effect is analysed (the crisis starting point can be thought of as a treatment). So, taking these individual effect sizes as pre-post contrasts does not seem to be a bad choice either. The decision made in the thesis is to use both approaches in parallel. As such, when individual effect sizes are treated as mean differences, this is referred to as Approach 1 in the following analysis, and when treating individual effect sizes as correlations it is referred to as Approach 2.

Computing weights start with calculating standard errors for individual effect sizes. For both the mean differences (gains) and the correlation coefficients as individual effect sizes that are used in the present analysis, the standard error formulations have been worked out and are available[17]. Using Approach 2 (taking effect sizes as correlations), in order to be able to find the weights for individual effect sizes, the individual effect sizes need to be altered a little to avoid problems in standard error formulations (such problems are discussed in more depth by Rosenthal 1994). A widely accepted modification method to transform the correlations is Fischer's Z_r-transformation (see Hedges and Olkin 1985):

$$ES_{Z_r} = 0.5\ln\left(\frac{1+r}{1-r}\right) \qquad (2)$$

where r is the correlation coefficient. In the present analysis the difference between post- and pre-crisis correlations is in the placement of r. So in

---

[17] The exact procedures for computing standard errors and weights for individual effect sizes are not discussed in the dissertation. One can see detailed information on the subject for example from Rosenthal (1994) or Hedges and Olkin (1985).

Approach 2, formula (2) is used instead of formula (1). Once the results are obtained (the meta-effect sizes are found), in order to interpret them, the Fischer Z-transformed meta-effect sizes are transformed back into standard correlation form by employing the inverse of the Z_r-transformation (Hedges and Olkin 1985):

$$r = \frac{e^{2ES_{Z_r}} - 1}{e^{2ES_{Z_r}} + 1}$$ (3)

After Fischer's z-transformation, the standard error formula for (correlation based (Approach 2)) the effect size mean is as follows:

$$SE_{Z_r} = \frac{1}{\sqrt{n-3}}$$ (4)

and inverse variance weights are therefore:

$$w_{z_r} = n - 3$$ (5)

where n in both equations is the sample size of the analysis from which correlation coefficients are obtained.

However, some of the data that is necessary to calculate weights when treating individual effect sizes as treatment effects (Approach 1) is not available. More specifically, information on the correlations between pre-treatment and post-treatment (pre-crisis and post-crisis in this case) asset prices in individual studies is missing, and this is needed for calculating the weights. These data problems make it impossible to calculate inverse variance weights in the standard manner. Therefore, when computing meta-effect size, sample size is designated as the proxy for weight instead.

Now, when suitable weights have been found, the overall meta-effect size can be calculated using the following formula:

$$\overline{ES} = \frac{\sum ES_i w_i}{\sum w_i}$$ (6)

where ES_i is the i-th individual effect size and w_i is the weight (inverse variance weight in the case of Approach 2 and sample size in the case of Approach 1) of the i-th effect size.

In the next step, the homogeneity of the effect size distribution is examined. This means investigating whether all of the effect sizes that are averaged into a mean value (meta-effect size) estimate the same population effect or not (see Hedges 1983, Rosenthal and Rubin 1982). If the distribution is homogeneous, the dispersion of the effect sizes around their mean is no greater than the dispersion expected from the sampling error alone[18].

Homogeneity testing is based on the Q-statistic[19], which is distributed as a chi-square with $k - 1$ degrees of freedom, where k is the number of individual effect sizes (Hedges and Olkin 1985). The formula for the Q-statistic is:

$$Q = \sum \left[w_i \left(ES_i - \overline{ES} \right)^2 \right] \tag{7}$$

where ES_i is the individual effect size for $i = 1$ to k (the number of individual effect sizes);

$\overline{ES}$ is the meta-effect size over the k individual effect sizes;

and w_i is the weight for ES_i.

If Q exceeds the critical value for a chi-square with $k - 1$ degrees of freedom, then the null hypothesis of homogeneity is rejected. A statistically significant Q therefore indicates a heterogeneous distribution and means that there are differences among the effect sizes that have some source other than a subject-level sampling error. That source is typically some study characteristic, which in the case of the present thesis may for example be the crisis under investigation, the destination country, the formula that is used for calculating post-crisis correlations or some other characteristic (see previous chapter for potential factors that may influence the results of contagion tests).

Before being able to run a meta-analysis, some independency concerns have to be dealt with. There are cases for multiple individual effect sizes within the same studies. This conflicts with the assumption of independence and overestimates the weights of studies with multiple effect

---

[18] the sampling error is associated with the subject samples upon which the individual effect sizes are based

[19] Alternative approach to homogeneity testing, so called 75% rule, is given by Hunter and Schmidt (1990). They partition the observed effect size variability into two components - the portion attributable to subject-level sampling error and the portion attributable to other between-study differences. According to their rule of thumb, the distribution is homogeneous if sampling error accounts for 75% or more of the observed variability.

sizes. The traditional way to deal with the situation is to choose only one effect size per study or per construct. However, this approach does not include some of the information contained in the primary studies, and it is not wished to lose any of the information available on different correlation measurement methodologies as possible moderators. It is well known that correlation coefficients adjusted for heteroscedasticity are lower than unadjusted coefficients, and therefore, the contagion seems to be more likely to occur in cases where there are unadjusted correlation coefficients (see chapter 2). Therefore, rather than dropping some of the data points, the weights of studies with multiple effect sizes per construct are diminished by dividing the sample size by the number of effect sizes per construct (For a discussion of multiple measurements within studies see also Rosenthal 1994).

3.2. Data and methodology for investigating contagiousness in the US 2008 crisis

3.2.1. Correlation coefficients based method

To investigate contagiousness in the US 2008 crisis, two alternative methodologies were used – one that is based on the differences between the post- and pre-crisis correlation coefficients of stock returns between countries and the ARCH-GARCH framework that studies mean and volatility spillovers. These two have been the most popular testing methodologies of financial contagion and as there are no alternatives that are generally agreed to be superior, these two were chosen.

Employing a correlation coefficients based analysis, the stock indexes of US, Estonian, Latvian and Lithuanian stock markets are analysed. The data set consists of daily returns on the closing prices of the S&P 500 (US), OMXT (Estonia), OMXR (Latvia) and OMXV (Lithuania) stock indexes from 3 March 2008 until 9 March 2009, and the bankruptcy of Lehman Brothers on 15 September 2008 is chosen as the starting point of the crisis. According to this approach, the period from 3 March 2008 to 15 September 2008 will be considered as a tranquil period and the period from 16 September 2008 to 9 March 2009 as a crisis period. Moving average two-day logarithmic returns[20] are used to control for the fact that the stock

---

[20] The moving average for period *i* is calculated as the arithmetic mean of the values for periods *i* and *i-1*.

markets in the US and the Baltic countries are not open during the same hours (for how to avoid the problem of non-synchronous trading periods for different markets, see Lin, Engle and Ito 1994).

The use of stock indexes is primarily pragmatic. Stock market index data can be accessed relatively easily compared to other variables that are sometimes used in financial contagion analyses (interest rates, bonds or exchange rates to name a few). Also, the stock market data is available on a daily basis, which decreases the probability of not having a reasonably large number of observations for the analysis. Also, equity holdings have become an increasingly significant source of wealth for people in many parts of the world, which means that changes in asset values could directly affect consumption levels and other real variables (Didier et al (2012)). The point selected as the start of a crisis is quite clear; commonly crises have been defined using the date of some relevant exogenous shock, and there is also higher variance in stock returns (which is sometimes used for determining a crisis period) after the Lehman Brothers bankruptcy,[21] but the chosen starting point of the tranquil period and the ending point of the crisis period need some further explanation. The ninth of March 2009 is chosen as the ending date for the crisis period because it was the local minimum for the S&P500 during the crisis. This kind of logic was previously used by Mishkin and White (2003) and Serwa (2005). The tranquil period cannot be considered to stretch for too long because structural breaks are not wanted during that time. There was quite a sharp fall in the S&P500 index at the end of February 2008, which stopped at the beginning of March. So, 3 March as the first trading day in March (1 and 2 March being the weekend) is taken as the starting date for the tranquil period. This approach also makes it possible to have a tranquil and crisis period with a relatively similar length. As shown by Dungey and Zhumabekova (2001), if the crisis period is a lot shorter than the tranquil period then a statistical significance test has very little power.

As said in the first chapter of the thesis, the correlation coefficients based method is most widely used in the field of financial contagion. One of the main reasons for the popularity of the method is relative simplicity, but it

---

[21] The author is well aware of the fact that the signs of the subprime crisis were evident already in 2007. Still, given the reasons explained in the text, 15 September 2008 as the starting point of the crisis seems more appropriate. Idier (2011) also did not choose the starting point in 2007, as the long-term volatility component did not jump to a high value at the time (although he chose 21 January 2008 not the bankruptcy of the Lehman Brothers).

also has other positive features. As noted by Billio and Pellizon (2003) and Forbes and Rigobon (2002), the correlation based analysis is more suitable than other approaches for shedding light on the issues of international diversification, the role of international institutions and bail-out funds, as well as propagation mechanisms.

This framework is used to test the hypothesis of whether the 2008 financial crisis spilled over contagiously from the US to Estonia, Latvia and Lithuania. The logic of the following tests is based on the assumption that contagion occurs when, if there is a crisis in the US, correlation is stronger because of some structural change in the international economy affecting the links across markets. Relying on this hypothesis and data sample, contagion is considered here as a significant increase in the correlation coefficient in stock returns between the country of the origin of the crisis (the US) and the country of destination (Estonia, Latvia or Lithuania) during the crisis compared to the non-crisis period.

As in many earlier papers (for example Forbes and Rigobon 2002), the thesis considers a model where stock returns on the country of the origin of the crisis is independent variable and influences returns on the country of destination. More specifically, the following linear model is used (see Forbes and Rigobon 2002 and Serwa and Bohl 2005):

$$y_t = \alpha + \beta x_t + u_t^y \tag{8}$$

$$x_t = u_t^x \tag{9},$$

where x_t are stock returns in the crisis market (US) that are exogenous and influence returns on the calm market y_t (Estonia, Latvia or Lithuania); and u_t^x and u_t^y are idiosyncratic shocks to the respective stock markets. *Alpha* and *beta* are model parameters.

The basic logic of the model is that the change in the relationship between x and y at some point is measured by a change in β. If the change in β is statistically significant, this is considered evidence of contagion.

It is assumed that the volatility of stock returns on the crisis market changes during crisis times, but the model parameters and the volatility of idiosyncratic shocks in the destination market remain constant. As in the move between a non-crisis and a crisis period, the volatility of the error term usually changes, violating the assumption of homoscedasticity, a respecification of the testing procedure is used and a statistically significant change in the correlation coefficient between the two periods is tested. The correlation coefficient is estimated in both tranquil and crisis times and then controlled for a significant increase in the correlation coefficient after the crisis hits.

The simple correlation coefficient is given by the equation (Chiang et al 2007)

$$\rho = Corr(x, y) = \frac{Cov(x, y)}{\sqrt{Var(x)Var(y)}} = \frac{\beta Var(x)}{\sqrt{[\beta^2 Var(x) + Var(u_y)]Var(x)}} = \left[1 + \frac{Var(u_y)}{\beta^2 Var(x)}\right]^{-\frac{1}{2}}$$

$$(10)$$

To obtain separate correlation coefficients for periods of calm and turmoil, the values of the respective period are used in the formula (10) above.

The author of the thesis agrees with Forbes and Rigobon (2002), who show that correlation is conditional on the volatility of stock returns in the crisis market, and therefore, the correlation between stock returns in the crisis and non-crisis country may rise even when contagion does not occur. Thus, it is not fully correct to test for contagion using simple correlations, as they do not take into account the increased volatility during crises. Therefore, it is considered that the testing approach with a heteroskedasticity adjustment in post-crisis correlations seems to be more reliable.

Thus, by estimating correlation coefficients, adjustments for heteroscedasticity are also made using the Forbes and Rigobon (2002) approach, who propose an adjustment so that the correlation coefficient does not depend on the volatility of returns in the crisis market:

$$\rho^* = \frac{\rho^{crisis}}{\sqrt{1 + \delta\left[1 - \left(\rho^{crisis}\right)^2\right]}}$$

$$(11),$$

where ρ^{crisis} is the simple correlation coefficient (calculated using formula 10) between the crisis and the non-crisis market observed during the crisis period.

The parameter δ represents the relationship between the variances of stock returns from the crisis country during the turmoil period, $Var^{crisis}(y_t)$ and during the calm period, $Var^{non-crisis}(y_t)$:

$$\delta = \frac{Var^{crisis}(y_t)}{Var^{non-crisis}(y_t)} - 1 \tag{12}.$$

One has to keep in mind the criticisms that Bartram and Wang (2005) and Corsetti et al (2005) have made of the Forbes and Rigobon methodology, claiming that their adjustments make results rely heavily on the particular assumptions about the stochastic process of idiosyncratic shocks, so that their adjustment may cause the correlation test to be severely biased towards the null hypothesis of no contagion. So the true values probably exist somewhere between unadjusted and adjusted correlations.

The analysis starts by estimating simple correlations with the adjustments proposed by Forbes and Rigobon (2002) subsequently implemented. The correlation coefficients (both not adjusted and adjusted) are transformed using a Fisher transformation[22], so that they are approximately normally distributed. This transformation is necessary in order to have relevant results from controlling the hypotheses (Dungey and Zhumabekova 2001, Jokipii and Lucey 2006, Lee *et al.* 2007). Finally, statistically significant difference between pre- and post-crisis correlations is tested using the following test suggested by Morrisson (1983):

$$T = \frac{0.5\ln(\frac{1+\rho^{non-crisis}}{1-\rho^{non-crisis}}) - 0.5\ln(\frac{1+\rho^{crisis}}{1-\rho^{crisis}})}{\sqrt{[1/(N^{non-crisis}-3)+1/(N^{crisis}-3)]}} \tag{13}$$

where $N^{non-crisis}$ and N^{crisis} are sample sizes in tranquil and crisis period respectively.

3.2.2. The ARCH-GARCH framework

Although easy to use and providing some other advantages, the correlation coefficients based methods also have several drawbacks. For example, as demonstrated by Baur (2003), contagion tests based on correlation coefficients can be misleading when the correlations are time-varying and volatility is contagious *per se*.

---

[22] Fischer transformation uses the following formula $r_z = 0.5\ln\left(\frac{1+r}{1-r}\right)$, where r is the correlation coefficient.

In order to check for the robustness of the empirical results, the thesis also implements the autoregressive conditionally heteroscedastic (ARCH) and generalized ARCH (GARCH) framework of statistical models to explore for possible contagion from the US stock market (S&P 500) to the Baltic stock markets. A similar framework to investigate contagion in emerging markets is used for example by Hamao et al (1990) and Edwards and Susmel (2001 and 2003).

This framework is used to investigate the two main hypotheses. Firstly, whether price changes on the US stock market influence prices in the Baltic stock markets, and secondly, whether changes in price volatility on the US stock market are related to changes in price volatility on the Baltic stock markets. In order to test these hypotheses, daily logarithmic stock returns are examined in the US and Baltic stock markets from 3 March 2008 to 9 March 2009. For the US stock market the Standard & Poors Composite Index is used, for Estonia OMXT, for Latvia OMXR and for Lithuania OMXV. The sample period used in the thesis includes September 2008, when one of the most severe stock market crashes in history took place. To investigate the contagion effect, the models are estimated over two sub-periods, before and after the Lehman Brothers bankruptcy on 15 September 2008.

The thesis uses many extensions of the basic ARCH model developed by Engle (1982) and generalized to the GARCH model by Bollerslev (1986). Firstly, it makes it possible for the conditional means to be a function of the conditional variance, which was first proposed by Engle, Lilien and Robins (1987). This extension gives the GARCH(1,1)-M model. According to French et al (1987), a member of the ARCH family, GARCH-M, is a good representation of the daily stock-return behaviour in the US because of its successful capture of the effects of time-varying volatility on an expected return of stock.

Secondly, the extension first given by French, Schwert and Stambaugh (1987) is used; they adjusted the conditional means return for a first-order moving average. This is done primarily because of the non-synchronous trading in the US and Baltic stock markets as this causes problems in the ARCH family of models (see for example Cohen et al 1980).

Third, a dummy variable is included in the model that helps to capture the fact that there are no price movements during weekends. The weekend influence that gives Mondays a somewhat special status is well known in the literature (see French 1980, Gibbons and Hess 1981 and others) and is called the Monday effect.

And finally, stock returns in the crisis market are included as an explanatory variable in the non-crisis market stock-return equation.

Thus, the thesis implements the MA (1) - GARCH (1, 1) - M model given by the formula:

$$X_t = \alpha + \beta b_t + \gamma D_t + \delta Y_t + \varepsilon u_{t-1} + u_t \tag{14}$$

$$b_t = a + b b_{t-1} + c u_{t-1}^2 + d D_t + f Z_t \tag{15},$$

where

X_t – stock index return in non-crisis market (Estonia, Latvia or Lithuania) at time t;

b_t – conditional variance of X at time t;

D – dummy variable for Monday effect (D takes value of 1 on days following weekends and holidays and is 0 otherwise);

Y_t – stock index return in crisis market (US) at time t;

u_t and u_{t-1} – error terms at time t and $t-1$ respectively;

Z_t – squared residual derived from an MA(1)-GARCH(1,1)-M model applied to the returns of the US stock market.

As Z_t is not available, the following equation has to be estimated first

$$Y_t = \alpha + \beta b_t + \delta D_t + \phi u_{t-1} + u_t \tag{16}$$

$$b_t = a + b b_{t-1} + c u_{t-1}^2 + d D_t \tag{17}$$

and from there the necessary squared residual can be derived (u_t^2).

The empirical results obtained using the abovementioned methodology are presented in sub-chapter 4.2.

4. EMPIRICAL RESULTS

4.1. Findings from the meta-analysis

4.1.1. Overall findings

The methodology described in sub-chapter 3.1 is used for the meta-analysis. Employing formulas (1) – (6) from sub-chapter 3.1, the following respective estimates of the meta-effect size are derived: 0.053 if Approach 1 is used and 0.072 if Approach 2 is used (these values are given in Table 2). The corresponding standard errors are 0.005 in both cases and the associated 95% confidence interval values are well above zero. The results for both approaches indicate that, relative to tranquil periods, asset price correlations are on average observably, albeit moderately, higher during turbulent periods. The Q-statistic (recall formula (7)), however, clearly exceeds the critical value, indicating that the dispersion of the individual effect sizes around their mean is greater than expected from a sampling error alone, and therefore, each effect size does not estimate a common population mean.

Because of heterogeneous distribution (indicated by the Q-statistic), the analysis continues by seeking moderators to explain the variabilities in effect sizes. As mentioned above, the correlation coefficient calculating methodology is widely accepted as a significant explaining variable for financial contagion. The logic behind this is that when not adjusting for heteroskedasticity, the post-crisis correlations are higher, and therefore, finding evidence for contagion is more probable. To check whether the correlation coefficient measurement performs as a potential moderator, the sample will be divided into two subsamples, differentiating heteroskedasticity adjusted (A) post-crisis correlation coefficients from their unadjusted (U) counterparts. In the sample with unadjusted correlation coefficients, the weighted mean effect size is found to be 0.168 using Approach 1 and 0.208 in the case of Approach 2 (see Table 2). In the sample with heteroskedasticity adjusted correlation coefficients, the respective values are 0.030 for both approaches 1 and 2. The difference is more than clear, and it can be concluded that whether correlation coefficients are heteroskedasticity adjusted or not significantly affects the results of financial contagion analyses. By dividing the overall Q-statistic into the within and between groups components, it is found that the between group Q is highly significant, which also indicates that the differences in correlation measurement (heteroskedasticity adjusted or not) accounts for a significant variability in effect sizes.

However, the Q-statistic indicates that there is still some heterogeneity left in the distribution. Therefore, it is necessary to also control for other potential moderator variables. The focus of interest is, for example, whether different crises have been contagious to differing extents.

For the Thai 1997 crisis the treatment effects based (Approach 1) weighted mean effect size[23] is 0.132 and 0.173 if the effect sizes are treated as correlation coefficients (Approach 2). For the Hong Kong 1997 crisis the same values are 0.100 and 0.098; for the Mexican 1994 crisis 0.141 and 0.160; for the Russian 1998 crisis -0.001 and 0.006; and for the Brazilian 1999 crisis -0.016 and -0.014 respectively. From these numbers, it is apparent that the Mexican, Thai and the Hong Kong crises were on average contagious, while the Russian and Brazilian crises were not. From among the less investigated crises, the US 1987 and the US 2002 crises were contagious, while the opposite is true for the Argentinean 2001 crisis, the Turkish 2001 crisis and the Indian 2004 crisis – asset prices correlations decreased during these crises; pre-World War II crises on average were not contagious, as neither were the Czech 1997 crisis and the US 2001 crisis with some albeit insignificant increase in average asset prices correlations. However, one has to keep in mind that the results regarding the contagiousness of crises are based on the average of the sample and may depend on the chosen destination countries in the individual studies. The given crisis as a grouping variable accounts for the significant variability in effect sizes, but there is still some heterogeneity left within the groups.

Table 2. The results of a meta-analysis of previous empirical findings in the field of financial contagion (whole sample of the study)

Samp le	Sam ple size	ESs as treatment effects (Approach 1)			ESs as correlation coefficients (Approach 2)		
		Meta-ES	Stand ard error	Q-statist ic	Meta-ES	Stand ard error	Q-statist ic
All	716*	0.053	0.005	2782.	0.072	0.005	5568.
U	159	0.168	0.007	956.7	0.208	0.007	3432.
A	545	0.030	0.007	668.0	0.030	0.007	716.1
Tha	86	0.132	0.007	853.9	0.173	0.007	3367.

---

[23] In the thesis "weighted mean effect size" and "meta-effect size" are used as synonyms.

HK	154	0.100	0.009	295.6	0.098	0.009	323.0
Rus	46	-	0.027	48.8	0.006	0.027	52.5
Bra	33	-	0.039	17.33	-	0.039	15.4
Prewa	344	0.045	0.026	165.8	0.059	0.028	197.3
Mex	372	0.141	0.038	45.7	0.160	0.045	39.0
US	70	0.185	0.062	5.8	0.181	0.071	4.7
Ind	68	-	0.028	122.0	-	0.031	153.5
Tur	19	-	0.055	22.2	-	0.066	19.3
US	82	0.014	0.055	22.4	0.019	0.066	17.8
Arg	33	-	0.015	126.6	-	0.015	156.6
US	33	0.126	0.055	12.8	0.133	0.066	10.3
Cze	45	0.057	0.039	26.2*	0.058	0.041	26.3*
Emerg	344	0.054	0.006	2254.	0.078	0.006	5116.
Devel	372	0.052	0.009	527.6	0.051	0.008	555.8

* denotes statistically significant results (in 95% confidence interval).

** the meta-sample, numbering 716, exceeds the sum of 159 (U) and 544 (A), since 12 observations in sample 'All' could not be categorized by either U or A.

ES - effect size.

All - all observations (data points) from the sample with all countries.

U – cases with unadjusted (for heteroskedasticity) correlation coefficients.

A – cases with adjusted (for heteroskedasticity) correlation coefficients.

Tha – Thai crisis; HK – Hong Kong crisis; Rus – Russian crisis; Bra – Brazilian crisis; Mex – Mexican crisis; US – United States crisis; Ind – Indian crisis; Tur – Turkish crisis; Arg – Argentinean crisis; Cze – Czech crisis; Prewar – average of 6 pre-World War II crises (Argentinean crisis 1890, Baring crisis (UK) 1890, US banking crisis 1893, US stock market crash 1929, Sterling crisis (UK) 1931, devaluation of the US dollar (US) 1933).

Emerg – cases reflect 152 emerging (developing) countries, numbered 31 through 182 per the Human Development Index 2008.

Devel – cases reflect 30 developed countries, numbered 1 through 30 per the Human Development Index 2008.

Source: author's calculations.

Using only data where correlation coefficients are adjusted for the presence of heteroskedasticity (see Appendix 5) the results do not change much. The Mexican, Thai and the Hong Kong crises are still contagious, although the weighted mean effect sizes are somewhat smaller. Also, the Russian and Brazilian crises are not contagious with weighted mean effect sizes slightly negative. The only notable change relates to the US 1987 crisis, which is no longer contagious at the 95% confidence interval. However, with the weighted mean effect size clearly above zero (0.17) and only slightly below the unadjusted (U) case, the reason seems to be mainly due to the small sample size.

As another possible moderator variable, whether the level of development in the destination country influences how susceptible a country is to the propagation of a financial crisis is also investigated. This kind of differentiation is suggested by some authors; for example, by Hartmann et al (2001), who find only very weak evidence of contagion in a sample of G5 countries, and speculated that this may be different for emerging economies. The Human Development Index (HDI) 2008 values are used for dividing countries as more or less developed. The top 30 countries in the HDI list are referred to as developed and all other countries as developing (emerging). This produces quite comparable sample sizes for both groups with 372 and 344 respectively. For the sample of less developed countries, the weighted mean effect size is 0.054 according to Approach 1 (effect sizes as treatment effects) and 0.077 according to Approach 2 (effect sizes as correlations). For the sample of more developed countries the corresponding values are 0.052 and 0.051 respectively. So with Approach 1, there is no difference in the susceptibility to the spread of crises between developed and developing countries, while according to Approach 2, less developed countries are somewhat more susceptible to the carryover of financial crises. The variability analysis reveals that the level of the development of the destination country does not account for significant variability in effect sizes. From this it may be judged that herding behaviour seems to be the more likely transmission force for financial crises than real and stable linkages. This finding is in line with that of Serwa (2005), who found that CEE stock markets are no more vulnerable to contagion than Western European markets. On the other hand, the finding contradicts that of Dungey and Tambakis (2003), who argue that developing countries are more affected by contagion than developed countries. Additionally, Billio and Caporin (2010) believe that developing economies are more sensitive to shocks because of their underdeveloped financial markets and their large public deficits. This is confirmed by their empirical analysis, which similar to that of Lee et al (2007), indicates that contagion effects are more obvious in developing financial markets than those of developed ones.

Developed and developing (emerging) country groups are also compared separately for adjusted (A) and unadjusted (U) cases and under Approach 1 (individual effect sizes as treatment effects) and Approach 2 (individual effect sizes as correlations). The findings are displayed in Appendix 5. Using Approach 1 for the unadjusted (U) cases, the respective meta-effect sizes are 0.12 for developed countries and 0.19 for developing countries, which is a significant difference, as the confidence intervals of the two point estimates do not overlap. Under Approach 2 for the unadjusted (U) cases, the disparity between meta-effect sizes for developed versus developing country groups is even more pronounced – 0.12 and 0.24 respectively. Accordingly, results using case U indicate that, relative to developed countries, developing countries are more susceptible to contagion of financial crises.

However, there are no significant differences between meta-effect sizes in these two subgroups for the adjusted (A) cases. Under both Approach 1 and Approach 2 the meta-effect sizes are 0.02 for developed countries and 0.04 for developing countries, but the differences in these values are not significant at the 95% confidence level.

As different financial markets are included in the sample, the analysis is also conducted separately for stock, bond, exchange rate and interest rate markets. The results are not presented in Table 2, but are available for heteroskedasticity adjusted cases in Appendix 5. It can be seen that on average contagion appears strongest in interest rate markets (where the meta-effect size is 0.14) with exchange rate markets closely behind (meta-effect size is 0.09). In stock markets, the meta-effect size is very small (0.02) but still statistically significantly different from zero. In bond markets, the meta-effect size is not statistically significantly positive, although higher than the respective value in stock markets (0.04 when Approach 1 is used and 0.06 in the case of Approach 2).

Two important remarks have to be made before drawing conclusions from the meta-analysis. As can be seen in Appendix 5, there is some heterogeneity left in the distribution in most of the subgroups even after these groups are based on two moderators together. This means that the results must be taken with caution, as all individual effect sizes inside groups may not estimate the same population mean. However, the author of the thesis is quite forced to be reconciled with the heteroskedasticity, as there are not enough studies in the sample to conduct a meta-regression, which typically may help in such situations. As a rule of thumb, there have to be ten studies per explanatory variable in a meta-regression, which the present analysis is clearly short of. Bringing in dummies for all crises in addition to those for the methodology (A or U) and development level of the destination country (developed or emerging) and also all cross-effects, makes the number of exogenous variables far too great for a meta-regression to be feasible.

A further remark should be made regarding the publication bias. Publication bias refers to the fact that studies with significant results are more likely to be published. In the field of financial contagion it is not clear which of the two types of results – supporting or contradicting the contagion hypothesis – is more interesting. Therefore, controlling for publication bias is not thought to be necessary in the thesis.

Summing up the results of the sub-chapter it can be concluded that on average asset market correlations have increased during turbulent periods, which provides some evidence in support of the financial contagion conception. Nevertheless, the increase is quite moderate and after controlling for heterogeneity in correlations in turbulent periods it is even smaller although still statistically significant at the 95% confidence level. Both the calculating methodology for the correlations (heteroskedasticity adjusted or not) and the crisis under observation are significant moderators explaining the heterogeneity in the distribution. From among the most important financial crises during the past two decades, the Mexican, Thai and Hong Kong crises are contagious, while the Russian and Brazilian crises are not. The level of development in the destination country does not account for significant variability in effect sizes.

4.1.2. Findings for CEE economies

Next, the meta-analysis is run for the CEE countries (as destination countries), and an attempt is made to compare the results (presented in Table 3) with those obtained on the basis of the whole sample (comprised of all 716 observations).

Table 3. The results of the meta-analysis of studies investigating financial contagion to CEE economies

Sample	Number of effect sizes	ESs as treatment effects (Approach 1)			ESs as correlation coefficients (Approach 2)		
		Meta-ES	Standard error	Q-statistic	Meta-ES	Standard error	Q-statistic
All	89	0.019	0.020	108.7	0.023	0.021	107.1
U	15	0.148*	0.034	32.6*	0.161*	0.034	35.0*
A	74	-0.051	0.025	53.6	-0.057	0.027	46.7
HK 1997	15	-0.004	0.037	14.9	-0.005	0.038	13.7
Rus 1998	19	0.057	0.039	35.4*	0.071	0.041	39.0*
Bra 1999	9	-0.084	0.075	5.3	-0.087	0.081	4.7
Tur 2001	9	-0.187	0.105	5.6	-0.203	0.126	5.1
US 2001	9	0.024	0.105	4.2	0.026	0.126	3.2
Arg 2001	9	-0.052	0.071	2.6	-0.053	0.079	2.3
US 2002	9	0.297*	0.105	2.8	0.308*	0.126	2.6
Cze 1997	10	0.056	0.045	22.2*	0.057	0.046	22.5*

* denotes statistically significant results (in 95% confidence level).

ES - effect size.

All - all observations (data points) from the sample with only CEE economies.

U - cases with unadjusted (for heteroskedasticity) correlation coefficients.

A - cases with adjusted (for heteroskedasticity) correlation coefficients.

HK – Hong Kong crisis; Rus – Russian crisis; Bra – Brazilian crisis; US – United States crisis; Tur – Turkish crisis; Arg – Argentinean crisis; Cze – Czech crisis.

Source: author's calculations.

In Table 3 'All' refers to the sample of 89 individual effect sizes affiliated with CEE economies, which includes eight financial crises: Hong Kong 1997, Czech 1997, Russian 1998, Brazilian 1999, Turkish 2001, US 2001, Argentinean 2001 and US 2002 and four CEE countries for which comparable data is available, namely Czech Republic, Estonia, Hungary and Poland.

The meta-effect size calculated for the sample of CEE countries based on 89 individual effect sizes is 0.019 according to Approach 1 (effect sizes as treatment effects) and 0.023 according to Approach 2 (effect sizes as correlation coefficients). Recall from Table 2 that corresponding meta-effect sizes for the whole sample were 0.053 under Approach 1 and 0.072 under Approach 2. Thus, on average, the rate of contagiousness with CEE transition economies as destination countries has been lower than average, although not statistically significantly so. Additionally, the meta-effect size in the sample of CEE transition economies is not statistically significantly above zero. This outcome bears some congruence with Serwa and Bohl (2005) and Serwa (2005), who argue that there is no evidence of CEE being more prone to financial contagion compared to western countries.

If only heteroskedasticity adjusted (A) correlation coefficients are included in the sample with CEE as destination countries, then the meta-effect sizes are negative at -0.051 and -0.057 according to Approach 1 and Approach 2 respectively. Thus, asset price correlations have, on average, even decreased during times of financial crisis. Also, compared to the corresponding meta-effect size value representing the whole sample, the meta-effect size value for CEE transition countries is statistically significantly lower.

Comparing different financial crises we can see that, on average, the US 2002 crisis (accounting scandals) has been the most contagious crisis for CEE countries with a weighted mean effect size of 0.30 according to Approach 1 and 0.31 according to Approach 2 with both values statistically significantly above zero. Next, in terms of contagiousness, come the Russian 1998 crisis and the Czech 1997 crisis with meta-effect sizes above 0.05, but statistically insignificant at a significance level of 0.05. Other crises do not seem to have spread significantly to CEE economies.

Compared to the average, CEE economies seem to have been affected more by both the Russian 1998 and the US 2002 crises, while the Hong Kong 1997 crisis has not propagated to CEE countries vigorously despite being contagious overall. This finding is in line with that of Weller and Morzuch (2000), who found that although the Asian financial crisis of 1997 spread to Russia and Brazil, the CEE transition economies remained largely unaffected.

If we narrow our focus to results obtained using only heteroskedasticity adjusted (A) data points, (results not reported in Table 3 but are available on request) then the US 2002 crisis emerges as the sole crisis contagiously propagating to CEE countries. The only other crisis during which heteroskedasticity adjusted asset price correlations have increased is the US 2001 crisis. For all other financial crises, asset price correlations have either remained constant or even decreased.

One of the most unanticipated finding that the meta-analysis returned is that CEE transition economies have, on average, been more susceptible to financial crises originating in the US as opposed to financial crises originating elsewhere, most notably Russia and the Czech Republic. One reason for this is large number of agents who are investing their money to the US. The other reason may be that the US is extremely influential both economically and politically around the world, and therefore, crises in the US are always resounded in the media worldwide. Therefore, investors are well informed about crises originating in the US, but may not be so about crises emerging elsewhere.

4.2. Contagion from the US 2008 financial crisis to the Baltic States

4.2.1. Some specific features of the Baltic States

In this sub-chapter two main approaches are employed to test for possible financial contagion from the US to Estonia, Latvia and Lithuania during the crisis that started in the US in 2008. First, the correlation coefficients based methods are implemented, and second, the ARCH-GARCH framework.

The events associated with the US 2008 crisis, which saw many countries falling into serious problems one after another like dominoes, reminded us once again that the phenomenon of financial contagion is a systematic component of financial risk. Small open economies like those in the Baltic States are particularly vulnerable to global economic developments. Therefore, financial contagion analysis is exceptionally important for these new EU member countries with their post-socialist path-dependence.

The three Baltic countries investigated in the chapter as destination countries have an interesting economic background. Since regaining their independence in 1991, the Baltic States have undergone similar processes of economic, political and social transformation. Under the Washington Consensus policy framework, these countries aimed to create stability and international trust as well as attractiveness for foreign direct investment through a fixed exchange rate, balanced state budget and comparatively low tax and administrative burdens. In the late 1990s, the transition and restructuring paradigms were replaced by the concepts of catching up and economic convergence to the level of the developed economies of the enlarged EU. Unfortunately, large amounts of foreign investment and private lending went into financing consumption and the real estate boom, and as a consequence, the export competitiveness of the Baltic economies started to weaken in the 2000s (see also Estonian Development Report 2008). Furthermore, the deepening downturn of the main trading partners of the Baltic States during the recent global crisis has remarkably weakened the economic outlook for these countries. Estonia is the only country among the three Baltic States that has joined the euro zone, doing so in 2011. Adopting the euro in itself is unlikely to trigger any major change in the pace of recovery, but it was expected during the joining that it may remove liquidity risks, add stability to the economy and help attract new investments. These small countries are facing a double challenge of simultaneously overcoming the recent economic downturn resulting from the global economic crisis as well as implementing national economic policies. The Baltic countries are particularly interesting to investigate as destination countries of the propagation of financial crises because of their small and open economies and post-socialist path-dependence. There are two main reasons why Baltic countries may differ from other countries in how they might be affected by contagion. On the one hand, the openness that has been taken almost to extremes in these countries and was one of the main reasons behind their noticeable success in the transition period, may have now performed a disservice, as a high level of openness may make a country more vulnerable to financial contagion. On the other hand, as argued by Weller and Morzuch (2000), there has been less speculative financing on the stock markets of the Baltic States as compared to many other countries, which decreases the likelihood of bubbles and should offer some protection against financial contagion. It would be an interesting finding to discover which of these two aspects prevail.

4.2.2. Results of the correlation coefficients based test

In the empirical section of the sub-chapter, the correlation coefficients between stock returns from the US (a crisis country) and the Baltic States (Estonia, Latvia and Lithuania) during non-crisis and crisis periods are compared first. Secondly, changes in volatility are measured to examine whether conditional means and conditional variances of financial variables are related to each other among these countries and whether these relations are stronger during the crisis.

The investigation of the correlation coefficients is based on the methodology outlined in chapter three (sub-chapter 3.2), and uses the data and time periods that are also explained in the same chapter. Two-day average[24] rolling logarithmic stock returns are used to control for the non-synchronous trading hours in the US and Baltic States. The number of

---

[24] To get more robust results also weekly rolling average logarithmic stock returns are investigated. The results do not change significantly, although correlations are lower in all periods for all three countries. These results are not reported in the dissertation but are available upon request.

observations used is 266. All stock indexes used are denominated in US dollars.

Unadjusted correlation coefficients are calculated using formula 10 in sub-chapter 3.2.1 separately for crisis and non-crisis periods using estimates and variances of the respective period. The results are given in the second (pre-crisis correlations) and third row (post-crisis correlations) in Table 4. The final row in Table 4 is obtained by adjusting the unadjusted post-crisis correlations given in the previous row using the adjustment procedure given in formulas 11 and 12 (see sub-chapter 3.2.1).

Table 4. Correlation coefficients between US and Baltic stoct markets before and during 2008. financial crisis period

Period	US and Estonia	US and Latvia	US and Lithuania
Pre-crisis	0.087	0.086	0.068
Post-crisis, unadjusted	0.345*	0.222	0.368*
Post-crisis, adjusted	0.231	0.146	0.248

* indicates statistically significant difference from pre-crisis value at 95% confidence level (sample size is 266 observations).
Source: author's calculations.

As seen in Table 4, the correlation coefficient for the pre-crisis period (after the Fischer transformation) between the US and Estonia is 0.087, between the US and Latvia 0.086 and between the US and Lithuania 0.068. The corresponding simple correlations for the crisis period are 0.345, 0.222 and 0.368. The post-crisis correlations are significantly higher, which is confirmed by the t-test in the cases of Estonia and Lithuania[25]. This finding supports the contagion hypothesis according to which linkages between

---

[25] For a remainder, test statistic suggested by Morrison (1983) is:

$$T = \frac{0.5\ln(\frac{1+\rho^{non-crisis}}{1-\rho^{non-crisis}}) - 0.5\ln(\frac{1+\rho^{crisis}}{1-\rho^{crisis}})}{\sqrt{1/(N^{non-crisis}-3)+1/(N^{crisis}-3)}}$$, where $N^{non-crisis}$ and N^{crisis} are sample

sizes in tranquil and crisis periods respectively.

crisis and non-crisis countries have become stronger after the starting point of the crisis. Therefore, there has to have been some changes in the structure of stock market linkages, which can be explained by herding behaviour or switches in investor expectations and attitude.

However, as pointed out in the previous chapter, the higher correlation coefficients in this simple model may be caused by the higher volatility that is present during crisis times. Because of this bias, correlations in crisis times are adjusted for the higher volatility bias. After doing this (adjusting post-crisis correlations for the presence of heteroskedasticity), the correlations are much lower, 0.231 for Estonia, 0.146 for Latvia and 0.248 for Lithuania. Comparing these values with the pre-crisis correlations, the differences are not statistically significant at the 95% confidence level. So it is clearly seen that not adjusting for heteroskedasticity increases the probability of finding supporting evidence for the existence of financial contagion. Still, in the case of Estonia and Lithuania, the post-crisis correlations are more than three times higher than pre-crisis correlations, and in the case of Latvia the difference is twofold, from which it can be deduced that there may have been some kind of structural break in the financial shocks' transmission mechanism, although not quite as strong as suggested by the simple unadjusted correlations. Furthermore, two aspects regarding statistical significance testing have to be kept in mind: firstly, the t-statistic used only takes into account absolute differences in correlation coefficients and not relative differences which arise much more clearly in the present case; and secondly, the adjustment methodology suggested by Forbes and Rigobon (2002) adjusts correlation coefficients only for heteroskedasticity, but there are also problems with omitted variables and simultaneous equations. Therefore, as subsequently claimed by some authors (for example Corsetti et al 2005), the adjusted correlations found using the methodology of Forbes and Rigobon (2002) tend to be biased towards the null hypothesis of no contagion. Therefore, it seems appropriate to conclude that as even adjusted post-crisis correlations were two or even three times higher than pre-crisis ones, at least some, albeit not very strong, evidence of financial contagion was found.

One additional aspect has to be mentioned. A characteristic of Baltic stock markets is that liquidity in all of them is in general rather low, which may decrease the probability of finding strong correlations of stock returns in the crisis period. For example, Didier et al (2010) have found that stock market illiquidity can explain a low degree of co-movement with the US. However, low liquidity levels should negatively affect both pre- and post-crisis correlations, so its impact on contagion effects is hardly important. This is in accordance with the findings by Grammatikos and Vermeulen (2011), who find intensified links between the US and countries with illiquid stock markets, while between the US and countries with more liquid stock markets links did not intensify during crisis periods.

4.2.3. Results of the MA (1) – GARCH (1, 1) - M model

It is understood that the level of volatility in these countries is likely to increase in more turbulent times. This means that conditional and unconditional variances may change over time. In order to capture a better picture of the contagion, it is assumed that there are two regimes in the volatility where one regime relates to lower volatility, tranquil times, and the other to high volatility, turbulent times. So, to test for contagion, an ARCH-GARCH framework for estimating the variance-covariance transmission mechanism is used across the countries as a second approach. The methodology is given in formulas 14–17 in sub-chapter 3.2.2. Table 4 shows the results of the model estimation.

Starting with the pre-crisis period, it is seen that statistically significant mean spillover effects (see values of sigma in the Table 5) are observed in the Estonian and Lithuanian but not in the Latvian stock markets. This means that the conditional mean return in Estonian and Lithuanian stock markets exhibits a positive spillover effect from the US stock market – a high (low) return in the S&P 500 index is followed by a high (low) return in the OMXT and OMXV, but such a relationship is not found between S&P 500 and OMXR. This result is similar to the one found using the correlation coefficients based method, which also showed a stronger increase in correlations between US and Estonia and US and Lithuania compared to the increase in correlation between US and Latvian stock returns. It is an interesting finding for which a good theoretical explanation still needs to be worked out.

Table 5. The results of estimating the MA (1) – GARCH (1, 1) - M model for contagion effects between the US and Baltic States stock markets during the US 2008 crisis.

	From US to		From US to		From US to	
	Non-	Crisis	Non-	Crisis	Non-	Crisis
α	-	-	0.002	-	-	-
β	11.53	16.24	-32.34	9.27	15.7	-0.99
γ	-	-	-0.002	-	-	-
δ	0.15*	0.20*	0.07	0.14	0.14	0.20
ε	0.13	0.06	-0.25*	-	0.09	0.03
a	-	0.000	0.000	0.00	0.00	0.00
b	1.05*	-0.17	0.68*	0.07	0.50	0.67
c	-	0.49*	0.08	0.32	0.38	0.27
d	0.000	0.000	0.000	0.00	0.00	0.00
f	-0.02	0.02	0.09	0.09	-0.08	-

The coefficients are estimated from the MA(1)-GARCH(1, 1)-M model

$$X_t = \alpha + \beta b_t + \gamma D_t + \delta Y_t + \varepsilon u_{t-1} + u_t$$

$$b_t = a + b b_{t-1} + c u_{t-1}^2 + d D_t + f Z_t$$

where

X_t – stock index return in a non-crisis market at time t;

b_t – conditional variance of the X_t at time t;

D – dummy variable for the Monday effect (D takes value of 1 on days following weekends and holidays and is 0 otherwise);

Y_t – stock index return in a crisis market at time t, u_t and u_{t-1} are error terms at time t and $t-1$ respectively;

Z_t – squared residual derived from an MA(1)-GARCH(1,1)-M model applied to the returns of US stock market.

Non-crisis period: 3 March 2008 – 14 September 2008.

Crisis period: 15 September 2008 – 9 March 2009.

* indicates statistically significant difference from zero at 95% confidence level.

Source: author's calculations.

Turning attention to the crisis period, it can be seen that mean spillover effects are now stronger in all three markets. In the crisis period, mean spillover effects are statistically significant even between US and Latvian stock markets if a 90% confidence level is used. This finding is in line with the contagion hypothesis, as post-crisis linkages seem to be stronger than those in the pre-crisis period, although the differences are quite moderate.

In addition to spillover effects in conditional mean also are investigated spillover effects in conditional variance (see values of f in Table 5). Unlike conditional mean, conditional variance does not exhibit statistically significant positive spillovers in any of the observed markets in the crisis period or the non-crisis period. The only statistically significant spillover effect is observed in the Estonian stock market in the pre-crisis period and it is negative. Therefore, high volatility in the S&P 500 index does not give any reason to expect that we will also see high volatility in Baltic stock markets. The conditional variance spillover effects are not stronger in the crisis period than in the non-crisis period. This means that no structural breaks in volatility transmission mechanisms are observed, and therefore, no support for the contagion hypothesis is found.

Summarising the findings of the empirical section, it can be said that the results of the correlation coefficients based and the volatility spillovers based methods are somewhat mixed. Correlations in returns on stock indexes between US and Baltic stock markets are clearly higher during the turmoil period compared to the tranquil period, which supports the contagion hypothesis. However, if post-crisis correlations are adjusted for heteroskedasticity the differences when compared to the pre-crisis period are much smaller and not statistically significant. The estimation results of the MA(1)-GARCH(1, 1)-M model, although showing some increase in spillover effects on the conditional mean, did not show any sign of positive spillover effects on conditional variance, neither did these spillover effects increase during crisis times. So changes in US stock market returns are likely to be followed by changes in the same direction in the Baltic stock markets, but the same cannot be said about changes in volatility. Thus, there is some evidence indicating contagious transmission of financial crisis of 2008 from the US to Baltic stock markets, but the contagion has been rather weak.

5. CONCLUSIONS AND DISCUSSION

The *financial contagion* puzzle has become one of the most newsworthy research tasks for economists in recent decades. This elevated attention was caused by the rapid transmission of initial country-specific shocks to other economies, some of which were very different in terms of their size and economic structure compared to the country of origin. The crises spread over the world like snowballs becoming larger and larger, and even countries far away from the crisis country and apparently with sound fundamentals were not left unaffected. The events a few years ago, with yet another financial crisis *snowballing* around the world, show that developing an understanding of financial contagion is clearly important for policy makers to help them manage and diminish the future spread of crises.

The aim of the study is to find out whether the propagation of financial crises in numerous past crisis episodes has been amplified by financial contagion or is based solely on stable fundamental linkages between countries. The importance of the research question emerges most clearly in the following aspects. Firstly, the existence or nonexistence of financial contagion is straightforwardly related to the merits of international diversification. Theoretical concepts postulate that international diversification should significantly reduce portfolio risk, but in the case of financial contagion, when cross-country correlations increase during crises, much of this rationale is undermined. In this case, the fundamentals of countries are overruled by the self-fulfilling expectations of financial agents, whose irrational actions at a collective level bring down even the soundest of countries. Secondly, at government level, it is important to know whether there is something that can be done in order to prevent crises from spilling over to other countries or to mitigate the negative consequences of such propagation. In the case of strong financial contagion, there is no good way to mount a defence against the propagation of crises, and therefore, countries should have tools at their disposal to deal with the consequences. One recommendation in this case could be to retain finances in reserve during the good times, even if there seems to be no particular reason to expect the economic outlook to worsen.

Practically, the dissertation is based on four published articles mentioned in the list of papers and presented in the appendices. However, as the research theme of financial contagion is extremely topical and new findings and theoretical ideas develop rapidly, the need to consider up-to-date information has resulted in the thesis being presented in the form of a monograph. In addition to updating those sections that have become out of date minor, shortcomings in the articles have also been corrected so the thesis as a monograph can be considered an improved version of the four base publications.

The thesis consists of four chapters, but there are no specific chapters for each article, instead the chapters and publications are somewhat intertwined. Study 1 (see the list of papers at the beginning of the introduction) is basically the sum of sub-chapter 1.1 and chapter 2 (with the exception of sub-chapter 2.7). Study 2 comprises the second half of both the third and fourth chapter (sub-chapters 3.2 and 4.2). The main parts of Studies 3 and 4 are covered in the first halves of the third and fourth chapters, with sub-chapters 3.1 and 4.1.1 being slight modifications of both these Studies, while sub-chapter 4.1.2 is based only on Study 3 (Study 3 is a follow up on Study 4). The sub-chapters not covered by the four base articles are 1.2 and 2.7. These sub-chapters are the product of the process of updating the findings in the articles.

The first chapter of the thesis provides the theoretical framework for the research problem by taking a look at alternative definitions of financial contagion and theories explaining the propagation of shocks and crises. It is shown in the chapter that financial crises and their contagion have long been studied and modelled by economists, and several alternative definitions of financial contagion have been used without coming to a unique definition that all authors agree on. The other contribution of the chapter is to separate the theories explaining the propagation of crises into two groups: theories that are in accordance with interdependence and not contagion – non-crisis-contingent theories – and theories that are in accordance with contagion – crisis-contingent theories.

The second chapter of the thesis provides an overview of the empirical literature in the field of financial contagion by introducing theoretical aspects that may influence the results of empirical studies and looking at previous empirical findings separately for four groups of studies based on the testing methodologies. This analysis is based on Study 1. The results that are based on around 75 empirical studies show that empirical studies provide heterogeneous results depending on the definitions and methods applied, the crises chosen, and the markets observed. These analyses contain both evidence confirming and evidence contradicting financial contagion. Summing up by simply counting all the relevant empirical findings, the results supporting the contagion hypothesis are clearly dominant, but this can be attributable to the broader definition used or having not adjusted for the presence of heteroskedasticity in the crisis period. Taking into account the differences in the definitions and testing methodologies, the qualitative analysis of previous studies of financial contagion did not reveal clear results as to which evidence dominates or should dominate.

One of the conclusions that can be made based on the second chapter of the thesis is that qualitative analysis of published research materials about previous financial crises does not give sufficient answers to the research question of whether the propagation of crises from one country to others is contagious in nature or not. Therefore, one contribution of the thesis is to suggest future research be conducted on the field of financial contagion with more emphasis on finding singular numerical values that are interpretable and comparable, and therefore, summarisable across all relevant studies, rather than trying to come out with some statistical significance measure of some contagion parameter. One potential measure of this kind is proposed in the third chapter and is used in the empirical analysis in the fourth chapter of the thesis.

The research results presented in the second chapter clearly showed that the multidimensionality of the financial contagion puzzle makes it almost impossible to obtain adequate findings based on a qualitative literature review. Therefore, the third and fourth chapter of the thesis are dedicated to quantitative analyses and are divided into two parts: meta-analysis of previous empirical findings (based on Studies 3 and 4) and a separate econometric analysis regarding the US 2008 crisis (based on Study 2). In the third chapter the data and methodology are introduced separately for both analyses, and in the fourth chapter the main findings obtained using these methods are presented in a similar fashion.

One of the contributions of the thesis regarding the meta-analysis is working out a quantitative measure that is interpretable across studies and permits meaningful numerical comparison and aggregation. As such the thesis proposes the use of an increase in cross-country asset price correlations between crisis and non-crisis country during crisis times relative to asset price correlations between the same countries during non-crisis times. Defined so the contagion measure is in accordance with the definition proposed by Forbes and Rigobon (2000, 2001 and 2002), according to which financial contagion is denoted as a structural break in the linear transmission mechanism of financial shocks during crisis times.

The given measure is used as an input in the meta-analysis with meta-effect size being the weighted average of the values of the measure.

The results of the meta-analysis, presented in the first part of the fourth chapter and in a nutshell given in Figure 1, indicate that on average asset market correlations have increased during turbulent periods, but the increase is rather moderate (see column *All* in Figure 1). Therefore, it seems that financial contagion has been present in past crisis episodes, but it has not been strong. Whether correlation coefficients are adjusted for the presence of heteroscedasticity or not in the individual studies is a clear moderating variable in explaining heterogeneity in distribution (see columns *Unadjusted* and *Adjusted*). In the case of adjusted correlation coefficients, the increase in correlations during turbulent periods is considerably smaller, but still statistically significant. It has been shown by many authors (e.g. Forbes and Rigobon 2001) that not adjusting for the presence of heteroskedasticity overestimates the contagion effects, and therefore, finding support for the contagion hypothesis is more likely than it should be. Now we can see for the first time how large the gap is between the estimation results of these two approaches (the difference in meta-effect size values is approximately 0.15), and thus how inadequate it is to mix them up in a qualitative analysis.

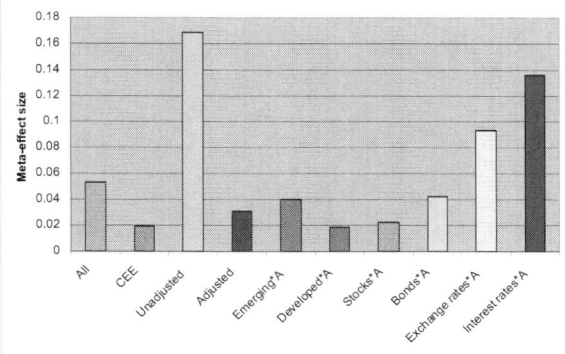

Figure 1. The main values for meta-effect sizes (using Approach 1[26] – individual effect sizes as treatment effects)

---

[26] The values of Appoach 2 do not differ much.

A – post-crisis correlations are adjusted for the presence of heteroskedasticity

Source: compiled by the author

Further results of the meta-analysis show that from the deepest financial crises in the last two decades (with the exception of the US 2008 crisis that was not included into the meta-analysis) the Mexican crisis of 1994, the Thai crisis of 1997 and the crisis in Hong Kong in 1997 were contagious, while the crisis in Russia in 1998, in Brazil in 1999 and the one in Argentina in 2001 were not[27]. The reasons behind this finding are not investigated in the thesis, so future investigation is needed in this respect.

Other findings indicate that the degree to which the destination country can be considered developed does not seem to be a significant contributory factor in determining whether a financial crisis will spread or not (see columns *Emerging*A* and *Developed*A*). The meta-effect size is a little bit higher in the case of emerging economies (compared to the developed ones) as destination countries but not statistically significantly so. This finding suggests that even economically strong economies are not protected if financial crises start to snowball.

In addition, whether the observed financial market affects the likelihood of finding evidence of contagion is also investigated. It turns out (see columns *Stocks*A*, *Bonds*A*, *Exchange rates*A* and *Interest rates*A*) that in interest rate markets contagion occurs more strongly than in stock markets. According to the meta-effect sizes, contagion effects also seem strong in exchange rate markets, but there is no statistically significant difference with any of the other three markets.

An important policy implication from the results of the meta-analysis is that potential benefits from international portfolio diversification are significantly lower than one might expect. If one country falls, others are not safe either, as herding behaviour or some other form of collectively irrational behaviour among financial agents can easily occur. At the government level, some guidelines for appropriate financial architecture that take into account the presence of financial contagion in international markets can be drawn. It may not be enough to have good policies and good macroeconomic fundamentals, as financial contagion can bring down

---

[27] These findings are not reflected in the Figure 1, but can be found in Table 2 in the fourth chapter and in the Appendix 5.

even strong countries. As closeting themselves behind an iron curtains seems neither realistic nor reasonable, nothing more than countries putting aside financial reserves during good times for use when financial contagion hits can really be suggested. This way a country can be better prepared and mitigate the negative consequences of crises. As there seems to be no good way to build a defence against the propagation of crises, countries should have tools at their disposal to deal with the consequences.

With respect to the CEE economies, the results indicate somewhat surprisingly that, on average, CEE economies are less susceptible to financial contagion compared to the average from the entire sample (compare columns *CEE* and *All*). The meta-effect size for CEE countries is statistically insignificant and, after adjusting for the presence of heteroskedasticity, takes on a negative value.

An interesting finding is that the CEE economies seem to be the most susceptible to the propagation of financial crises that originate in the US. Crises originating elsewhere, most notably in Russia and the Czech Republic, seem not to have contagiously propagated to CEE countries. The reason behind this may well be the fact that the US has been extremely influential financially, economically and politically around the world. Therefore, a lot of agents are investing their money in the US, and most of them are well aware of every crisis episode almost immediately after its occurrence. At the same time, small crises in less influential countries may be of no interest for the international media, and given the smaller number of investors losing investments, it is less likely for such local crises to become global. Here it is worth remembering that this does not mean that crises like those in Russia in 1998 and the Czech Republic in 1997 do not affect other Central and Eastern European countries. Rather the propagation of these crises happens through stable fundamental linkages, and breaks in transmission channels do not occur.

One of the most important limitations of the sub-chapters regarding the meta-analysis is that the analysis is restricted to empirical studies based exclusively on correlation coefficients. The majority of studies use this methodology, and it is no simple task to construct the comparable individual effect sizes necessary for the meta-analytic approach using other methodologies as well. Nonetheless, this might be one subject future research could focus on, if the authors of subsequent studies provide numerical findings that can be used in future meta-analyses. Another limitation is associated with the heterogeneity that is left in the data even after dividing the sample into several subgroups. Thus, one has to keep in mind that the numerical values of some meta-effect sizes are of questionable validity because all individual effect sizes within the groups may not represent the common population, and the groups could be divided even further. Studies investigating the US 2008 crisis should also be included in the sample in any future meta-analyses on the subject.

At the time of writing the papers that the dissertation is based on, there was not a single study that investigated the contagiousness of the US 2008 crisis. This made it impossible to add the mentioned crisis to the articles utilising a meta-analysis (Studies 3 and 4). Therefore, a separate analysis was conducted to examine contagiousness from the US 2008 crisis. This analysis was published as Study 2 and is presented as an improved version at the end of the third (where the model is presented) and fourth chapter (where the results are given and discussed) of the thesis. The more recent analyses that investigate the US 2008 crisis are considered in the second chapter of the thesis, and more specifically in sub-chapter 2.7, which is one improvement the thesis provides in addition to the four base articles.

In regard to the US 2008 crisis, the thesis examines whether there has been financial contagion from the US to the three Baltic States during the 2008 financial crisis using data on two-day rolling average stock returns during the period from 3 March 2008 to 9 March 2009. As with the definition used in the meta-analysis, financial contagion is defined as a structural break in the linear transmission mechanism of financial shocks during the crisis and is tested by applying both correlation coefficients based tests and the ARCH-GARCH framework.

The logic of the correlation coefficients based tests is to measure the correlation in stock returns between the US (crisis country) and the Baltic States (destination countries) during the period before the bankruptcy of Lehman Brothers (stable period), and then test for a significant increase in this correlation coefficient during the period after the bankruptcy of Lehman Brothers (crisis period). A significant increase in the correlation coefficient after the starting point of the crisis is considered evidence of contagion. Correlation coefficients based testing reveals some but not strong supporting evidence for financial contagion. The unadjusted (for the presence of heteroskedasticity) post-crisis correlation between the US and all three Baltic countries is clearly higher than the pre-crisis correlation (the pre-crisis correlations were 0.087, 0.086 and 0.068 in case of Estonia, Latvia and Lithuania respectively and the respective values for the post-crisis period were 0.345, 0.222 and 0.368), and in the case of Estonia and Lithuania the increase is statistically significant. This finding supports the contagion hypothesis and indicates that linkages between the US (crisis country) and Estonia and Lithuania (non-crisis countries) have become stronger after 15 September 2008, which was agreed upon as the starting date of the crisis.

Because of the bias of unadjusted correlation coefficients towards overestimating contagion effects, the correlations in crisis times are adjusted for the presence of heteroskedasticity. Using these adjusted correlations, the differences between pre- and post-crisis correlations are much smaller and statistically insignificant in the case of all three Baltic countries (the values of adjusted post-crisis correlations were 0.231, 0.146 and 0.248 in the case of Estonia, Latvia and Lithuania respectively). To obtain a complete picture, it should nevertheless be mentioned that the differences are still two or three times in favour of post-crisis correlations, and given the slight downward bias of the adjusted correlation coefficients, the general conclusion of the analysis is in favour of some weak contagion effects.

Within the framework of the ARCH-GARCH models, the MA(1)-GARCH(1,1)-M model is estimated to analyse both mean and volatility spillovers from the US to the Baltic countries. Significantly stronger spillovers in the crisis period compared to the tranquil period are considered as evidence of financial contagion. The results obtained using that model are mixed. The mean spillover effects from the US to Estonia, Latvia and Lithuania are stronger during the crisis period compared to the tranquil period. During crisis times the conditional mean return in all three Baltic stock markets exhibits a positive spillover effect from the US stock market. However, this is not true for the conditional variance, which does not exhibit statistically significant positive spillovers in any of the observed markets. Furthermore, there is no sign of spillovers of conditional variance becoming stronger during crisis times.

Summarising the results of the two alternative testing methodologies, some evidence of financial contagion was found, but it seems to have not been particularly strong. These results also confirm once again that financial contagion is a complex phenomenon, and examining it requires further investment in the employment and development of study methods, probably with future meta-analysis in mind.

The transmission of the crisis from the US to the Baltic stock markets (and economies), that the unadjusted correlation coefficients based testing indicated, shows the risks that small open economies have to face. However, although the Baltic States in 2009 faced similar problems as Greece is undergoing in the recent crisis, they managed to overcome this problem by reducing human resources costs. The rating agency Standard & Poor's has increased the rating outlook for all three countries, on the basis of their success in decreasing the budget. Thus, as shown by the analysis of adjusted correlation coefficients, one can judge that the infection was not especially difficult for the Baltic countries, as many countries with less open economies are facing even larger problems. The low level of susceptibility (to financial contagion) among the Baltic countries was even more clearly indicated by the meta-analysis and testing the spillover effects of the conditional mean and conditional variance. The latter revealed that, in spite of being extremely open economies, the Baltic stock markets exhibit only a slightly stronger mean spillover effect from the US stock market during the crisis, they do not exhibit a positive variance spillover effect from the US stock market and the presence of the 2008 crisis in the US did not make variance spillovers significantly stronger.

Thus, small open economies like those in the Baltic States do not seem to be more susceptible to financial crises than other countries, and should probably continue to be as open as possible for foreign trade and investments, an aspect which has been one of the main reasons for their success so far. In order to deal with some unavoidable contagion from elsewhere, government intervention to direct knowledge and innovation based development, which could enable better mitigation of the negative consequences of crises, are probably necessary.

As the analysis of the US 2008 crisis is restricted to two methodological approaches, and the results of these approaches are somewhat mixed, this can be considered as one of the main limitations of this analysis. Therefore, further analysis using different methodological frameworks is one way to continue in future research.

REFERENCES

1. **Abeysinghe, T.** (2001). Thai Meltdown and Transmission of Recession within ASEAN4 and NIE4. In S. Claessens and K.Forbes (eds) *International Financial Contagion*. Boston, Kluwer Academic Publishers, pp. 225-240.

2. **Agenor, P.-R., Aizenman, J. and Hoffmaister, A.** (1998). Contagion, Bank Lending Spreads and Output Fluctuations. - *NBER Working Paper No. W6850.*

3. **Agenor, P.-R., and Aizenman, J.** (1997). Contagion and volatility with imperfect credit markets – *NBER Working Paper* No. 6080.

4. **Alba, P., Bhattacharya, A., Claessens, S., Ghosh, S. and Hernandez, L.** (1998), Volatility and Contagion in a Financially-Integrated World: Lessons from East Asia's Recent Experience. World Bank and Central Bank of Chile. [http://www.worldbank.org/html/dec/Publications/Workpapers/wps20 00series/wps2008/wps2008.pdf].

5. **Aloui, R., Aissa, M. S. B. And Nguyen, D. K.** (2011). Global financial crisis, extreme interdependences and contagion effects: The role of economic structure? – *Journal of Banking & Finance*, Vol. 35, Issue 1, pp. 130-141.

6. **Alvarez-Plata, P. and Schrooten, M.** (2003). Latin America After the Argentine Crisis: Diminishing Financial Market Integration. – *Economic Bulletin*, Volume 40, Number 12 / December, 2003.

7. **Arestis, P., Caporale, G.M., Cipollini, A. and Spagnolo, N.** (2005). Testing for financial contagion between developed and emerging markets during the 1997 East Asian crisis. – *International Journal of Finance & Economics.* Volume 10, Issue 4, pages 359-367.

8. **Arias, E. F., Hausmann, R. and Rigobon, R.** (1998). Contagion on Bond Markets: Preliminary Notes. Mimeo, MIT.

9. **Bae, K, Karolyi, A. and R. Stulz, R.** (2003). A new approach to measuring financial contagion. - *Review of Financial Studies* 16, pp. 717–763.

10. **Baig, T. and Goldfajn, I.** (1999). Financial market contagion in the Asian crisis. - *IMF Staff Papers* 46 (1999), pp. 167–195.

11. **Bartram, S. M. and Wang, Y.** (2005). Another look at the relationship between cross-market correlation and volatility. – Finance Research Letters, Vol. 2, pp. 75-88.

12. **Baur, D.** (2003). Testing for contagion – mean and volatility contagion. – *Journal of Multinational Financial Management*, Volume 13, Issues 4-5, December 2003, Pages 405-422.

13. **Basu, A**. (2003). How to conduct a meta-analysis. [http://www.pitt.edu/~super1/lecture/lec1171].

14. **Bayoumi, T., Fazio, G., Kumar, M. and MacDonald, R.** (2007). Fatal attraction: Using distance to measure contagion in good times as well as bad. – *Review of Financial Economics, Volume 16, Issue 3, 2007*, Pages 259-273.

15. **Billio, M. and Caporin, M.** (2010). Market linkages, variance spillovers, and correlation stability: Empirical evidence of financial contagion. – *Computational Statistics & Data Analysis*, Vol. 54, Issue 11, pp. 2443-2458.

16. **Billio, M. and Pelizzon, L.** (2003). Contagion and Interdependence in Stock Markets: Have they been misdiagnosed? - *Journal of Economics and Business 55*, 405 – 426.

17. **Bollerslev, T.** (1986). Genaralized autoregressive conditional heteroskedasticity. - *Journal of Econometrics*, 31, pp. 307-327.

18. **Bordo, M.D. and Murshid, A.P.** (2000a). The International Transmission of Financial Crises before World War II: Was There Contagion? [http://www.cfr.org/content/thinktank/Depression/Bordo_1.pdf].

19. **Bordo, M. D. and Murshid, A.P.** (2000b). Are financial crises becoming increasingly more contagious? What is the historical evidence on contagion? NBER Working Paper Series, WP 7900.

20. **Boschi, M. and Goenka, A.** (2012). Relative risk aversion and the transmission of financial crises. - *Journal of Economic Dynamics and Control*, Vol. 36, Issue 1, pp. 85-99.

21. **Boyer, B., Gibson, M. and Loretan, M.** (1999). Pitfalls in tests for changes in correlations. - *Federal Reserve Board Working Paper* vol. 597.

22. **Burdekin, C. K. and Siklos, P. L.** (2012). Enter the dragon: Interactions between Chinese, US and Asia-Pasific equity markets, 1995-2010. – *Pacific-Basin Finance Journal*, Vol. 20, Issue 3, pp. 521-541.

23. **Calvo, G.A.** (1996). Capital flows and macroeconomic management: Tequila lessons. – *International Journal of Finance & Economics*. Vol. 1, Issue 3, pp. 207-223.

24. **Calvo, G. A.** (2005). Contagion in emerging markets: When Wall Street is a carrier. In: G. Calvo, Editor, *Emerging capital markets in*

90

turmoil: Bad luck or bad policy?, MIT Press, Cambridge (2005), pp. 313–328.

25. **Calvo, G. and Mendoza, E.** (2000). Rational Contagion and the Globalization of Securities Markets - *Journal of International Economics*, Vol. 51, No. 1, June 2000, pp. 79-113.

26. **Calvo, S. and Reinhart, C.** (1996). Capital Flows to Latin America: Is There Evidence of Contagion Effects? in *Private Capital Flows to Emerging Markets After the Mexican Crisis* (G. A. Calvo, M. Goldstein and E. Hochreiter, eds.), Institute for International Economics, Washington, D. C.

27. **Candelon, B, Hecq, A. and Verschoor, F.C.** (2005). Measuring common cyclical features during financial turmoil: Evidence of interdependence not contagion. – *Journal of International Money and Finance*, Volume 24, Issue 8, December 2005, Pages 1317-1334.

28. **Caramazza, F., Ricci, L. and Salgado, R,F.** (2004) International financial contagion in currency crises. - *Journal of International Money and Finance* 23 (2004), pp. 51–70.

29. **Caramazza, F., Ricci, L. and Salgado, R.** (2000). Trade and Financial Contagion in Currency Crises. - *IMF Working Paper*.

30. **Cerra, V. and Saxena S.C.** (2002). Contagion, Monsoons and Domestic Turmoil in Indonesia's Currency Crisis. – *Review of International Economics*. Volume 10, Issue 1, Pages 36-44.

31. **Cheung, L.; Tam, C. and Szeto, J.** (2009). Contagion of financial crises: a literature review of theoretical and empirical frameworks. Hong Kong Monetary Authority, Research Note 02/2009.

32. **Chiang, T.C., Jeon, B.N. and Li, H.** (2007). Dynamic correlation analysis of financial contagion: Evidence from Asian markets. – *Journal of International Money and Finance, Volume 26, Issue 7, Novenber 2007,* Pages 1206-1228.

33. **Chiang, M. and Wang, L.** (2011). Volatility contagion: a range-based volatility approach. – *Journal of Econometrics*, Vol. 165, Issue 2, pp. 175-189.

34. **Choe, K., Choi, P., Nam, K. and Vahid, F.** (2012). Testing financial contagion on heteroskedastic asset returns in time-varying conditional correlation. – *Pacific-Basin Finance Journal*, Vol. 20, Issue 2, pp. 271-291.

35. **Chou, R., Ng, V. and Pi, L.** (1994). Cointegration of international stock market indices. – *IMF Working Paper* WP/94/94.

36. **Claessens, S., Dornbusch, R. and Y.C. Park. Y.C.** (2001). Contagion: why crises spread and how this can be stopped. In: S. Claessens and K. Forbes, Editors, *International Financial Contagion*, Kluwer Academic Publishers, Boston (2001), pp. 19–42.

37. **Cohen, K, Hawaeini, G., Maier, S., Schwartz, R., Whitcomb, D.** 1980. Implications of Microstructure Theory for Empirical Research to Stock Price Behaviour, - *Journal of Finance*, 35, pp. 249-257.

38. **Corsetti, G., Pericoli, M. and Sbracia, M.** (2005) Some contagion, some interdependence: more pitfalls in tests of financial contagion. - *Journal of International Money and Finance* 8 (2005), pp. 1177–1199.

39. **Costinot, A.; Roncalli, T. and Teiletche, J.** (2000). Revisiting the dependence between financial market with copulas. – *SSRN Working PaperSeries.* [http://papers.ssrn.com/sol3/papers.cfm?abstract_id=1032535].

40. **Craig, A., Dravid, A. and Richardson, M.** (1995). Market efficiency around the clock: some supporting evidence using foreign-based derivatives. – *Journal of Financial Economics*, Volume 39, Issues 2-3, October-November 1995, Pages 161-180.

41. **De Dominicis, L; de Groot, H and Florax, R**. 2006. Growth and inequality: a meta-analysis. [http://www.tinbergen.nl/discussionpapers/06064.pdf].

42. **De Gregorio, J and Valdes, R.O.** (2001) Crisis transmission: Evidence from the debt, tequila, and Asian flu crises, *World Bank Economic Review* 15 (2001), pp. 289–314.

43. **Didier, T., Love, I. and Martinez Peria, M. S.** (2010). What explains stock markets' vulnerability to the 2007-2008 crisis? – *World Bank Policy Research Working Paper* 5224.

44. **Didier, T., Love, I. and Martinez Peria, M. S.** (2012). What explains comovement in stock market returns during the 2007-2008 crisis? – *International Journal of Finance & Economics,* Vol. 17, Issue 2, pp. 182-202.

45. **Didier, T., Mauro, P. and Schmukler, S. L.** (2008). Vanishing financial contagion? – *Journal of Policy Modeling.* Volume 30, Issue 5, September-October 2008, Pages 775-791.

46. **Diwan, I. and Hoekman, B.** (1999). Competition, Complementarity and Contagion in Asia. - In: Pierre-Richard Agenor, Marcus Miller, David Vines and Axel Weber, Editors, *The Asian financial crises: Causes, contagion and consequences*, Cambridge University Press, Cambridge (1999), pp. 425, ISBN 0 521 77080 7.

47. **Dornbusch, R., Park Y.C. and Claessens S.** (2000a) Contagion: Understanding how it spreads. - *World Bank Research Observer* 15 (2000), pp. 177–197.

48. **Dornbusch, R., Park Y.C. and Claessens S.** (2000b) Contagion: How it spreads and how it can be stopped. http://www1.worldbank.org/economicpolicy/managing %20volatility/contagion/documents/Claessens-Dornbusch-Park.pdf.

49. **Drazen, A.** (1999). Political contagion in currency crises – *NBER Working Paper 7211*, Cambridge.

50. **Dungey, M. and Dambakis, D.** (2003). Financial contagion: What do we mean? What do we know? [http://www.g24.org/Dungey-Tambakis2003.pdf].

51. **Dungey, M. and Zhumabekova, D.** (2001). Testing for contagion using correlations: some words of caution. - *Working Paper No. PB01-09, Pacific Basin Working Paper Series*, Federal Reserve Bank of San Francisco.

52. **Dungey, M., Fry, R., Gonzalez-Hermosillo, B., Martin, V. and Tang, C.** (2010). Are financial crises alike? – IMW Working Paper, No. 10/14, 58 p.

53. **Edwards, S.** (1998). Interest rate volatility, capital controls, and contagion. - *NBER Working Paper 6756*.

54. **Edwards, S.** (2000). Contagion. [http://www.anderson.ucla.edu/faculty/sebastian.edwards/world_econo my5.pdf].

55. **Edwards, S., Susmel, R.** (2001). Volatility Dependence and Contagion in Emerging Markets. - *Journal of Development Economics*, 66, 505-532.

56. **Edwards, S., Susmel, R.** (2003). Interest-Rate Volatility in Emerging Markets. - *The Review of Economics and Statistics*, 85, 328-348.

57. **Eichengreen, B. and Rose A.** (1999). Contagious currency crises: Channels of conveyance. In: T. Ito and A. Krueger, Editors, *Changes*

in exchange rates in rapidly developing countries: Theory, practice, and policy issues, University of Chicago Press (1999), pp. 29–50.

58. **Eichengreen, B.; Rose A.K. and Wyplosz C.** (1996). Contagious currency crises: First tests, *The Scandinavian Journal of Economics* 98 (1996), pp. 463–484.

59. **Engle, R.F.** (1982). Autoregressive conditional heteroskedasticity with estimates of the variance of United Kingdom inflation. - *Econometrica*, 50, pp. 987-1997.

60. **Engle, R.F.; Lilien, D. and Robins, R.** (1987). Estimating time varying risk premia in the term structure: the ARCH-M model. - *Econometrica,* 55, pp. 391-407.

61. Estonian Development Fund Report 200; available: www.arengufond.ee

62. **Fazio, G.** (2007). Extreme interdependence and extreme contagion between emerging markets. – *Journal of International Money and Finance, Volume 26, Issue 8, December 2007*, Pages 1261-1291.

63. **Favero, C. A. and Giavazzi**, F. (1999). Looking for Contagion: Evidence from the 1992 ERM Crisis. http://www1.worldbank.org/economicpolicy/managing %20volatility/contagion/documents/fg.pdf.

64. **Forbes, K.** (1999). How are shocks propagated internationally? Firm-level evidence from the Russian and Asian crises. [http://www.frbsf.org/economics/conferences/990923/papers/forbes.pd f].

65. **Forbes, K.** (2001). Are trade links important determinants of country vulnerability to crises? - *NBER working paper no. 8194*. Cambridge, Massachusetts: National Bureau of Economic Research.

66. **Forbes, K.** (2004). The Asian flu and Russian virus: The international transmission of crises in firm-level data. - *Journal of International Economics* 63 (1) (2004), pp. 59–92.

67. **Forbes, K. and Rigobon, R.** (2000). Contagion in Latin America: Definitions, Measurement, and Policy Implications. National Bureau of Economic Research Working Paper No. 7885.

68. **Forbes, K. and Rigobon, R.** (2002). No Contagion, Only Interdependence: Measuring Stock Market Co-Movements. – *The Journal of Finance*, 57, No. 5, pp. 2223-2261.

69. **Forbes, K. and Rigobon, R.K.** (2001). Measuring contagion: Conceptual and empirical issues. In: S. Claessens and K. Forbes, Editors, *International financial contagion*, Kluwer Academic Publishers (2001), pp. 43–66.

70. **Frankel, J. and Schmukler, S.** (1998). Crisis, Contagion, and Country Fund: Effects on East Asia and Latin America. – *Managing Capital Flows and Exchange Rates, edited by R.Glick, Cambridge University Press.*

71. **French, K.R.** (1980). Stock returns and the weekend effect. - *Journal of Financial Economics*, 8, pp. 55-69.

72. **French, K.R., G.W. Schwert and R.F. Stambaugh.** (1987). Expected Stock Returns and Volatility. - *Journal of Financial Economics,* 19, 3-30.

73. **Fry, R., Martin, V. L. and Tang, C.** (2010). A new class of tests of contagion with applications. – *Journal of Business & Economic Statistics*, Vol. 28, Issue 3, pp. 423-437.

74. **Gelos, R. G. and Sahay, R.** (2001). Financial market spillovers in transition economies. - *Economics of Transition* 9, 53 – 86.

75. **Gerlach, S. and Smets, F.** (1995), Contagious speculative attacks. - *European Journal of Political Economy* 11 (1995), pp. 45–63.

76. **Gibbons, M.R. And Hess, P.** (1981). Day of the week effects and asset returns. - *Journal of Business,* 54, pp. 579-596.

77. **Gilmore, C. G. and McManus, G. M.** (2002). International portfolio diversification: US and central European equity markets. – *Emerging Markets Review*, Vol. 3, pp. 69-83.

78. **Glass, G. V.** (1976). Primary, secondary and meta-analysis of research. – *Educational Researcher*, 5, p. 3-8.

79. **Glick R. and Rose, A.K.** (1999) Contagion and trade: Why are currency crises regional? - *Journal of International Money and Finance* 18 (1999), pp. 603–617.

80. **Goldstein, M.** (1998) The Asian financial crisis: Causes, cures, and systemic implications. - *Policy analyses in international economics* Vol. 55, Institute for International Economics, Washington.

81. **Goldsein, M. and Hawkins, J.** (1998). The origin of the Asian financial turmoil – RBA Research Discussion Papers, rdp9805, Reserve Bank of Australia.

82. **Grammatikos, T. and Vermeulen, R.** (2012). Transmission of the financial and sovereign debt crises to the EMU: Stock prices, CDS spreads and exchange rates. – *Journal of International Money and Finance*, Vol. 31, Issue 3, pp. 517-533.

83. **Gravelle, T., Kichian, M. and Morley, J.** (2003). Shift-contagion in asset markets. – *Bank of CAnada Working Paper 2003-5.*

84. **Haile, F. and Pozo, S.** (2008). Currency crisis contagion and the identification of transmission channels. - *International Review of Economics & Finance, Volume 17, Issue 4, October 2008, Pages 572-588.*

85. **Hamao, Y., Masulis, R. and Ng, V.** (1990). Correlations in price changes and volatility across international stock markets. - *The Review of Financial Studies*, 3(2):281—307.

86. **Hartmann, P., Straetmans, S. and de Vries, C.G.** (2001). Asset Market Linkages in Crisis Periods. – *Tinbergen Institute Discussion Paper*, TI 2001-071/2.

87. **Hedges, L. V., and Olkin, I.** (1985). Statistical methods for meta-analysis. Orlando, FL: Academic Press Inc. Harcourt, Brace, Jovanovich publishers.

88. **Hedges, L.V.** (1982). Fitting categorical models to ESs from a series of experiments. – Journal of Educational Statistics, 7, 119-137.

89. **Hernandez, L.F. and Valdes, R.O.** (2001) What drives contagion: Trade, neighborhood, or financial links? - *International Review of Financial Analysis* 10 (2001), pp. 203–218.

90. **Hon, M.T., Strauss, J. and Yong, S.** (2004). Contagion in financial markets after September 11: myth or reality? – *Journal of Financial Research*. Volume 27, Issue 1, pages 95-114.

91. **Horta, P., Mendes, C. and Vieira, I.** (2010). Contagion effects on the subprime crisis in the European NYSE Euronext markets. – *Portuguese Economic Journal*, Vol. 9, Number 2, pp. 115-140.

92. **Hunter, J. E., Schmidt, F. L.** (1990). Methods of meta-analysis: Correcting error and bias in research findings. Newbury Park, CA: Sage.

93. **Idier, J.** (2011). Long-term vs. short-term comovements in stock markets: the use of Markov-switching multifractal models. – *European Journal of Finance*, Vol. 17, Issue 1. pp. 27-48.

94. **Iwatsubo, K. and Inagaki, K.** (2006). Measuring Financial Market Contagion using Dually-Traded Stocks of Asian Firms. – *CEI Working paper Series*, No. 2006-14.

95. **Jeanne, O.** (1997). Are currency crises self-fulfilling? A test – *Journal of International Economics*, Vol. 43 (No ¾), pp. 263-286.

96. **Jeanne, O. and Masson, P.** (2000). Currency crises and Markov-switching regimes. - *Journal of International Economics* 50 2 , pp. 327–350.

97. **Jokipii, T. and Lucey, B.** (2006). Contagion and interdependence: measuring CEE banking sector co-movements. - *Bank of Finland Research Discussion Papers*, No. 15, 47p.

98. **Kali, R. and Reyes, J.** (2005). Financial Contagion on the International Trade Network. http://wcob.uark.edu/rkali/networkcontagion.pdf.

99. **Kallberg, J. and Pasquariello, P.** (2008). Time-series and cross-sectional excess comovement in stock indexes. – *Journal of Empirical Finance*, Volume 15, Issue 3, June 2008, Pages 481-502.

100. **Kaminsky, G.L. and Reinhart, C.M.** (1998). Financial Crisis in Asia and Latin America: Then and now. - *American Economic Review papers and proceedings*, 88, May, 444-448.

101. **Kaminsky, G.L. and Reinhart, C.M.** (2000). On crises, contagion, and confusion. - *Journal of International Economics* 51 (2000), pp. 145–168.

102. **Kaminsky, G.L. and Schmukler, S.** (2003). Short-run pain, long-run gain: the effects of financial liberalization. NBER Working Paper 9787, 63 pages.

103. **Kelejian, H.H., Tavlas, G.S. and Hondroyiannis, G.** (2006). A Spatial Modelling Approach to Contagion Among Emerging Economies. – *Open Economic Review, Volume 17, Numbers 4-5 / December, 2006.*

104. **King, M.A. and Wadhwani, S.** (1990). Transmission of Volatility between Stock Markets. - *Review of Financial Studies* 3 (1): pages 5–33.

105. **Kleimeier, S., Lehnert, T. and Verschoor, W.F.C.** (2008). Measuring financial contagion using time-aligned data: the importance of the speed of transmission of shocks. – *Oxford Bulletin of Economics and Statistics*. Volume 70, Issue 4, Pages 493-508.

106. **Kodres, L.E. and Pritsker, M.** (2002). A rational expectations model of financial contagion. – Vol. 57, Issue 2, pp. 769-799.

107. **Lee, H.; Wu, H. And Wang, Y.** (2007). Contagion effect in financial markets after the South-East Asia Tsunami. – *Research in International Business and Finance, Volume 21, Issue 2, June 2007*, Pages 281-296.

108. **Lee, S.B. and Kim, K.J.** (1993). Does the October 1987 crash strengthen the co-movements among national stock markets. - *Review of Financial Economics* 3, pp. 89–104.

109. **Lin, W.; Engle, R. And Ito, T.** (1994). Do bulls and bears move across borders? Transmission of international stock returns and volatility. - *Review of Financial Studies*, 7, pp. 507-538.

110. **Lipsey, Mark, W. and Wilson, David, B.** (2001). Practical meta-analysis. Applied Social Research Methods Series, Volume 49. SAGE Publications.

111. **Lomakin, A. and Paiz S.** (1999). Measuring Contagion in the Face of Fluctuating Volatility. MIT-Sloan Project, 15.036.

112. **Longin, F.M. and Solnik, B.** (1995). Is the Correlation in International Equity Returns Constant: 1960-1990? - *Journal of International Money and Finance* 14:1 (1995), pages 3-26.

113. **Longin, F.M. and Solnik, B.** (2001) Extreme correlation of international equity markets. - *The Journal of Finance* 56 (2001), pp. 649–676.

114. **Longstaff, F. A.** (2010). The subprime credit crisis and contagion in financial markets. – *Journal of Financial Economics*, Vol. 97, Issue 3, pp. 436-450.

115. **Loretan, M. and English, W.** (2000) Evaluation "correlation breakdowns" during periods of market volatility. - *In Bank of International Settlements (BIS), International Financial Markets and the Implications for Monetary and Financial Stability*, BIS, Switzerland.

116. **Lucey, B. M. and Voronkova, S.** (2008). Russian equity market linkages before and after the 1998 crisis: Evidence from stochastic and regime-switching cointegration tests. – *Journal of International Money and Finance*, Vol. 27, pp. 1303-1324.

117. **Masson, P.** (1999). Multiple equilibria, contagion and the emerging market crises. – *IMF Working Paper* 99/164.

118. **Masson, P.** (2004) Contagion: Monsoonal effects, spillovers, and jumps between multiple equilibria. In: Pierre-Richard Agenor, Marcus Miller, David Vines and Axel Weber, Editors, *The Asian financial crises: Causes, contagion and consequences*, Cambridge University Press, Cambridge.

119. **McAleer, M. and Nam, J.C.W.** (2005). Testing for contagion in ASEAN exchange rates. – *Mathematics and Computers in Simulation, Volume 68, Issues 5-6, 26 May 2005*, Pages 517-525.

120. **Mishkin, F. and White, E.N.** (2003). US stock market crashes and their aftermath: implications for monetary policy, in William C. Hunter, George G. Kaufmann, and Michael Pomerleano, eds., Asset price bubbles: the implications for monetary, regulatory and international policies. The MIT Press, pp. 53-79.

121. **Mishkin, F. S.** (1991). Asymmetric Information and Financial Crises: A Historical Perspective, in Hubbard et altri, *Financial Markets and Financial Crises*, University of Cgicago Press.

122. **Morrison, D.** (1983). Applied Linear Statistical Methods. Prentice-Hall, Inc., New Jersey.

123. **Moussalli, C.B.** (2007). Financial Crises, Panic and Contagion: Evidence from a Cross-country Comparison Using Two Time Frames. – *Business and Public Affairs*, ISSN 1934-7219, Volume 1, Issue 2, 2007.

124. **Mullainathan, S.** (2002). A memory-based model of bounded rationality. – *The Quarterly Journal of Economics*. Vol. CXVII, Issue 3.

125. **Neill, J.** 2006. Meta-analysis research methodology. [http://wilderdom.com/research/meta-analysis.html].

126. **Park, Y.C. and Chi-Young, S.** (1998). Financial Contagion in the East Asian Crisis - With Special Reference to the Republic of Korea. [http://209.85.129.132/search? q=cache:1qvSxEOt3Q4J:www1.worldbank.org/economicpolicy/mana ging%2520volatility/contagion/documents/Park-Song.pdf+Financial+Contagion+in+the+East+Asian+Park+Song&cd= 1&hl=et&ct=clnk&gl=ee].

127. **Pearson, K.** (1904). Mathematical contributions to the theory of evolution. [http://visualiseur.bnf.fr/Visualiseur? Destination=Gallica&O=NUMM-55992].
99

128. **Pericoli, M. and Sbracia, M.** (2003) A primer on financial contagion - *Journal of Economic Surveys* 17 (2003), pp. 571–608.

129. **Pindyck, R. and J. Rotemberg, J.** (1990) The excess comovement of commodity prices. - *Economic Journal* 100 (1990), pp. 1173–1189.

130. **Pindyck, R. and J. Rotemberg, J.** (1993) The comovement of stock prices. - *Quarterly Journal of Economics* 108 (1993), pp. 1073–1104.

131. **Rigobon, R.** (2000). Identification Through Heteroskedasticity: Measuring 'Contagion' between Argentinian and Mexican Sovereign Bonds. - *National Bureau of Economic Research Working Paper* No. 7493.

132. **Ramirez, M., and Martinez, C.** (2011). International propagation of shocks: An evaluation of contagion effects for some Latin American countries. – Macroeconomics and Finance in Emerging Market Economies, Vol. 4, Issue 2, pp. 213-233.

133. **Rigobon, R.** (2002). Contagion: How to measure it? In: S. Edwards and J. Frankel, Editors, Preventing currency crises in emerging markets, The University Chicago Press, Chicago, pp. 269–334.

134. **Rigobon, R.** (2003). On the measurement of the international propagation of shocks: is the transmission stable? – *Journal of International Economics. Volume 61, Issue 2, December 2003, Pages 261-283.*

135. **Rosenthal, R.** (1994). Statistically describing and combining studies. – The handbook of research synthesis, Eds. H. Cooper & L. V. Hedges. New York: Russell Sage Foundation, pp. 231-244.

136. **Rosenthal, R. and Rubin, D. B.** (1982). A simple, general purpose display of magnitude of experimental effect. - Journal of Educational Psychology, 74, pp. 166-169.

137. **Rothschild, M. and Stiglitz, J.** (1976) Equilibrium in Competitive Insurance Markets: An Essay on the Economics of Imperfect Information. - *Quarterly Journal of Economics* 90, 629-649.

138. **Sachs, J., Tornell, A. and Velasco, A.** (1996). Financial Crises in Emerging Markets: The Lessons from 1995. - *Brooking Papers on Economic Activity* 1, 147-215.

139. **Sander, H. and Kleimeier, S.** (2003). Contagion and Causality: An Empirical Investigation of Four Asian Crisis Episodes. - *Journal of International Financial Markets, Institutions & Money 13*, 171 – 186.

140. **Schleicher, M.** (2001). The comovements of stock markets in Hungary, Poland and Czech Republic. – *International Journal of Finance and Economics*, Vol. 6, pp. 27-39.

141. **Schotman, P. C. and Zalewska, A.** (2006). Non-synchronous trading and testing for market integration in Central European emerging markets. – *Journal of Empirical Finance*, Vol. 13, pp. 462-494.

142. **Serwa, D.** (2005). Empirical evidence on financial spillovers and contagion to international stock markets. [http://opus.kobv.de/euv/volltexte/2007/20/pdf/serwa.dobromil.pdf].

143. **Serwa, D. and Bohl, M.** (2005). Financial contagion vulnerability and resistance: a comparison of European capital markets. - *Economic Systems*, Vol. 29, Issue 3, September, pp. 344-365.

144. **Schultze, R.** (2004). Meta-Analysis. A Comparison of Approaches. Hogrefe & Huber Publishers, 242 p.

145. **Sola, M., Spagnolo, F. and Spagnolo, N.** (2002). A test for volatility spillovers. – *Economics Letters* 76, pp. 77 – 84.

146. **Syllignakis, M. and Kouretas, G. P.** (2010). German, US and Central and Eastern European stock market integration. – *Open Economies Review*, Vol. 21, pp. 607-628.

147. **Syllignakis, M. and Kouretas, G. P.** (2011). Dynamic correlation analysis of financial contagion: Evidence from the central and Eastern European markets. – *International Review of Economics & Finance*, Vol. 20, Issue 4, pp. 717-732.

148. **Syriopoulos, T.** (2004). International portfolio diversification to Central European stock markets. – *Applied Financial Economics*, Vol. 14, pp. 1253-1268.

149. **Syriopoulos, T.** (2007). Dynamic linkages between emerging European and developed stock markets: has the EMU any impact? – *International Review of Financial Analysis*, Vol. 16, pp. 41-60.

150. **Tornell, A.** (1999). Common fundamentals in the Tequila and Asian crises. – *NBER Working Paper Series, Working Paper 7139*.

151. **Valdes, R.** (1997). Emerging Markets Contagion: Evidence and Theory. In: S. Edwards and J. Frankel, Editors, *Preventing currency crises in emerging markets*, The University Chicago Press, Chicago (2002), pp. 269–334.

152. **Van Rijckeghem, C. and Weder, B.** (2001) Sources of contagion: Is it finance or trade? - *Journal of International Economics* 54 (2001), pp. 293–308.

153. **Wang, K. and Thi T.N.** (2006). Does Contagion Effect Exist Between Stock Markets of Thailand and Chinese Economic Area (CEA) during the „Asian Flu"? – *Asian Journal of Management and Humanity Sciences, Vol. 1, No. 1*, pp. 16-36.

154. **Wang, P. and Moore, T.** (2008). Stock market integration for the transition economies: time-varying conditional correlation approach. – *The Manchester School, Volume 76, Issue s1*, Pages 116-133.

155. **Weller, C. E. and Morzuch B.** (2000). International Financial Contagion: Why are Eastern Europe's banks not failing when everybody else's are? – Economics of Transition, Vol. 8 Issue 3, pages 639-663.

156. **Villar Frexedas, O. And Vaya, E.** (2005). Financial contagion between Economies: an exploratory spatial analysis. - *Estudios de Economia Aplicada*, Vol. 23-1, ISSN 1697-5731

157. **Voronkova, S.** (2004). Equity market integration in Central European emerging markets: A cointegration analysis with shifting regimes. – *International Review of Financial Analysis*, Vol. 13, pp. 633-647.

158. **Wolf, H.C.** (1996). Comovements among emerging equity markets. http://www1.worldbank.org/economicpolicy/managing %20volatility/contagion/documents/comove.pdf.

159. **Woo, W. T., Carleton, P. D. and Rosario, B. P.** (2000). The unorthodox origins of the Asian Currency crisis: Evidence from logit estimation. - *ASEAN Economic Bulletin, 17*, pages 120-134.

160. **Woo, W.T.** (2000). Coping with accelerated capital flows from the globalization of financial markets. - *ASEAN Economic Bulletin, 17*, 193-204.

161. **World Bank Group** (2009). Contagion of financial crises website. http://www1.worldbank.org/economicpolicy/managing %20volatility/contagion/index.html.

162. **Xue, Y., He, Y. and Shao, X**. (2012). Butterfly effect: the US real estate market downturn and the Asian recession. – *Finance Research Letters*, Vol. 9, Issue 2, pp. 92-102.

APPENDICES

Appendix I. Studies investigating financial contagion: correlation coefficients based tests

Author(s)	Year	Method; Definition	Result*	Data	Observed market
King, Wadhwani	1990	Shift-contagion	Yes	US, UK and Japan after 1987 US crash	Stocks, bonds
Pindyck, Rotemberg	1990	Excess comovement	Yes	US, 1960-1985	Commodity prices
Lee, Kim	1993	Shift-contagion	Yes	12 major markets after US 1987 crash	Stocks
Pindyck, Rotemberg	1993	Excess comovement	Yes	42 companies, 1969-1984	Stocks
Calvo, Reinhart	1996	Shift-contagion	Yes	1994 Mexican peso crisis, Asian and Latin American emerging markets	bonds and equities
Valdes	1997	Excess comovement	Yes	7 Latin-American countries, 1986-1994	secondary market debt prices and credit ratings
Frankel, Schmukler	1998	Correlation coefficient based tests	Yes	Mexican 1994, to Asia and Latin-America	Country fund prices
Baig and	1999	Shift-contagion,	Mixed	emerging markets	Stocks, interest

103

Goldfaj n		adjusted		during the 1997-98 East Asian crisis	rates
Baig and Goldfaj n	199 9	Shift-contagion	Yes	1997-98 East Asian crisis	Sovereig n spreads, currencie s
Boyer, Gibson, Loretan	199 9	Shift-contagion, adjusted	No	Germany, Japan; 1991-1998	Exchang e rates
Loretan, English	200 0	Shift-contagion, adjusted	No	Germany and GB (Germany and Japan in case of exchange rates)	Equities, bonds, foreign exchange
Forbes, Rigobon	200 0	Shift-contagion, adjusted	No	Latin American crises in 1990s	Bonds, stocks
Bordo, Murshid	200 0b	Shift-contagion, adjusted	No / Weak	Different historical and current crises	Bonds, interest rates
Gelos, Sahay	200 1	Shift-contagion	Yes	from the Czech Republic, Asia, and Russia to CEE	Exchang e rates
Gelos, Sahay	200 1	Shift-contagion	No	from the Czech Republic, Asia, and Russia to CEE	Stocks

Forbes, Rigobon	2001	Shift-contagion, adjusted	No	28 countries, 1987 US stock market crash, 1994 Mexican peso collapse, 1997 East Asian crisis	Stocks
Sander, Kleimei er	2003	Shift-contagion using Granger-causality methodolo gy	Yes	Asian crisis, 1996-2000	Bonds
Alvarez-Plata, Schroot en	2003	Shift-contagion	No	7 Latin-American countries, 2001-02 Argentinean crisis	Stocks, interest rates
Gravelle , Kichian, Morley	2003	Shift-contagion	No	4 emerging-market countries 1991-2001	Brady bonds
Gravelle , Kichian, Morley	2003	Shift-contagion	Yes	7 developed countries 1985-2001	Currenci es
Hon, Strauss, Yong	2004	Shift-contagion, adjusted	Yes	2001 terrorist attack, 25 economies: OECD and Asia	Stocks
Serwa	2005	Shift-contagion,	Weak	7 crises, 1997-2002;	stocks

		adjusted		17 Western Europe and CEE countries	
McAleer, Nam	2005	Shift-contagion, adjusted	Yes	6 Asian countries, Asian crisis 1997	Exchange rates
Arestis, Caporale, Cipollini, Spagnolo	2005	Shift-contagion, adjusted	Mixed	1997 Asian crisis; from Thailand, Indonesia, Korea, Malaysia to Japan, UK, Germany, France	Stocks
Corsetti, Pericoli, Scrabcia	2005	Shift-contagion, adjusted	Yes	Hong Kong crisis 1997, 17 countries	Stocks
Wang, Thi	2006	Increase in dynamic correlation coefficient	Yes	Asian crisis 1997, Thailand, China, Hong Kong, Taiwan	Stocks
Chiang, Jeon, Li	2007	Dynamic conditional correlation	Yes	9 Asian countries, 1990-2003	Stocks
Bayoumi, Fazio, Kumar, MacDonald	2007	Correlations and distance relationships	Yes	15 countries, 1991-2001	Stocks, exchange rates
Lee, Wu, Wang	2007	Shift-contagion, adjusted	No	earthquake in South-East Asia on Dec	Stocks

			Yes*	26, 2004, 26 international stock indexes	
Lee, Wu, Wang	2007	Shift-contagion, adjusted	Yes	earthquake in South-East Asia on Dec 26, 2004, 26 international stock indexes	Exchange market
Kleimeier, Lenhert, Verschoor	2008	Shift-contagion, adjusted, time-aligned data	Yes	Asian crisis, Thailand + 14 countries	Stocks
Wang, Moore	2008	Dynamic conditional correlation	Yes	three CEE countries, 1994-2006	Stocks
Kallberg, Pasquariello	2008	Excess comovement, adjusted	Yes	82 US industry indexes, 1976-2001	Stocks

* Result column indicates whether evidence in favor of financial contagion was found or not.

Source: compiled by the author.

Appendix II. Studies investigating financial contagion: conditional probability based tests

Author	Year	Method; Definition	Result*	Data	Observed market
Eichengreen, Rose and Wyplosz	1996	Probit model	Yes	20 industrial countries, 1959-1983	Currencies
Park, Song	1998	Conditional probability	Yes	Asian crisis, 8 Asian countries	Exchange rates, stocks, interests
Lomakin, Paiz	1999	Probit analysis	No	Various countries	Bonds
De Gregorio, Valdes	2001	Conditional probability	Yes, but funda-mentals more important	1982 debt crisis, Mexican 1994, 1997 Asian	Exchange rates, credit ratings
Glick, Rose	1999	Multivariate probit model	Yes (broad definition)	5 crises and 161 countries	Currencies
Woo, Carleton, Rosario	2000	Logit model	Yes	Asian crisis; 6 Asian countries 1990-1998	Currencies
Kaminsky and Reinhart	2000	Probit model	Yes	Mexican 1994 and Asian 1997 20	Assets

				countries, 1970-1998	
Hartmann, Straetmans, de Vries	2001	Extreme value analysis	Weak	G5 countries	Asset prices
Caramazza, Ricci, Salgado	2004	Panel probit model	Yes	Mexican 1994, Asian 1997, Russian 1998; 41 emerging countries	Currencies
Fazio	2007	Probit model	Weak	1990-1999, 14 emerging market economies	Currencies
Haile, Pozo	2008	Panel probit model	Yes	37 advanced and emerging market economies, quarterly data 1960-1998	Currencies

* Result column indicates whether evidence in favor of financial contagion was found or not.
Source: compiled by the author.

Appendix III. Studies investigating financial contagion: tests measuring changes in volatility

Author	Year	Method; Definition	Result *	Data	Observed market
Eichengreen, Rose and Wyplosz	1996	Probit model	Yes	20 industrial countries, 1959-1983	Currencies
Park, Song	1998	Conditional probability	Yes	Asian crisis, 8 Asian countries	Exchange rates, stocks, interests
Lomakin, Paiz	1999	Probit analysis	No	Various countries	Bonds
De Gregorio, Valdes	2001	Conditional probability	Yes, but fundamentals more important	1982 debt crisis, Mexican 1994, 1997 Asian	Exchange rates, credit ratings
Glick, Rose	1999	Multivariate probit model	Yes (broad definition)	5 crises and 161 countries	Currencies
Woo, Carleton, Rosario	2000	Logit model	Yes	Asian crisis; 6 Asian countries 1990-1998	Currencies
Kaminsky and Reinhart	2000	Probit model	Yes	Mexican 1994 and Asian 1997	Assets

				20 countries, 1970-1998	
Hartmann, Straetmans, de Vries	2001	Extreme value analysis	Weak	G5 countries	Asset prices
Caramazza, Ricci, Salgado	2004	Panel probit model	Yes	Mexican 1994, Asian 1997, Russian 1998; 41 emerging countries	Currencies
Fazio	2007	Probit model	Weak	1990-1999, 14 emerging market economies	Currencies
Haile, Pozo	2008	Panel probit model	Yes	37 advanced and emerging market economies, quarterly data 1960-1998	Currencies

* Result column indicates whether evidence in favor of financial contagion was found or not.

Source: compiled by the author.

Appendix IV. Studies investigating financial contagion: other tests

Author	Year	Method	Result*	Data	Observed market
Craig, Dravid and Richardson	1995	CDR approach	No	US and Japanese stocks	Stocks
Kali, Reyes	2005	Network approach	Yes	Tequila Crisis Mexican 1994), the Asian Flu, and the Russian Virus	Stocks
Kali, Reyes	2005	Network approach	No	Venezuelan and Argentine crises	Stocks
Wolf	1996	Granger-causality	Weak	21 sectors of 24 developing countries, 1976-1995	Equities
Frankel, Schmukler	1998	Granger-causality	Yes	Mexican 1994, to Asia and Latin-America	Country fund prices
Alba, Bhattacharya, Claessens, Ghosh, Hernandez	1998	Qualitative analysis	Unclear, probably Yes	Asian crisis	stocks, exchange rates, sovereign bonds
Abeysinghe	2001	Structural full trade model	Yes	Asian crisis, East-Asian countries	Stocks
Tornell	1999	Regression analysis	No	Mexican 1995 and Asian 1997	Currencies
Woo	200	Qualitati	Yes	Asian crisis;	Bonds

	0	ve analysis		from Thailand to 4 Asian countries	
Sola, Spagnolo, Spagnolo	2002	Markov switching framework	Yes	Asian crisis 1997; from Thailand to South-Korea	Stocks
Sola, Spagnolo, Spagnolo	2002	Markov switching framework	No	Asian crisis 1997; from South-Korea to Brazil	Stocks
Cerra, Saxena	2002	Markov switching framework	Yes	Indonesian currency crisis	stocks, currencies
Serwa	2005	Markov switching framework	No	HSI and Nikkei 225; 1997 Asian crisis	Stocks
Serwa	2005	Markov switching framework	Weak / No	US, UK , Japan, Germany	Stocks
Candelon, Hecq, Verschoor	2005	Serial correlation common feature	No	Mexican 1994, Asian 1997	Stocks
Agenor, Aizenman, Hoffmaiste	1998	VAR model	Yes	Mexico and Argentina, 1993-1998	Interest rates

r					
Favero, Giavazzi	1999	VAR model and full-information approach	Yes	7 European countries; ERM crisis, 1988-1992	Interest rates
Gelos, Sahay	2001	VAR model and Granger causality	Mixed at best	Czech, Asian and Russian crisis to CEE	Stocks
Gelos, Sahay	2001	VAR model and Granger causality	Mixed / Some support	Czech, Asian and Russian crisis to CEE	Exchange rates
Serwa	2005	VAR model	Yes	Asian crisis 1997	Capital markets
Kelejian, Tavlas, Hondroyiannis	2006	Spatial modelling	Yes	6 crisis; 25 developing countries	Currencies
Iwatsubo, Inagaki	2006	CDR approach (EGARCH model)	Yes	22 Asian firms and 7 indeces, Asian crises	Stocks
Moussalli	2007	OLS and the bootstrap method	Yes	Asian, Russian, Brazilian crisis; Asian, East-European, Latin-American countries	Stocks
Didier, Mauro,	2008	Theoretical	Yes		

Shmukler		analysis			

* Result column indicates whether evidence in favor of financial contagion was found or not.
Source: compiled by the author.

Appendix V. Results of meta-analysis for subgroups based on two moderators

	Sample size	ESs as treatment effects (Approach 1)			ESs as correlation coefficients (Approach 2)		
		Meta-ES	Standard error (ES)	Q-stat.	Meta-ES	Standard error (ES)	Q-stat.
Emerg and	237	0.04*	0.009	261	0.04*	0.009	280*
Emerg and	95	0.19*	0.008	846	0.24*	0.008	3257
Devel and	308	0.02	0.010	404	0.02	0.011	433*
Devel and	64	0.12*	0.014	92*	0.12*	0.015	92*
Mex and A	41	0.12*	0.044	30	0.15*	0.050	28
Mex and U	27	0.20*	0.075	15	0.22*	0.103	10
HK and A	116	0.04*	0.012	167	0.04*	0.012	173*
HK and U	38	0.17*	0.026	78*	0.17*	0.013	93*
US87 and	9	0.17	0.108	1.7	0.18	0.131	1.2
US87 and	10	0.19*	0.04	4.0	0.18	0.084	3.4
Ind04 and	41	-	0.040	70*	-	0.044	98
Ind04 and	10	-	0.040	52	-	0.044	55
Cze97 and	7	0.01	0.056	9.1	0.01	0.058	9.0
Cze97 and	7	0.10	0.056	16*	0.11	0.058	16*
Stocks and	416	0.02*	0.007	420	0.02*	0.008	435
Bonds and	48	0.04	0.029	129	0.06	0.031	163*
Exchange rates and A	23	0.09*	0.046	21	0.09	0.050	21
Interest rates and A	36	0.14*	0.033	49	0.14*	0.036	48

* denotes statistically significant results (in 95% confidence level)

There are no data points for Brazilian, Turkish, US01, Argentinean and US02 crisis with U (all the data points in case of these crises are calculated using heteroscedasticity adjusted post-crisis correlations).
Source: compiled by the author.

Appendix VI. Studies and constructs used in the meta-analysis

Author(s)	Year	Within study distinction	No. of effect sizes
Bordo and Murshid	2000	na	106
Forbes and Rigobon	1999	U	63
Forbes and Rigobon	1999	A	63
King and Wadhwani	1995	U	1
Lee, Wu and Wang	2006	U, stocks	23
Lee, Wu and Wang	2006	A, stocks	23
Lee, Wu and Wang	2006	U, interest rates	18
Lee, Wu and Wang	2006	A, interest rates	18
Wang, Thi	2006	Conditional	3
Wang, Thi	2006	Unconditional	3
Kleimeier, Lenhert, Verschoor	2008	Closing prices	28
Kleimeier, Lenhert, Verschoor	2008	Matched intra day prices	28
Baig, Goldfajn	1999	Exchange rates	4
Baig, Goldfajn	1999	Stocks	4
Baig, Goldfajn	1999	Interest rates	4
Baig, Goldfajn	1999	Sovereign spreads	4
Corsetti, Pericoli, Sbracia	2005	Na	17
Serwa	2005	Forbes-Rigobon methodology	76
Serwa	2005	Corsetti-Pericoli-Sbracia methodology	76

Serwa	2005	Residuals based methodology	76
Alvarez-Plata, Schrooten	2003	Stocks	6
Alvarez-Plata, Schrooten	2003	Interest rates	6
Chiang, Jeon, Li	2007	Adjusted	14
Chiang, Jeon, Li	2007	Unadjusted	14
Gelos, Sahay	2001	Stocks, unadjusted	12
Gelos, Sahay	2001	Stocks, adjusted	12
Gelos, Sahay	2001	Exchange rates, U	9
Gelos, Sahay	2001	Exchange rates, A	5

Source: compiled by the author.

Appendix VII. Author's publications

Appendix 7.1. Paas, T., Kuusk, A. (2011). Contagion of financial crises: what does the empirical evidence show? *Baltic Journal of Management*, Vol. 7(1), pp. 25-48.

 The current issue and full text archive of this journal is available at www.emeraldinsight.com/1746-5265.htm

Contagion of financial crises: what does the empirical evidence show?

Tiiu Paas and Andres Kuusk

Faculty of Economics and Business Administration, University of Tartu, Tartu, Estonia

Received 20 October 2009
Revised 2 April 2010
13 May 2010
Accepted 12 October 2010

Abstract

Purpose – The purpose of this paper is to give an overview of variability of empirical results of several financial contagion studies, taking into account the role of financial markets, data sets and the applied definitions and methods that may explain the variability of empirical evidence.

Design/methodology/approach – The authors used qualitative analysis of published research materials about previous financial crises and analyzed the variability of empirical results of around 75 studies of financial contagion, taking into account the particularities of financial markets, data sets and tests methods.

Findings – The results of the analysis show that empirical studies provide heterogeneous results depending on applied definitions and methods, as well as chosen crises, destination countries and financial indices. Summing up all the relevant empirical findings the results supporting the contagion hypothesis are in clear dominance, but taking into account differences in definitions and testing methodologies the research did not reveal clear results as to which evidence dominates or should dominate.

Research limitations/implications – The authors conclude that solely qualitative analysis of published research materials about previous financial crises does not give sufficient information to elaborate proper management measures to prevent serious consequences of financial crises. The authors propose that it is possible to obtain a more adequate picture of financial contagion by using a meta-analysis, which the authors are planning to do in future studies.

Practical implications – The paper provides information about some reasons that explain the variability of the results that are presented in the empirical studies about financial contagion. This information can be used for elaborating policy proposals and regulations that can help alleviate possible negative consequences of financial contagion. The paper shows the way for future articles summarising financial contagion.

Originality/value – The study sums up previous findings on the field of financial contagion and shows the insufficiency of the traditional literature review to accomplish that task.

Keywords Economics research, Research work, Financial analysis, Financial contagion, Financial crises

Paper type Literature review

1. Introduction

Contagion of financial crisis, which can be considered as a systematic component of financial risks, makes the crisis management in financial institutions and on national level fairly unique and complex. The recent financial crisis, which started from the USA, is a typical example emphasizing the importance of improvements in activities of financial institutions and their management. When seeking to improve the financial institutions activities, the possible transmission channels of crises, the role of monitoring and data quality as well as systematic analysis of the lessons of previous crises and their contagion should be taken into account. The results of such analyses

Baltic Journal of Management
Vol. 7 No. 1, 2012
pp. 25-48
© Emerald Group Publishing Limited
1746-5265
DOI 10.1108/17465261211196883

offer additional information to improve countries' policies and institutional environment and thereby enhance risk management. It should be mentioned, that the main interest of contagion studies is associated with the merits of international diversification of risks. Therefore, the results of financial contagion analysis are particularly important for the Baltic states, the countries with small very open economies that are extremely vulnerable to external shocks.

Without doubt, financial contagion has become increasingly popular research task in the recent decades. Several crisis in 1980s, 1990s and in the present century were transmitted rapidly to other countries that were sometimes quite different in their size and economic structure as compared to the country of origin and being even located on the other side of the globe. Borrowing the phrase from epidemiology this phenomenon has been called contagion in the economic literature. The phenomenon of contagion is not historic. According to Rigobon (2002), the issue of contagion has been one of the most debated topics in international finance since the Asian crises. As argued by Didier *et al.* (2008), the factors underlying the channels that generated contagion during the crises of the 1990s seem to be potentially at least as strong today as they were a decade ago. One of the main interests of contagion studies is associated to the merits of international diversification. The rationale being that theoretically international diversification should significantly reduce the portfolio risk, but when cross-country correlations increase during crises much of the rationale is undermined. Besides, questions about appropriate financial architecture and investment opportunities and risks to local markets can be answered by studies of financial contagion.

The paper aims to give an overview of variability of empirical results of several financial contagion studies (Appendix 1) taking into account the role of financial markets, data sets and the applied definitions and methods that may explain a significant part of the variability of empirical evidence. We seek the answer on the question whether a qualitative analysis of economic literature allows us to get a relevant picture of the real consequences of financial crises and their contagion. We suppose that empirical results may be affected depending on several reasons including definitions of contagion, test methods and heterogeneity of samples. The main contribution of the paper is to clearly show the multidimenionality of the financial contagion puzzle and the heterogeneity in the results of previous empirical studies because of that. Unlike previous literature reviews which have mainly focused on alternative theoretical and empirical frameworks used, we concentrate mainly to the concrete results found by previous empirical literature. The Word Bank Group (2009) provides comprehensive information about several approaches to the concept of "financial contagion" and the transmission channels of financial crisis, as well as also about the results of empirical studies focused on financial contagion in their special web site. In our analysis we rely on the World Bank Group web site information and also on other data sources allowing us to create a comprehensive picture of the consequences and possible contagion of the previous financial crises. We apply qualitative analysis for examining previous literature about empirical evidence of financial contagion classifying the literature sources in four groups according to the methodology applied for testing of contagion (e.g. cross-market correlation, conditional probability, volatility changes, other approaches).

The paper consists of four main parts. The next section of the paper examines some concepts related to financial contagion and its transmission channels. Section 3 focuses on explaining empirical evidence of financial contagion taking into account the variability of tests and data sets used in empirical studies. This part of the paper is based on the qualitative analysis of around 75 empirical studies. The last section of the paper shortly concludes.

2. Financial contagion and its transmission channels

In spite of significant theoretical and empirical interest on the topic there is still no consensus on neither the definition nor transmission channels of financial contagion. Economic literature offers conceptually different definitons of financial contagion. According to our opinion there does not exist clear definitions allowing explaining the complexity of this phenomenon. Using the contagion of financial crises web site summary (The World Bank Group, 2009), we can distinguish at least three different definitions of financial contagion:

- *Definition 1.* The broadest definition considers contagion as the cross-country transmission of shocks or as the general cross-country spillover effects. Unlike other definitions it includes fundamental linkages as a channel of contagion.

- *Definition 2.* The second definition makes the restriction that only the transmission of shocks to other countries beyond any fundamental link among the countries and beyond common shocks is considered financial contagion. For example, Masson (1999) defines contagion to mean only those transmissions of crises that cannot be identified with observed changes in macroeconomic fundamentals. Going for somewhat other testing methodology Eichengreen *et al.* (1996) argue that there is contagion if the probability of a crisis in a given country increases conditional on the occurrence of a crisis elsewhere, after controlling for the standard set of macroeconomic fundamentals. This definition is sometimes referred as excess co-movement (Edwards, 2000) – a correlation that remains even after controlling for fundamentals and common shocks. Herding behavior is usually argued to be responsible for that more-than-expected co-movement.

- *Definition 3.* According to the most restrictive approach contagion occurs when not only there exist transmissions of shocks to other countries but also these transmissions are stronger during crisis times as compared to tranquil times. This definition is sometimes referred as shift-contagion (term coined by Forbes and Rigobon (2001)) and it excludes a constant high degree of co-movement in a crisis period. In the latter case, markets are just interdependent.

Additionally to the above-mentioned approaches to the explaining financial contagion, we can also rely on some other and even more extreme definitions of this phenomenon. For example, according to Sola *et al.* (2002) there is contagion if the probability of having a crisis at home equals one if the crisis hits another market; on the other hand Bae *et al.* (2003) consider coincidence of extreme return shocks across countries as evidence for contagion.

The understanding of the phenomenon financial contagion is closely related to its transmission channels. But the authors of the papers considering financial crises have not yet achieved consensus on the channels through which contagion spreads. Several trade issues, macro environment, common lender, market psychology, etc. have been considered as the determinants of the degree of contagion. Different opinions are well summarized by The World Bank Group (2009):

Some claim that contagion is explained by real links, while others provide a financial explanation. At the same time, other studies argue that herding behavior is the key element to understand the recent contagious episodes. Although one can show that these factors are present in the cross-country transmission of crises, an even more difficult problem is to determine the relative importance of each component.

This summary accords with the statement pointed out by Dornbusch *et al.* (2000b): "not only the exact causes and channels of contagion are not known, neither are the precise policy interventions which can most effectively reduce it".

In the last decade a distinction has been made between contagion and interdependence according to the transmission channels (Rigobon, 2002; Kleimeier *et al.*, 2008). If crises are transmitted through stable fundamental linkages, then only countries with weak economic fundamentals will be affected and good fundamentals can offer protection. On the other hand, if the irrational behavior by the agents (in the form of speculative attacks, financial panic and/or herd behavior) is the transmission force, then even countries with good fundamentals can be seriously affected. In the former case we have only interdependence and not contagion between countries, while in the latter case we have true contagion. Considering this distinction the first definition presented above may be only interdependence and not contagion.

In sum, it is possible to distinguish at least three fundamental links that explain transmission channels (The World Bank Group, 2009). These links are:

- financial;
- real; and
- political.

There are financial links between countries when these countries are connected through international financial system. According to Didier *et al.* (2008) financial links appear to have been the main transmission channel of the Mexican 1994 crisis. Also Baig and Goldfajn (1999), Caramazza *et al.* (2004), Kaminsky and Reinhart (2000) and Van Rijckeghem and Weder (2001) have argued that the financial links were the main channel of transmission of shocks across countries during the 1990s. (For those models see Calvo (2005), Calvo and Mendoza (2000) and Kaminsky and Reinhart (2000).)

Fundamental economic relationships between countries are labeled real links. The most commonly considered economic relationships are when countries are connected through international trade. Eichengreen and Rose (1999), Forbes (2001, 2004) and Glick and Rose (1999) investigated the 1992-1993 European exchange rate mechanism (ERM) crisis, the 1994 Mexican crisis, the 1997 Asian crisis, and the 1999 Brazilian crisis and have argued that trade links are primary channel through which crises were transmitted to other countries. On the other hand Didier *et al.* (2008) argue that although the trade channel seems to have played a role, to different degrees, in the crises of the 1990s, it does not explain the contagion observed in the context of the 1998 Russian crisis, where trade links, either bilateral trade or third party competition, among the affected countries were quite limited. Thus, the experience of the Russian crisis suggests that trade is unlikely to be the only channel of contagion and also other channels are necessary to account for the evidence. (For models of contagion based on trade linkage and macroeconomic similarities, see Eichengreen *et al.* (1996), Goldstein (1998) and Gerlach and Smets (1995)).

Political links label the situation when there are political relationships among countries. Usually that means that countries' exchange rates are closely tied.

Hernandez and Valdes (2001) investigate the relative importance of alternative fundamental links during the Thai, Russian, and Brazilian crises. Results are different according to whether crises are measured by changes in sovereign bond spreads or by stock market returns. In the former case financial links seem to be clearly dominant transmission channel. In the latter case both trade links and neighborhood effects appear to be relevant contagion channels during the Thai and Brazilian crises, while financial competition remains the only relevant channel in the case of the Russian crisis.

Many authors have found that fundamental links (and commons shocks) do not fully explain the relationship and changes in relationships among countries. That being the case, herding behavior is suggested as reason for spillover effects between countries. Herding behavior arises when information about countries' fundamentals is incomplete and asymmetric, there are no serious restrictions for investors choosing their moves and information is too costly for the less informed investors (For a good overview of financial crises based on asymmetric information approach, see Mishkin (1991), for more general overview of information asymmetry, see Rothschild and Stiglitz (1976).) So instead of making expenses for getting lacking information these not well-informed investors are watching the actions of other, supposedly well informed, investors and try to follow them as they think these actions reflect the future price changes. It follows that all the market moves jointly. In reality those supposedly well-informed investors may not act based on their information about countries' fundamentals but rather just adjust their portfolio after being damaged by crisis elsewhere. In the circumstances of that kind of herd behavior and the world of multiple equilibria even countries with sound fundamentals are not protected. According to Alvarez-Plata and Schrooten (2003) the pull effect caused by investors all behaving in the same way makes economic fundamentals unimportant and lead to the rapid withdrawal of capital from the economies concerned or possibly even from entire regions. Claessens et al. (2001) argue that as spreads are directly reflecting the risk perception of financial markets, pure contagion may be solely the result of the behavior of investors or other financial agents.

Evidence of herding behavior-based transmission of crises have been found by many authors. Eichengreen et al. (1996) highlight that the countries that came under speculative attack during the ERM crisis had heterogeneous macroeconomic fundamentals, and only in some cases could the attack be justified by the fundamentals. Pindyck and Rotemberg (1990, 1993) find that after taking into account common fundamentals there is still residual co-movement across stocks with very different industry and idiosyncratic fundamentals. These results point on the important role played during the crisis by irrationally behaving investors and speculators. Also Moussalli (2007), Alvarez-Plata and Schrooten (2003) and Woo (2000) have argued that herding is the main channel for spillover effects between countries.

Somewhat ironically, at a private level, it might be rational to follow the herd for the same reason that information is too costly for the individual investor, so looking at the market reaction or to opt for general investment strategies may be the rational solution. But as said, at a public level, however, contagion can be very costly. And to do things even worse asymmetric information seems not to be absolutely necessary condition for multiple equilibria to occur. Jeanne and Masson (2000) have pointed out, that there can be multiple equilibria even with complete and symmetric information if investors are sufficiently forward looking.

Thus, economic literature provides heterogenous views on financial contagion and its transmission channels and therefore it is understandable that also the results of empirical studies may vary depending on theoretical and empirical frameworks for considering the concept of financial contagion as well as on several other reasons. In the next part of our paper we analyse the variability of empirical evidence of financial contagion relying on the results of the relevant economic literature.

3. Analysis of financial contagion empirical evidence

3.1 Literature overview: some main reasons explaining variability of empirical evidence
Drawing some finite conclusions on financial contagion based on empirical evidence is not easy. Empirical analyses differ on chosen conceptual definition of contagion and even in the most widely used approach of focusing on co-movements in asset prices, there are substantial differences whether correlations are adjusted for the presence of heteroskedasticity or not. We are aware that chosen crises, time periods, destination countries and even the financial market under investigation may affect the results of empirical studies. In addition, the problems of omitted variables, feedback dependencies between stock markets, different time zones, and arbitrary choices of the crisis window can all affect tests of contagion (Billio and Pelizzon (2003) and Dungey and Zhumabekova (2001) for good study on the subject). Naively counting numbers examining several aspects of contagion we can conclude that evidence for contagion during financial crises has been found more often than not. On the other hand, this result is mostly being obtained when the presence of heteroskedasticity is not taken into account; the papers that control for heteroskedasticity find evidence for financial contagion far less often. This diversity of results is well illustrated by the research by Serwa (2007) who used four different testing methodologies and different samples to achieve mixed results. According to his findings contagion is a rather rare phenomenon, but patterns of capital and information flow to stock markets still change during turbulent periods.

There is also no consensus on the issue whether the recent crises have been more contagious than those before 1990s. While some authors (Haile and Pozo, 2008) argue that currency crises prior to 1990s did not appear to spread across countries with the virulence and speed observed recently, the others (Bordo and Murshid, 2000a, b) have found no evidence to confirm that.

And finally there are also other problems measuring contagion (Cheung *et al.*, 2009). Rigobon (2002, 2003) pointed out that contagion has been associated with high-frequency events; it has been measured on stock market returns, interest rates, exchange rates, or linear combinations of them. Rigobon argues that these data are plagued with simultaneous equations, omitted variables, conditional and unconditional heteroskedasticity, serial correlation, non-linearity and non-normality problems. We fully agree with these viewpoints and follow some of them in our analysis. Unfortunately, no such procedure has been found yet that can handle all these problems at the same time.

We have followed the footsteps of some earlier papers (Dornbusch *et al.*, 2000b) and have divided recent empirical analyses into following categories according to the testing methodology: tests based on cross-market correlation coefficients, tests based on the conditional probabilities of currency crisis and tests measuring changes in volatility.

Furthermore, there are some more seldom used tests we discuss under label "other tests". The overview of the papers investigating financial contagion and the results of previous empirical studies is presented in Appendix 1. By compiling this overview we focused on empirical evidence found in the papers (contagion or not), particularities of data sets (variability of countries, time periods, types of crises), financial markets (stocks, bounds, exchange rates, etc.), and applied methods.

3.2 Tests based on cross-market correlation coefficients

Tests based on cross-market correlation coefficients are the most common and widely used approach to test for contagion. These tests measure the correlation in returns between two markets during a stable period and then test for a significant increase in this correlation coefficient after a shock. A significant increase in the correlation coefficient after a crisis in one of these markets is considered as evidence of contagion. These tests are mainly consistent with the third definition of financial contagion. The overview of the contagion studies that implement correlation coefficients-based tests is presented in Appendix 1.

Majority of studies that estimate correlations among markets and do not adjust for the presence of heteroskedasticity found evidence for contagion. For instance, King and Wadhwani (1990) found that correlations between some relevant economic indicators of the USA, UK and Japan increased significantly after the US 1987 crisis. Lee and Kim (1993) came to the same conclusion on the sample of 12 major markets. Baig and Goldfajn (1999) found the evidence for contagion between emerging markets during the 1997-1998 East Asian crises.

Several authors have found that the Mexican crisis in 1994 was contagious. Evidence for contagion has been found by Calvo and Reinhart (1996) and Frankel and Schmukler (1998) on the sample of Asian and Latin American emerging markets; by Valdes (1997) on the sample of Latin America; by Agenor et al. (1998) on the sample of Argentina.

However, Forbes and Rigobon (2002) and Rigobon (2002, 2003) argue that simple correlations are biased due to the presence of heteroskedasticity, endogeneity, and omitted variables. Therefore, an increase in correlations among different countries' markets may not be contagion but only interdependence. Forbes and Rigobon (2002) show that in the presence of heteroskedatisticity of asset price movements an increase in correlation could be just a continuation of strong transmission mechanisms, which exist also in tranquil times. Given that usually volatility increases during a crisis, the heteroskedasticity is actually likely and expected. If there is historically high cross-correlation among markets, then a rapid and extensive change in one market will lead to significant changes in the other markets also and according to Forbes and Rigobon (2002) these changes should not be counted as evidence of contagion. Forbes and Rigobon (2002) also show that an increase in correlations of asset prices may result when changes in economic fundamentals, risk perception, and preferences are correlated without any additional contagion being present. They argue that because of this endogeneity, estimation of correlations must control for co-movement of these variables during the so-called normal times and for the effects of fundamentals in order to be able identify pure contagion.

A deeper explanation to why it is necessary to distinguish contagion from interdependence is amongst others given by Forbes and Rigobon (2002), Rigobon (2002), Boyer et al. (1999), Loretan and English (2000) and Corsetti et al. (2005). When two random variables X and Y are positively correlated, their correlation coefficient may be an increasing function of the variance of each of them. In particular, this is always the case if X and Y are normally distributed or if one variable is a linear function of the other variable. Pericoli and Sbracia (2003) conclude that in general, correlation coefficients in specific subsamples tend to be biased in the presence of heteroskedasticity and endogeneity or if some variables are omitted. Therefore, they argue, when comparing correlation coefficients over a specific subsample, one needs to correct the bias in the coefficients generated by the different variances assumed by the variables in that subsample. For instance, during the crisis periods, economic variables generally show an increase in volatility. Hence, empirical tests that do not correct for the bias typically tend to favor the hypothesis of excessive transmission.

Unfortunately, to adjust for the effects of heteroskedasticity some restrictive assumptions have to be made. Still it may be the lesser evil. Forbes and Rigobon (2002), first version of the paper 1999 show that correlation coefficients across multi-country returns are not significantly higher during crisis periods (1987 US stock market crash, the 1994 Mexican peso crisis, and the 1997 East Asian crisis), if the problems of endogenous variables, omitted variables and changes in the variance of residuals are properly corrected for. Their famous result of no contagion, only interdependence means that large cross-market linkages after a shock are simply a continuation of strong transmission mechanisms that exist in more stable periods and has been an object of large discussion and controversy since then. Forbes and Rigobon (2000) find no clear evidence of contagion in stock and bond markets during Latin American crises in 1990s. Similarly Arias et al. (1998) find only limited evidence for contagion. Boyer et al. (1999) and Loretan and English (2000) use slightly refined methodology (by calculating corrected correlation coefficients under the assumption of normally distributed variables) and also find no evidence for contagion.

Gelos and Sahay (2001) apply a simplified version of this methodology and find no contagion from the Czech Republic, Asia, and Russia to CEE stock markets. However, they find significant changes in the relationship between exchange markets in the crisis-origin country (Russia and Czech Republic) and other markets during crisis times. Serwa (2007) uses the extension of the models presented by Forbes and Rigobon (2002) and Corsetti et al. (2005) to investing seven crises on the sample of some CEE and Western European countries and found that contagion occurred hardly ever or not frequently during the investigated crises.

However, some authors have found evidence of financial contagion even after controlling for heteroskedasticity. For example, Favero and Giavazzi (1999) find that, after controlling for normal interdependence in the context of ERM crisis there was still evidence of contagion in interest rates residuals. Hon et al. (2004) show that even after correcting for between sample heteroskedasticity and within-sample GARCH effects the terrorist attack in the USA on September 11, 2001, resulted in a contagion. Baig and Goldfajn (1999) find clear evidence for contagion with regards to sovereign spreads (however, evidence with regards to exchange rate, stock markets and interest rates co-movements is mixed as best). Kleimeier et al. (2008) use time-alignment-of-data approach and also find evidence of contagion[1]. The same result is found by Kallberg and Pasquariello (2008) who investigate excess co-movement in US stock indexes using adjustments proposed by Forbes and Rigobon (2002) and Sander and Kleimeier (2003) extend the measurement methodology by directly investigating changing causality patterns by using the Granger causality methodology and find that Asian crisis episodes were contagious.

Corsetti *et al.* (2005) show that the no "contagion, only interdependence" result obtained by Forbes and Rigobon (2002) is due to some arbitrary assumptions that concerned the variance of the market-specific noise in the country where the crisis originated. These assumptions cause that the tests are biased towards the null hypothesis of interdependence and against the hypothesis of contagion. And indeed, Corsetti *et al.* (2005) find evidence for contagion from Hong Kong to the stock markets in Singapore, Philippines, France, Italy and the UK. Also Serwa (2007) shows that the adjusted correlation coefficients of Forbes and Rigobon (2002) (and its extension by Corsetti *et al.* (2005)), that may have different values in stable and crisis periods, may in some situations be biased. For now, it is a well-known fact that the "no contagion, only interdependence" result of Forbes and Rigobon (2002) is due to the poor size properties of their methodology (Kleimeier *et al.*, 2008).

Bordo and Murshid (2000a) examine the contagiousness of financial crises over the past 120 years and find some evidence that correlations among markets were higher during crisis periods. However, as the volatility in correlation coefficients is quite high in turbulent periods, they (using the same reasoning as given by Forbes and Rigobon (2002)) find no solid evidence that contagion has been increasing over time.

In sum, the overview of the previous empirical studies applying the tests based on cross-market correlation analysis confirm our opinion that empirical evidence of financial contagion is very sensitive to the data sets and testing methods. When the correlations are not adjusted for the presence of heteroskedasticity, evidence for contagion is found in the case of majority of studies and time periods, but when the heteroskedasticity is taken into account the results of the studies are more mixed.

3.3 Tests based on the conditional probabilities

Rather than using raw correlations some authors study conditional correlation or probabilities to test financial contagion. The overview of the main contagion studies that base on implementing of conditional probability to test evidences of financial contagion is presented in Appendix 2.

The most commonly used methodology, introduced by Eichengreen *et al.* (1996) and Sachs *et al.* (1996), is examining whether the likelihood of crisis is higher in a given country when there are crises in one country or several countries by estimating the probability of a crisis conditional on information of the occurrence of crisis elsewhere. This approach has some clear advantages: first, it allows statistical tests of the existence of contagion, and second, these tests can also try to investigate the channels through which contagion may occur (Dornbusch *et al.*, 2000a).

Using a probit model and a sample of 20 industrial economies from 1959 through 1993, Eichengreen *et al.* (1996) show that the probability of a domestic currency crisis increases with a speculative attack elsewhere. Using a similar methodology, De Gregorio and Valdes (2001) found that the 1994 Mexican crisis was less contagious than the 1982 debt crisis and the Asian crisis. They also concluded that debt composition and exchange rate flexibility limit the extent of contagion, whereas capital controls do not appear to curb it. Caramazza *et al.* (2000, 2004) on the other hand have found that the contagious nature of the Mexican, Asian and Russian crises does not differ much.

Haile and Bozo (2008) use quarterly data (1960-1998) for a set of 37 advanced and emerging market economies and find that countries face currency crises because of both unsustainable macroeconomics fundamentals and contagion. Other important findings of their work are that contagion is regional and more specifically it operates through the trade channel. Glick and Rose (1999) apply a similar approach to five episodes of currency crises and 161 countries and find that trade linkages are important in propagating a crisis. They argue that contagion tends to be rather regional than global because trade tends to be more intra-regional than inter-regional (Diwan and Hoekman, 1999). Kaminsky and Reinhart (2000) find some evidence for contagion but conclude it has been a primarily regional phenomenon (Calvo and Reinhart, 1996; Kaminsky and Schmukler, 1998).

Alba *et al.* (2008) argue that the effects of competitive devaluations alone could not have explained the large depreciation of other regional currencies after the Thai devaluation, they therefore hint at some evidence for contagion. For transition economies, Gelos and Sahay (2001) find that correlations in exchange market pressures can be explained by direct trade linkages, but not by measures of other fundamentals. Shock propagation mechanisms were weak during the Asian and Czech crises, but strong during the Russian crisis. Forbes (1999, 2004) finds that country-specific effects and trade are all important transmission mechanisms during Asian and Russian crises. Using closed-end country fund data, Frankel and Schmukler (1998) test whether adverse shocks from the Mexican crisis were transmitted directly to other Latin American and East Asian countries or through New York. They find that the Mexican crisis was spread through Wall Street to East Asian countries, but was directly transmitted to other Latin-American countries. Lomakin and Paiz (1999) use a probit analysis and find that after adjustment for heteroskedasticity the strength of cross-country linkages are significantly reduced.

Analoguous to the conditional probability approach is taken by Hartmann *et al.* (2001) who derive non-parametric estimates for the expected number of market crashes given that at least one market crashes. Using G5 countries as a sample they find only very weak evidence for contagion and suggest it may be advisable to differentiate between the various types of countries on the future research.

Thus, also the results of empirical analyses applying tests based on the conditional probabilities of crises confirm our opinion that evidence of contagion is mixed and concrete testing results are very sensitive to the research methodology.

3.4 Tests measuring changes in volatillity and other tests
Tests measuring changes in volatility examine whether conditional variances of financial variables are related to each other among countries during the crisis period. It means using ARCH or GARCH framework to estimate changes in the variance-covariance matrix (Hamao *et al.*, 1990; Edwards, 1998) or co-integrating vector across countries (Chou *et al.*, 1994; Longin and Solnik, 1995). The overview of the main contagion studies that measure changes in volatility examining whether conditional variances of financial variables are related to each other among countries during the crisis period is presented in Appendix 3.

Using this procedure Chou *et al.* (1994) and Hamao *et al.* (1990) find evidence of contagion after the 1987 US stock market crisis. Using an augmented GARCH model, Edwards (1998) focuses on the 1994 Mexican crisis and finds that there was strong evidence for contagion from Mexico to Argentina, but not from Mexico to Chile. Park and Chi-Young (1998) apply a GARCH model and find that the effects of the crisis in Indonesia and Thailand were transmitted to the Korean foreign exchange market, while the Korean crisis was not contagious to the two Southeast Asian countries. Longin and Solnik (1995) find that the correlation of monthly excess returns for seven major countries over the period 1960-1990 rises in periods of high volatility.

By the way, we stress to the fact that authors using these testing approaches usually have not controlled for fundamentals and thus the tests do not enable to distinguish between pure and fundamental-based contagion, not to mention they do not allow to test for shift-contagion. This remark was also done groundedly by Dornbusch *et al.* (2000a).

There are also many more tests that are used less often (Appendix 4). Sola *et al.* (2002) use Markov switching framework and find some support for financial contagion from Thailand to South Korea during the 1997 Asian crisis. However, in the case of South Korea and Brazil independent model is preferred to the contagion interpretation. Serwa (2007) introduces the concept of causality on the same framework and finds no evidence for contagion between the Japanese (Nikkei 225) and the Hong Kong (HSI) markets during the Asian crisis.

Abeysinghe (1999) applies a full trade model for crisis-affected East Asian countries and finds that, although transmission through trade played an important role, the immediate economic contractions are largely a result of direct shocks that are attributable to pure contagion (Dornbusch *et al.*, 2000a). Serwa (2007) employs threshold vector autoregressive model to investigate the 1997 Asian crisis and finds evidence for financial contagion according to both following definitions: financial crisis spilling over from one market to other markets and a break in the interdependency structure between countries. Baur (2003) introduces a test that concentrates on the transmission mechanism of shocks directly and differentiates between mean contagion and volatility contagion in an asymmetric way. Empirical results for 11 Asian stock markets show that there is mean and volatility contagion in the Asian crisis.

Gravelle *et al.* (2003) developed a methodology to detect shift-contagion in pairs of asset returns using bootstrap procedure. Their findings suggest that shift-contagion occurs among currency markets of developed countries (in the time period 1985-2001) but not bond markets of emerging market countries (1991-2001). Kali and Reyes (2005) use quite original methods that they call network approach. Their main finding is that the network effect of the crisis epicenter country was substantially higher for the 1994 Mexican crisis, the 1997 Asian crisis and the 1998 Russian crisis than for the Venezuelan and Argentine crises. That was the reason, they argue, why these first three crises were highly contagious while the other two were not.

Craig *et al.* (1995) and Iwatsubo and Inagaki (2006) propose alternative (to the mainstream) measures (we call it CDR approach in the following) for identifying financial contagion between non-synchronous trading markets. Craig *et al.* (1995) find that Japanese Nikkei index-based futures traded in the USA provide complete information about contemporaneous overnight Japanese returns. Iwatsubo and Inagaki (2006) investigate the bilateral contagion effects between US and Asian stock markets and find that there exist significant bilateral contagion effects in returns and return volatility between US and Asian markets and the intensity of contagion was significantly greater during the Asian financial crisis than after the crisis.

Villar Frexedas and Vaya (2005) and Kelejian *et al.* (2006) have used spatial econometric tools to investigate the financial contagion phenomenon. Both papers detect that contagion seems to have a clearly regional component.

Tornell (1999) does not actually test for the presence of contagion, but rather how the crisis, if occurs, spreads across emerging markets. His findings suggest that crises do not spread to the countries with strong fundamentals, which of course is not supporting for the contagion hypothesis (at least if we speak about more restrictive definitions of contagion).

In sum, the results of empirical studies investigating financial crises and applying different test methods are very heterogeneous and do not allow to provide a clear and synthesized picture of financial contagion and its spread. Thus, the application of additional methodological approaches allowing systematically analyze and adequately summarize the consequences of previous financial crises for examining the phenomenon of financial contagion is necessary.

3.5 Summary of variability of empirical evidence

Appendixes 1-4 summarize empirical results on the field on financial contagion presenting information about the method implemented for analysis, data, observed markets as well as about the results concerning evidence of contagion (Yes, No, Mixed). As it can be seen from the tables in Appendixes 1-4 and from the preceding literature review, the results obtained in the financial contagion studies are very much heterogeneous. One should keep in mind that in many cases the chosen result in favor of Yes, No or Mixed in appendixes is not clear-cut. For example, in correlation coefficients-based tests, there are mostly different results – some correlations have increased significantly during crises, some have not changed much and some have even decreased. Also note that not all selected papers presented in this overview actually test for the presence for financial contagion. So in some cases the results presented in the fourth column of the table (whether evidence for contagion have been found or not) may be somewhat disputable (see also different definitions of financial contagion). So simply summing up the results for one yes or no conclusion may not be the perfect way for the contagion analysis.

Next we shortly summarise the main results from four main groups of studies which are separated according to the financial contagion testing methodologies.

Appendix 1 summarises the results obtained by the studies using correlation coefficients-based methodologies. As it can be seen the results supporting the contagion hypothesis are clearly prevailing being twice as frequent as the no-contagion results. However, Yes-results are undermined by the later papers because of the questionability of the applied testing methodologies. As pointed out earlier it is found that not adjusting for the presence of heteroskedasticity may affect the results and the findings tend to be biased towards the supporting contagion. If only papers with heteroskedasticity adjusted post-crises correlations are taken into account Yes and No results are being found quite evenly.

Going on to Appendix 2 and papers using conditional probability-based tests it is clearly seen that results supporting the contagion hypothesis are dominating. From 11 studies seven have found clear evidence of contagion and three more have found some support to the contagion hypothesis. Still, one has to keep in mind that these papers investigate broader definitions of financial contagion than the ones that investigate shift-contagion, which makes finding supporting evidence more likely.

Appendix 3 summarises the results from studies that investigate volatility changes to test for contagion. Again great majority of studies using this methodology have found evidence of contagion with only a few studies with mixed results. But, of course, this may be attributable to the fact that these studies only test for the two broader definitions of financial contagion and most of them even do not control for fundamentals.

Appendix 4 summarises results from the studies that use some other methodologies than those presented in Appendixes 1-3. From these studies the methodology of Markov switching framework has been used the most. Both results supporting and contradicting the contagion hypothesis have been found evenly by using this methodology. From studies using other methodologies also both results have been found many times with slight edge to the contagion supporting ones.

There are almost no pairs of studies that are identical in all their definition of financial contagion, testing methodology, chosen crises, financial markets, and destination countries, but all of these aspects may influence the results of the analysis. So drawing some final conclusions based on the qualitative literature review is probably too much to ask. If we forget for a moment all these heterogeneities we can conclude that results supporting the financial contagion hypothesis are clearly dominating. However, if one wants to specify the definition of contagion and clearly separate it from interdependence, the completely different picture arises and the debate over the existence of financial contagion is still pretty much open.

4. Conclusion

Financial contagion has become increasingly popular research task in the recent decades and there is a large amount of economic literature examining the concept of "financial contagion" and the transmission channels of financial crisis, as well as analyzing empirical evidence of this phenomenon. But despite of all these activities and study results, there is still no clear consensus among the researchers in order to elaborate proper policy measures allowing alleviating serious consequences of possible financial contagion. We analysed the variability of empirical results of around 75 studies of financial contagion taking into account the particularities of financial markets, data sets and tests methods. The results of the analysis show that empirical studies provide heterogeneous results depending on applied definitions and methods, also chosen crises, destination countries and observed markets may have an impact to the results. Recent empirical analyses contain both, the evidence confirming and the evidence contradicting financial contagion. Summing up all the relevant empirical findings the results supporting the contagion hypothesis are in clear dominance, but taking into account differences in definitions and testing methodologies our research which is based on the qualitative analysis of previous studies about financial contagion did not reveal clear results as to which evidence dominates or should dominate. We are aware that in many cases the results of empirical analyses may be biased and serious additional investments into examining possible consequences of financial crises are still necessary. We conclude that qualitative analysis of published research materials about previous financial crises does not give sufficient information to elaborate proper management measures allowing to prevent serious consequences of financial crises. We propose that it is possible to obtain more adequate picture of financial contagion by using more quantitative approach, for example a meta-analysis, which we are planning to do in our next studies. Still, as even in the case of most restrictive definition of financial contagion, there is at least as much support as contradiction to the contagion hypothesis, the financial contagion phenomenon cannot be ignored. That means the regulations that try to alleviate the harmful consequences of possible future financial crises have to have much more global orientation than they have had so far and they should be strongly coordinated between the countries and country groups as well as large international organisations like the World Bank, International Monetary Fund, etc.

Note

1. Kleimeier *et al.* (2008) make an important step forward investigating synchronized data. Whether this kind of data needs to be time aligned or not may be one of the main discussion objects in the future research.

References

Abeysinghe, T. (1999), "Thai meltdown and transmission of recession within ASEAN4 and NIE4", mimeo.

Agenor, P.-R., Aizenman, J. and Hoffmaister, A. (1998), "Contagion, bank lending spreads and output fluctuations", NBER Working Paper No. W6850.

Alba, P., Bhattacharya, A., Claessens, S., Ghosh, S. and Hernandez, L. (2008), "Volatility and contagion in a financially-integrated world: lessons from east Asia's recent experience", World Bank and Central Bank of Chile, available at: www.worldbank.org/html/dec/Publications/Workpapers/wps2000series/wps2008/wps2008.pdf

Alvarez-Plata, P. and Schrooten, M. (2003), "Latin America after the Argentine crisis: diminishing financial market integration", *Economic Bulletin*, Vol. 40 No. 12.

Arestis, P., Caporale, G.M., Cipollini, A. and Spagnolo, N. (2005), "Testing for financial contagion between developed and emerging markets during the 1997 East Asian crisis", *International Journal of Finance & Economics*, Vol. 10 No. 4, pp. 359-67.

Arias, E.F., Hausmann, R. and Rigobon, R. (1998), "Contagion on bond markets: preliminary notes", mimeo, MIT Press, Cambridge, MA.

Bae, K., Karolyi, A. and Stulz, R. (2003), "A new approach to measuring financial contagion", *Review of Financial Studies*, Vol. 16, pp. 717-63.

Baig, T. and Goldfajn, I. (1999), "Financial market contagion in the Asian crisis", *IMF Staff Papers*, Vol. 46, pp. 167-95.

Baur, D. (2003), "Testing for contagion – mean and volatility contagion", *Journal of Multinational Financial Management*, Vol. 13 Nos 4/5, pp. 405-22.

Bayoumi, T., Fazio, G., Kumar, M. and MacDonald, R. (2007), "Fatal attraction: using distance to measure contagion in good times as well as bad", *Review of Financial Economics*, Vol. 16 No. 3, pp. 259-73.

Billio, M. and Pelizzon, L. (2003), "Contagion and interdependence in stock markets: have they been misdiagnosed?", *Journal of Economics and Business*, Vol. 55, pp. 405-26.

Bordo, M.D. and Murshid, A.P. (2000a), "Are financial crises becoming increasingly more contagious? What is the historical evidence on contagion?", NBER Working Paper Series, WP 7900.

Bordo, M.D. and Murshid, A.P. (2000b), "The international transmission of financial crises before world war II: was there contagion?", available at: www.cfr.org/content/thinktank/Depression/Bordo_1.pdf

Boyer, B., Gibson, M. and Loretan, M. (1999), "Pitfalls in tests for changes in correlations", Federal Reserve Board Working Paper, Vol. 597.

Calvo, G.A. (2005), "Contagion in emerging markets: when wall street is a carrier", in Calvo, G. (Ed.), *Emerging Capital Markets in Turmoil: Bad Luck or Bad Policy?*, MIT Press, Cambridge, MA, pp. 313-28.

Calvo, G.A. and Mendoza, E. (2000), "Rational contagion and the globalization of securities markets", *Journal of International Economics*, Vol. 51 No. 1, pp. 79-113.

Calvo, S. and Reinhart, C. (1996), "Capital flows to Latin America: is there evidence of contagion effects?", in Calvo, G.A., Goldstein, M. and Hochreiter, E. (Eds), *Private Capital Flows to Emerging Markets after the Mexican Crisis*, Institute for International Economics, Washington, DC.

Candelon, B., Hecq, A. and Verschoor, F.C. (2005), "Measuring common cyclical features during financial turmoil: evidence of interdependence not contagion", *Journal of International Money and Finance*, Vol. 24 No. 8, pp. 1317-34.

Caramazza, F., Ricci, L. and Salgado, R.F. (2000), "Trade and financial contagion in currency crises", IMF working paper.

Caramazza, F., Ricci, L. and Salgado, R.F. (2004), "International financial contagion in currency crises", *Journal of International Money and Finance*, Vol. 23, pp. 51-70.

Cerra, V. and Saxena, S.C. (2002), "Contagion, monsoons and domestic turmoil in Indonesia's currency crisis", *Review of International Economics*, Vol. 10 No. 1, pp. 36-44.

Cheung, L., Tam, C. and Szeto, J. (2009). "Contagion of financial crises: a literature review of theoretical and empirical frameworks", Research Note 02/2009, Hong Kong Monetary Authority, Central.

Chiang, T.C., Jeon, B.N. and Li, H. (2007), "Dynamic correlation analysis of financial contagion: evidence from Asian markets", *Journal of International Money and Finance*, Vol. 26 No. 7, pp. 1206-28.

Chou, R., Ng, V. and Pi, L. (1994), "Cointegration of international stock market indices", IMF Working Paper WP/94/94.

Claessens, S., Dornbusch, R. and Park, Y.C. (2001), "Contagion: why crises spread and how this can be stopped", in Claessens, S. and Forbes, K. (Eds), *International Financial Contagion*, Kluwer Academic, Boston, MA, pp. 19-42.

Corsetti, G., Pericoli, M. and Sbracia, M. (2005), "Some contagion, some interdependence: more pitfalls in tests of financial contagion", *Journal of International Money and Finance*, Vol. 8, pp. 1177-99.

Craig, A., Dravid, A. and Richardson, M. (1995), "Market efficiency around the clock some supporting evidence using foreign-based derivatives", *Journal of Financial Economics*, Vol. 39 Nos 2/3, pp. 161-80.

De Gregorio, J. and Valdes, R.O. (2001), "Crisis transmission: evidence from the debt, tequila, and Asian flu crises", *World Bank Economic Review*, Vol. 15, pp. 289-314.

Didier, T., Mauro, P. and Schmukler, S.L. (2008), "Vanishing financial contagion?", *Journal of Policy Modeling*, Vol. 30 No. 5, pp. 775-91.

Diwan, I. and Hoekman, B. (1999), "Competition, complementarity and contagion in Asia", in Agenor, P.-R., Miller, M., Vines, D. and Weber, A. (Eds), *The Asian Financial Crises: Causes, Contagion and Consequences*, Cambridge University Press, Cambridge, p. 425.

Dornbusch, R., Park, Y.C. and Claessens, S. (2000a), *Contagion: How it Spreads and How it can be Stopped*, available at: www1.worldbank.org/economicpolicy/managing%20volatility/contagion/documents/Claessens-Dornbusch-Park.pdf

Dornbusch, R., Park, Y.C. and Claessens, S. (2000b), "Contagion: understanding how it spreads", *World Bank Research Observer*, Vol. 15, pp. 177-97.

Dungey, M. and Zhumabekova, D. (2001), "Testing for contagion using correlations: some words of caution", Working Paper No. PB01-09, Pacific Basin Working Paper Series, Federal Reserve Bank of San Francisco, San Francisco, CA.

Edwards, S. (1998), "Interest rate volatility, capital controls, and contagion", NBER Working Paper 6756.

Edwards, S. (2000), *Contagion*, available at: www.anderson.ucla.edu/faculty/sebastian.edwards/world_economy5.pdf

Eichengreen, B. and Rose, A.K. (1999), "Contagious currency crises: channels of conveyance", in Ito, T. and Krueger, A. (Eds), *Changes in Exchange Rates in Rapidly Developing Countries: Theory, Practice, and Policy Issues*, University of Chicago Press, Chicago, IL, pp. 29-50.

Eichengreen, B., Rose, A.K. and Wyplosz, C. (1996), "Contagious currency crises", NBER Working Paper 5681.

Favero, C.A. and Giavazzi, F. (1999), "Looking for contagion: evidence from the 1992 ERM crisis", available at: www1.worldbank.org/economicpolicy/managing%20volatility/contagion/documents/fg.pdf

Fazio, G. (2007), "Extreme interdependence and extreme contagion between emerging markets", *Journal of International Money and Finance*, Vol. 26 No. 8, pp. 1261-91.

Forbes, K. (1999), "How are shocks propagated internationally? Firm-level evidence from the Russian and Asian crises", available at: www.frbsf.org/economics/conferences/990923/papers/forbes.pdf

Forbes, K. (2001), "Are trade links important determinants of country vulnerability to crises?", NBER Working Paper No. 8194, National Bureau of Economic Research, Cambridge, MA.

Forbes, K. (2004), "The Asian flu and Russian virus: the international transmission of crises in firm-level data", *Journal of International Economics*, Vol. 63 No. 1, pp. 59-92.

Forbes, K. and Rigobon, R.K. (2000), "Contagion in Latin America: definitions, measurement, and policy implications", NBER Working Paper No. 7885.

Forbes, K. and Rigobon, R.K. (2001), "Measuring contagion: conceptual and empirical issues", in Claessens, S. and Forbes, K. (Eds), *International Financial Contagion*, Kluwer Academic Publishers, Boston, MA, pp. 43-66.

Forbes, K. and Rigobon, R.K. (2002), "No contagion, only interdependence: measuring stock market co-movements", *The Journal of Finance*, Vol. 57 No. 5, pp. 2223-61.

Frankel, J. and Schmukler, S. (1998), "Crisis, contagion, and country fund: effects on East Asia and Latin America", in Glick, R. (Ed.), *Managing Capital Flows and Exchange Rates*, Cambridge University Press, Cambridge.

Gelos, R.G. and Sahay, R. (2001), "Financial market spillovers in transition economies", *Economics of Transition*, Vol. 9, pp. 53-86.

Gerlach, S. and Smets, F. (1995), "Contagious speculative attacks", *European Journal of Political Economy*, Vol. 11, pp. 45-63.

Glick, R. and Rose, A.K. (1999), "Contagion and trade: why are currency crises regional?", *Journal of International Money and Finance*, Vol. 18, pp. 603-17.

Goldstein, M. (1998), "The Asian financial crisis: causes, cures, and systemic implications", *Policy Analyses in International Economics*, Vol. 55, Institute for International Economics, Washington, DC.

Gravelle, T., Kichian, M. and Morley, J. (2003), "Shift contagion in asset markets", Bank of Canada Working Paper 2003-5.

Haile, F. and Pozo, S. (2008), "Currency crisis contagion and the identification of transmission channels", *International Review of Economics & Finance*, Vol. 17 No. 4, pp. 572-88.

Hamao, Y., Masulis, R. and Ng, V. (1990), "Correlations in price changes and volatility across international stock markets", *The Review of Financial Studies*, Vol. 3 No. 2, pp. 281-307.

Hartmann, P., Straetmans, S. and de Vries, C.G. (2001), "Asset market linkages in crisis periods", Tinbergen Institute Discussion Paper, TI 2001-071/2.

Hernandez, L.F. and Valdes, R.O. (2001), "What drives contagion: trade, neighborhood, or financial links?", *International Review of Financial Analysis*, Vol. 10, pp. 203-18.

Hon, M.T., Strauss, J. and Yong, S. (2004), "Contagion in financial markets after September 11: myth or reality?", *Journal of Financial Research*, Vol. 27, pp. 95-114.

Iwatsubo, K. and Inagaki, K. (2006), "Measuring financial market contagion using dually-traded stocks of Asian firms", CEI Working Paper Series, No. 2006-14.

Jeanne, O. and Masson, P. (2000), "Currency crises and Markov-switching regimes", *Journal of International Economics*, Vol. 50 No. 2, pp. 327-50.

Kali, R. and Reyes, J. (2005), "Financial contagion on the international trade network", available at: http://wcob.uark.edu/rkali/networkcontagion.pdf

Kallberg, J. and Pasquariello, P. (2008), "Time-series and cross-sectional excess comovement in stock indexes", *Journal of Empirical Finance*, Vol. 15 No. 3, pp. 481-502.

Kaminsky, G.L. and Reinhart, C.M. (2000), "On crises, contagion, and confusion", *Journal of International Economics*, Vol. 51, pp. 145-68.

Kaminsky, G.L. and Schmukler, S. (1998), *On Booms and Crashes: Stock Market Cycles and Financial Liberalization*, George Washington University, Economics Department, Washington, DC.

Kelejian, H.H., Tavlas, G.S. and Hondroyiannis, G. (2006), "A spatial modelling approach to contagion among emerging economies", *Open Economic Review*, Vol. 17 Nos 4/5.

King, M.A. and Wadhwani, S. (1990), "Transmission of volatility between stock markets", *Review of Financial Studies*, Vol. 3 No. 1, pp. 5-33.

Kleimeier, S., Lehnert, T. and Verschoor, W.F.C. (2008), "Measuring financial contagion using time-aligned data: the importance of the speed of transmission of shocks", *Oxford Bulletin of Economics and Statistics*, Vol. 70 No. 4, pp. 493-508.

Lee, H., Wu, H. and Wang, Y. (2007), "Contagion effect in financial markets after the South-East Asia Tsunami", *Research in International Business and Finance*, Vol. 21 No. 2, pp. 281-96.

Lee, S.B. and Kim, K.J. (1993), "Does the October 1987 crash strengthen the co-movements among national stock markets", *Review of Financial Economics*, Vol. 3, pp. 89-104.

Lomakin, A. and Paiz, S. (1999), "Measuring contagion in the face of fluctuating volatility", MIT-Sloan Project, 15.036.

Longin, F.M. and Solnik, B. (1995), "Is the correlation in international equity returns constant: 1960-1990?", *Journal of International Money and Finance*, Vol. 14 No. 1, pp. 3-26.

Longin, F.M. and Solnik, B. (2001), "Extreme correlation of international equity markets", *The Journal of Finance*, Vol. 56, pp. 649-76.

Loretan, M. and English, W. (2000), "Evaluation 'correlation breakdowns' during periods of market volatility", International Finance Discussion Paper No. 658, BIS, Basel.

McAleer, M. and Nam, J.C.W. (2005), "Testing for contagion in ASEAN exchange rates", *Mathematics and Computers in Simulation*, Vol. 68 Nos 5/6, pp. 517-25.

Masson, P. (1999), "Contagion: monsoonal effects, spillovers, and jumps between multiple equilibria", in Agenor, P.-R., Miller, M., Vines, D. and Weber, A. (Eds), *The Asian Financial Crises: Causes, Contagion and Consequences*, Cambridge University Press, Cambridge, p. 425.

Mishkin, F.S. (1991), "Asymmetric information and financial crises: a historical perspective", in Hubbard, R.G. (Ed.), *Financial Markets and Financial Crises*, University of Chicago Press, Chicago, IL.

Moussalli, C.B. (2007), "Financial crises, panic and contagion: evidence from a cross-country comparison using two time frames", *Business and Public Affairs*, Vol. 1 No. 2.

Park, Y.C. and Chi-Young, S. (1998), "Financial contagion in the East Asian crisis: with special reference to the Republic of Korea", available at: http://209.85.129.132/search?q=cache:1qvSxEOt3Q4J:www1.worldbank.org/economicpolicy/managing%2520volatility/contagion/documents/Park-Song.pdf+Financial+Contagion+in+the+East+Asian+Park+Song&cd=1&hl=et&ct=clnk&gl=ee

Pericoli, M. and Sbracia, M. (2003), "A primer on financial contagion", *Journal of Economic Surveys*, Vol. 17, pp. 571-608.

Pindyck, R. and Rotemberg, J. (1990), "The excess comovement of commodity prices", *Economic Journal*, Vol. 100, pp. 1173-89.

Pindyck, R. and Rotemberg, J. (1993), "The comovement of stock prices", *Quarterly Journal of Economics*, Vol. 108, pp. 1073-104.

Rigobon, R. (2000), "Identification through heteroskedasticity: measuring 'contagion' between Argentinian and Mexican sovereign bonds", National Bureau of Economic Research Working Paper No. 7493.

Rigobon, R. (2002), "Contagion: how to measure it?", in Edwards, S. and Frankel, J. (Eds), *Preventing Currency Crises in Emerging Markets*, The University Chicago Press, Chicago, IL. pp. 269-334.

Rigobon, R. (2003), "On the measurement of the international propagation of shocks: is the transmission stable?", *Journal of International Economics*, Vol. 61 No. 2, pp. 261-83.

Rothschild, M. and Stiglitz, J. (1976), "Equilibrium in competitive insurance markets: an essay on the economics of imperfect information", *Quarterly Journal of Economics*, Vol. 90, pp. 629-49.

Sachs, J., Tornell, A. and Velasco, A. (1996), "Financial crises in emerging markets: the lessons from 1995", *Brooking Papers on Economic Activity*, Vol. 1, pp. 147-215.

Sander, H. and Kleimeier, S. (2003), "Contagion and causality: an empirical investigation of four Asian crisis episodes", *Journal of International Financial Markets, Institutions & Money*, Vol. 13, pp. 171-86.

Serwa, D. (2007), *Empirical Evidence on Financial Spillovers and Contagion to International Stock Markets*, available at: http://opus.kobv.de/euv/volltexte/2007/20/pdf/serwa.dobronil.pdf

Sola, M., Spagnolo, F. and Spagnolo, N. (2002), "A test for volatility spillovers", *Economics Letters*, Vol. 76, pp. 77-84.

Tornell, A. (1999), "Common fundamentals in the tequila and Asian crises", NBER Working Paper Series, Working Paper 7139.

Valdes. R. (1997), "Emerging markets contagion: evidence and theory", in Edwards, S. and Frankel, J. (Eds), *Preventing Currency Crises in Emerging Markets*, University Chicago Press, Chicago, IL. pp. 269-334.

Van Rijckeghem, C. and Weder, B. (2001), "Sources of contagion: is it finance or trade?", *Journal of International Economics*, Vol. 54, pp. 293-308.

Villar Frexedas, O. and Vaya, E. (2005), "Financial contagion between economies: an exploratory spatial analysis", *Estudios de Economía Aplicada*, Vol. 23 No. 1.

Wang, K. and Thi, T.N. (2006), "Does contagion effect exist between stock markets of Thailand and Chinese Economic Area (CEA) during the 'Asian Flu'?", *Asian Journal of Management and Humanity Sciences*, Vol. 1 No. 1, pp. 16-36.

Wang, P. and Moore, T. (2008), "Stock market integration for the transition economies: time-varying conditional correlation approach", *The Manchester School*, Vol. 76, s1, pp. 116-33.

Wolf, H.C. (1996), "Comovements among Emerging Equity Markets", available at: www1.worldbank.org/economicpolicy/managing%20volatility/contagion/documents/comove.pdf

Woo, W.T. (2000), "Coping with accelerated capital flows from the globalization of financial markets", *ASEAN Economic Bulletin*, Vol. 17, pp. 193-204.

Woo, W.T., Carleton, P.D. and Rosario, B.P. (2000), "The unorthodox origins of the Asian currency crisis: evidence from logit estimation", *ASEAN Economic Bulletin*, Vol. 17, pp. 120-34.

(The) World Bank Group (2009), "Contagion of financial crises website", available at: www1.worldbank.org/economicpolicy/managing%20volatility/contagion/index.html

Further reading

Kaminsky, G. and Reinhart, C. (1998), "Financial crisis in Asia and Latin America: then and now", *American Economic Review Papers and Proceedings*, Vol. 88, May, pp. 444-8.

(Appendices follow overleaf.)

Corresponding author
Andres Kuusk can be contacted at: hakeem@mtk.ut.ee

Appendix 1

Author (year)	Method; definition	Correlation coefficients-based tests		Observed market
		Contagion	Delta	
King and Wadhwani (1990)	Shift contagion	Yes	USA, UK and Japan after 1987 US crash	Stocks, bonds
Pindyck and Rotemberg (1990)	Excess co-movement	Yes	USA, 1960-1985	Commodity prices
Lee and Kim (1993)	Shift-contagion	Yes	12 major markets after US 1987 crash	Stocks
Pindyck and Rotemberg (1993)	Excess co-movement	Yes	42 companies, 1969-1984	Stocks
Calvo and Reinhart (1996)	Shift-contagion	Yes	1994 Mexican peso crisis, Asian and Latin American emerging markets	Bonds and equities
Valdes (1997)	Excess co-movement	Yes	Seven Latin-American countries, 1986-1994	Secondary market debt prices and credit ratings
Frankel and Schmukler (1998)	Correlation coefficient-based tests	Yes	Mexican 1994, to Asia and Latin-America	Country fund prices
Baig and Goldfajn (1999)	Shift-contagion, adjusted	Mixed	Emerging markets during the 1997-1998 East Asian crisis	Stocks, interest rates
Baig and Goldfajn (1999)	Shift contagion	Yes	1997,1998 East Asian crisis	Sovereign spreads, currencies
Boyer et al. (1999)	Shift-contagion, adjusted	No	Germany, Japan, 1991-1998	Exchange rates
Loretan and English (2000)	Shift contagion, adjusted	No	Germany and GB (Germany and Japan in case of exchange rates)	Equities, bonds, foreign exchange
Forbes and Rigobon (2000)	Shift contagion, adjusted	No	Latin American crises in 1990s	Bonds, stocks
Bordo and Murshid (2000a)	Shift-contagion, adjusted	No/weak	Different historical and current crises	Bonds, interest rates
Gelos and Sahay (2001)	Shift-contagion	Yes	from the Czech Republic, Asia, and Russia to CEE	Exchange rates
Gelos and Sahay (2001)	Shift-contagion	No	From the Czech Republic, Asia, and Russia to CEE	Stocks
Forbes and Rigobon (2001)	Shift-contagion, adjusted	No	28 countries, 1987 US stock market crash, 1994 Mexican peso collapse, 1997 East Asian crisis	Stocks
Sander and Kleimeier (2003)	Shift-contagion using Granger causality methodology	Yes	Asian crisis, 1996-2000	Bonds

(continued)

Table AI.
Studies investigating
financial contagion:
correlation
coefficients-based tests

Author (year)	Method; definition	Correlation coefficients-based tests		Observed market
		Contagion	Data	
Alvarez-Plata and Schrooten (2003)	Shift-contagion	No	Seven Latin-American countries, 2001-2002 Argentinean crisis	Stocks, interest rates
Gravelle et al. (2003)	Shift-contagion	No	Four emerging market countries 1991-2001	Brady bonds
Gravelle et al. (2003)	Shift-contagion	Yes	Seven developed countries 1985-2001	Currencies
Hon et al. (2004)	Shift-contagion, adjusted	Yes	2001 terrorist attack, 25 economies: OECD and Asia	Stocks
Serwa (2007)	Shift-contagion, adjusted	Weak	Seven crises, 1997-2002, 17 Western Europe and CEE countries	Stocks
McAleer and Nam (2005)	Shift-contagion, adjusted	Yes	Six Asian countries, Asian crisis 1997	Exchange rates
Arestis et al. (2005)	Shift-contagion, adjusted	Mixed	1997 Asian crisis; from Thailand, Indonesia, Korea, Malaysia to Japan, UK, Germany, France	Stocks
Corsetti et al. (2005)	Shift-contagion, adjusted	Yes	Hong Kong crisis 1997, 17 countries	Stocks
Wang and Thi (2006)	Increase in dynamic correlation coefficient	Yes	Asian crisis 1997, Thailand, China, Hong Kong, Taiwan	Stocks
Chiang et al. (2007)	Dynamic conditional correlation	Yes	Nine Asian countries, 1990-2003	Stocks
Bayoumi et al. (2007)	Correlations and distance relationships	Yes	15 countries, 1991-2001	Stocks, exchange rates
Lee et al. (2007)	Shift-contagion, adjusted	No	Earthquake in South-East Asia on December 26, 2004, 26 international stock indexes	Stocks
Lee et al. (2007)	Shift-contagion, adjusted	Yes	Earthquake in South-East Asia on December 26, 2004, 26 international stock indexes	Exchange market
Kleimeier et al. (2008)	Shift-contagion, adjusted, time-aligned data	Yes	Asian crisis, Thailand + 14 countries	Stocks
Wang and Moore (2008)	Dynamic conditional correlation	Yes	Three CEE countries, 1994-2006	Stocks
Kallberg and Pasquariello (2008)	Excess co-movement, adjusted	Yes	82 US industry indexes, 1976-2001	Stocks

Table AI.

Appendix 2

Author (year)	Method; definition	Conditional probability-based tests		Observed market
		Contagion	Data	
Eichengreen et al. (1996)	Probit model	Yes	20 industrial countries, 1959-1993	Currencies
Park and Chi-Young (1998)	Conditional probability	Yes	Asian crisis, eight Asian countries	Exchange rates, stocks, interests
Lomakin and Paiz (1999)	Probit analysis	No	Various countries	Bonds
De Gregorio and Valdes (1999)	Conditional probability	Yes, but fundamentals more important	1982 debt crisis, Mexican 1994, 1997 Asian	Exchange rates, credit ratings
Glick and Rose (1999)	Multivariate probit model	Yes (broad definition)	Five crises and 161 countries	Currencies
Woo et al. (2000)	Logit model	Yes	Asian crisis, six Asian countries 1990-1998	Currencies
Kaminsky and Reinhart (2000)	Probit model	Yes	Mexican 1994 and Asian 1997 20 countries, 1970-1998	Assets
Hartmann et al. (2001)	Extreme value analysis	Weak	G5 countries	Asset prices
Caramazza et al. (2004)	Panel probit model	Yes	Mexican 1994, Asian 1997, Russian 1998; 41 emerging countries	Currencies
Fazio (2007)	Probit model	Weak	1990-1999, 14 emerging market economies	Currencies
Haile and Bozo (2008)	Panel probit model	Yes	37 advanced and emerging market economies, quarterly data 1960-1998	Currencies

Table AII.
Studies investigating financial contagion: conditional probability-based tests

Author (year)	Method; definition	Tests measuring changes in volatility Contagion	Data	Observed market
Hamao et al. (1990)	GARCH framework	Yes	1987 US stock market crash; Japan, UK, USA	Stocks
Chou et al. (1994)	Variance-covariance transmission mechanisms	Yes	1987 US stock market crash	Stocks
Longin and Solnik (1995)	GARCH framework	Yes	Seven OECD countries from 1960 to 1990	Stocks
Edwards (1998)	GARCH framework	No	Mexican peso crisis, Mexico to Chile	Bonds
Edwards (1998)	GARCH framework	Yes	Mexican peso crisis, Mexico to Argentina	Bonds
Agenor et al. (1998)	VAR model	Yes	Mexico and Argentina, 1993-1998	Interest rates
Favero and Giavazzi (1999)	VAR model and full-information approach	Yes	Seven European countries; ERM crisis, 1988-1992	Interest rates
Rigobon (2000)	Variance-covariance matrix	No	Mexican, Russian, Asian crisis; Argentina, Mexico 1994-1999	Brady bonds
Longin and Solnik (2001)	GARCH framework extreme value theory	Yes	USA, UK, France, Germany, Japan; 1959-1996	Stocks
Gelos and Sahay (2001)	VAR model and Granger causality	Mixed at best	Czech, Asian and Russian crisis to CEE	Stocks
Gelos and Sahay (2001)	VAR model and Granger causality	Mixed/some support	Czech, Asian and Russian crisis to CEE	Exchange rates
Rigobon (2002)	Determinant of the change in the covariance matrix test	Unclear	14 countries; 1993-1998	Stocks
Rigobon (2002)	Determinant of the change in the covariance matrix test	No	Seven countries, 1994-1998	Bonds
Rigobon (2003)	Determinant of the change in the covariance matrix test	No	Mexican, Asian, Russian crises; 36 countries	Stocks
Hon et al. (2004)	GARCH framework	Yes	2001 terrorist attack, 25 economies: OECD and Asia	Stocks
Serwa (2007)	VAR model	Yes	Asian crisis 1997	Capital markets

Table AIII.
Studies investigating
financial contagion: tests
measuring changes
in volatility

Appendix 4

Author (year)	Method	Contagion	Other tests Data	Observed market
Craig et al. (1995)	CDR approach	No	USA and Japanese stocks	Stocks
Kali and Reyes (1995)	Network approach	Yes	Tequila Crisis Mexican 1994), the Asian flu, and the Russian virus	Stocks
Kali and Reyes (1995)	Network approach	No	Venezuelan and Argentine crises	Stocks
Wolf (1996)	Granger causality	Weak	21 sectors of 21 developing countries, 1976-1995	Equities
Frankel and Schmukler (1998)	Granger causality	Yes	Mexican 1994, to Asia and Latin-America	Country fund prices
Alba et al. (2008)	Qualitative analysis	Unclear, probably Yes	Asian crisis	Stocks, exchange rates, sovereign bonds
Abeysinghe (1999)	Structural full trade model	Yes	Asian crisis, East Asian countries	Stocks
Tornell (1999)	Regression analysis	No	Mexican 1995 and Asian 1997	Currencies
Woo (2000)	Qualitative analysis	Yes	Asian crisis from Thailand to four Asian countries	Bonds
Sola et al. (2002)	Markov switching framework	Yes	Asian crisis 1997; from Thailand to South Korea	Stocks
Sola et al. (2002)	Markov switching framework	No	Asian crisis 1997; from South Korea to Brazil	Stocks
Cerra and Saxena (2002)	Markov switching framework	Yes	Indonesian currency crisis	Stocks, currencies
Baur (2003)	Tests based on a regression model	Yes	Asian crisis, 11 Asian markets	Stocks
Serwa (2007)	Markov switching framework	No	HSI and Nikkei 225; 1997 Asian crisis	Stocks
Serwa (2007)	Markov switching framework	Weak/no	USA, UK, Japan, Germany	Stocks
Candelon et al. (2005)	Serial correlation common feature	No	Mexican 1994, Asian 1997	Stocks
Kelejian et al. (2006)	Spatial modelling	Yes	Six crisis, 25 developing countries	Currencies
Iwatsubo and Inagaki (2006)	CDR approach (EGARCH model)	Yes	22 Asian firms and seven indices, Asian crises	Stocks
Moussalli (2007)	OLS and the bootstrap method	Yes	Asian, Russian, Brazilian crisis; Asian, East-European, Latin-American countries	Stocks
Didier et al. (2008)	Theoretical analysis	Yes		

Table AIV.
Studies investigating
financial contagion:
other tests

Appendix 7.2. Kuusk, A., Paas, T., Viikmaa, K. (2011) Financial contagion of the 2008 crisis: is there evidence of financial contagion from the US to the Baltic States. *Eastern Journal of European Studies*, 2(2), pp. 61-76.

Financial contagion of the 2008 crisis: is there any evidence of financial contagion from the US to the Baltic states

Andres KUUSK[*], Tiiu PAAS[**], Karmen VIIKMAA[***]

Abstract

The paper aims to investigate the research question whether the US 2008 crisis spilled over contagiously to the Baltic States as small open economies. In order to examine the evidence of financial contagion as a systematic component of financial risks in the case of the Baltic States, we employ several testing methodologies like correlation coefficients based methods adjusting also with possible heteroskedasticity and ARCH-GARCH framework. The results are somewhat mixed. On the one hand, stock returns' correlations between US and Baltic States increased during crisis times, confirming the financial contagion hypothesis. On the other hand, volatility has not spilled over from US to Estonia, Latvia and Lithuania, neither have volatility spillovers become stronger after the crisis hit.

Keywords: financial crisis, financial contagion, crisis management, Baltic states

JEL Classification: F36, P34

1. Introduction

The events associated with the US 2008 crisis, which saw many countries falling into serious problems one after another like domino stones, reminded us

[*] Andres Kuusk is PhD student at University of Tartu, Faculty of Economics and Business Administration, Tartu, Estonia; e-mail: hakeem@mtk.ut.ee.
[**] Tiiu Paas is professor of Econometrics at University of Tartu, Factulty of Economics and Business Administration, Tartu, Estonia; e-mail: tiiu.paas@ut.ee.
[***] Karmen Viikmaa is PhD student at University of Tartu, Faculty of Economics and Business Administration, Tartu, Estonia, e-mail: karmen_viikmaa@yahoo.com.
Acknowledgements: The authors of the paper are grateful to the Estonian Ministry of Education and Science (grant No SF0180037s08) and the Estonian Science Foundation (research grant No 7756) for their financial support. The views expressed in the paper are solely those of the authors and, as such, should not be attributed to other parties.

once again of the phenomenon of financial contagion as a systematic component of financial risks. Financial contagion in the broadest view means the transmission of a crisis from one economy to others which has often been quite unrelated to the fundamental problems of the countries and markets under observation. Contagious nature of financial crises undermines the risk-reducing potential of international portfolio diversification of international investors and makes countries vulnerable to the crises originating elsewhere. In the conditions of a highly global world the events that occur in one part of the world can have enormous impact on all markets and countries around the globe.

Small open economies like the Baltic States are particularly vulnerable to global economic development. Therefore financial contagion analysis is exceptionally important for these countries – EU new member countries with post-socialist path-dependence.

Since regaining their independence in 1991, the Baltic States have undergone similar processes of economic, political and social transformation. Under the Washington Consensus policy framework these countries aimed to create stability and international trust as well as attractiveness for foreign direct investments through a fixed exchange rate, balanced state budget and comparatively low tax and administrative burdens. In the late 1990s, the transition and restructuring paradigms were replaced by the concepts of catching up and economic convergence to the level of the developed economies of the enlarged EU. Unfortunately, large amounts of foreign investment and private lending went into financing consumption and the real estate boom, and as a consequence the export competitiveness of the Baltic economies started to weaken in the 2000s (see also Estonian Development Report 2008. Also, the deepening downturn in the main trading partners of the Baltic States during the recent global crisis has remarkably weakened the economic outlook for these countries. Estonia is the only country among the three Baltic States that joined the euro zone in 2011. Adopting the euro in itself is unlikely to trigger any major change in the pace of recovery, but it was expected during the joining that may remove liquidity risks, add stability to the economy and help attract new investments. These small countries are facing a double challenge to simultaneously overcome recent economic downturn as consequences of global economic crises as well as national economic policies.

The paper aims to investigate the research question of whether the US 2008 crisis spilled over contagiously to the Baltic States as small open economies. The essential aim of this study is to provide additional information for elaborating proposals mitigating or even avoiding some negative consequences of possible future crises' spreading.

In order to explore the evidence of financial contagion in the case of the Baltic States, we employ alternative testing methodologies like the correlation coefficients based methods and ARCH-GARCH framework. We focus on examining the evidence of financial contagion from the US to the Estonian, Latvian and Lithuanian stock markets. The data set employed for the analysis includes daily closing prices of the US (Standard & Poor's 500), Estonian (OMX Tallinn), Latvian (OMX Riga) and Lithuanian (OMX Vilnius) stock markets' indices over the time period from February 29th 2008 to March 9th 2009.

This paper is structured as follows. In the following part of the paper we give a short overview of several considerations and discussions regarding the concept of financial contagion. The next parts of the paper present information about data and research methodology and the main research results. The paper ends with conclusions and discussion.

2. Financial contagion

The concept "contagion" is borrowed from epidemiology. In economic literature it is ordinarily considered as the transmission of crisis from on economy to others and usually some further restrictions have been made (see alternative definitions below). Financial contagion has become increasingly popular research task in the recent decades when several crises transmitted rapidly to other countries in 1980's, 1990's and in the current century. Many of the countries that have got hit by the crisis' snowball are rather different in terms of size and economic structure as compared to the country of origin of a crisis.

The most comprehensive information about several approaches to the concept of "financial contagion", the transmission channels of financial crisis, and the results of empirical studies focused on financial contagion is provided by the Word Bank Group (2009) on their special website. According to the World Bank approach there are three main alternative definitions of financial contagion:

- Contagion is the cross-country transmission of shocks or the general cross-country spillover effects which have been emphasized during the crisis times. Contagion can be observed through co-movements of different financial indices in different countries or rising probabilities of default if crisis occurs elsewhere. So, unlike other definitions this one includes fundamental linkage as a channel of contagion.
- Contagion is the transmission of shocks to other countries or the cross-country correlation, beyond any fundamental link among the countries and beyond common shocks. For example Masson (2004) defines contagion as only those transmissions of crises that cannot be identified with observed changes in macroeconomic fundamentals. Going for somewhat other testing methodology Eichengreen et al (1996) argue that there is contagion if the probability of a crisis in a given country increases conditional on the occurrence of a crisis elsewhere, if the standard set of macroeconomic fundamentals is taken into account. This definition is sometimes referred as

excess co-movement – a correlation that remains even after controlling for fundamentals and common shocks. Herding behaviour is usually argued to be responsible for that more-than-expected co-movement. Fundamental linkages are distinguished from contagion by most of the literature.

• Contagion occurs when cross-country correlations increase during "crisis times" relative to correlations during "tranquil times." Or as Forbes and Rigobon (2001) put it: contagion is a significant increase in cross-market linkages after a shock. This definition is sometimes referred as shift-contagion. Forbes and Rigobon (2001 and 2002) stress that this notion of contagion excludes a constant high degree of co-movement in a crisis period. In this case, markets are just interdependent.

As argued by Didier, Mauro and Schmukler (2008), the factors underlying the channels that generated contagion during the crises of the 1990s seem to be potentially at least as strong today as they were a decade ago. One of the main interests of contagion studies is associated to the merits of international diversification. Although the rationale is that theoretically international diversification should significantly reduce the portfolio risk, when cross country correlations increase during crises much of the rationale is undermined. Besides, questions about appropriate financial architecture and investment opportunities and risks to local markets can be answered by studies of financial contagion.

The results of previous empirical studies about empirical evidence of financial contagion (see also overview of Kuusk and Paas 2011) are heterogeneous. They differ depending on several circumstances, like chosen conceptual definition of contagion and even in the most widely used approach of focusing on co-movements in asset prices. There are also substantial differences in study results depending on whether correlations are adjusted for the presence of heteroskedasticity or not. Chosen crisis, time periods, destination countries and even the financial market under investigation may affect the results of empirical studies. In addition, the problems of omitted variables, feedback dependencies between stock markets, different time zones, and arbitrary choices of the crisis window can all affect tests of contagion (see also Billio and Pellizon (2003) and Dungey and Zhumabekova (2001)).

The variability of empirical results of studies on financial contagion can also be explained by several measuring problems. For instance, Rigobon (2002) points out that contagion have been associated with high frequency events; it has been measured on stock market returns, interest rates, exchange rates, or linear combinations of them. Rigobon argues that the data is plagued with simultaneous equations, omitted variables, conditional and unconditional heteroskedasticity, serial correlation, non-linearity and non-normality problems. Naively counting numbers examining several aspects of contagion we can conclude that evidence for contagion during financial crises has been found more often than not. On the other hand, this result is mostly being obtained when the presence of heteroskedasticity is not taken into account. The studies that account for heteroskedasticity find evidence for financial contagion far less often. This diversity of results is well illustrated by the research by Daniel Serwa (2005) who used four different testing methodologies and different samples to achieve mixed results. According to his findings contagion is a rather rare phenomenon, but patterns of capital and information flow to stock markets still change during turbulent periods.

In addition, the previous literature relating to issues of financial contagion does not always have consensus on the issue whether the recent crises have been more contagious than those before 1990's. While some authors (Haile and Pozo 2008) argue that currency crises prior to 1990s did not appear to spread across countries with the virulence and speed observed recently, the others (Bordo and Murshid 1999 and 2000) have found no evidence to confirm that.

We agree with the problems stressed in the literature considering financial contagion and rely on the viewpoints presented in the analysed studies discussing some of them in the next part of our paper. We rely on the definition given by Forbes and Rigobon (2002) who distinguish between contagion and interdependence and define contagion as an excessive transmission of shocks from crisis stock market to other stock markets, beyond any idiosyncratic disturbances and fundamental links among them. According to the definition used in this paper, financial contagion, unlike interdependence, means that there are breaks in the international transmission mechanism owing to financial panics, herding or switches of investors' expectations. Accordingly, contagion requires a change in the structure of stock market linkages and in the case of contagion the increase in these linkages during crises has to be statistically significant.

3. Data and methodology

3.1. The correlation coefficients based method

In the empirical part of our paper we employ two main approaches for testing hypotheses regarding possible financial contagion from the US to the Baltic States Estonia, Latvia and Lithuania during the crisis that started in US in 2008. First, we implement the correlation coefficients based methods, and second, the ARCH-GARCH framework.

Employing the correlation based analysis we investigate stock indices from March 3-rd 2008 until March 9-th 2009 and choose the bankruptcy of Lehman Brothers in September 15, 2008 as the starting point of the crisis. According to this approach, the period from March 3-rd 2008 to September 15-th 2008 will be considered as a tranquil period and the period from September 16-th 2008 to March 9-th 2009 as crisis period. The use of stock indices is mainly based on pragmatic reasons. Stock market indices are relatively easily accessible data compared to other variables such as comparable interest rates, bonds or exchange rates. Also, the stock market data is available on a daily basis, which makes it easier to have reasonable number of observations for the analysis.

As our choice of the starting point of a crisis is clear, the chosen starting point of a tranquil period and the ending point of a crisis period need some further explanation. We have chosen March 9-th 2009 as the ending date of a crisis period, because it was the local minimum for S&P500 during crisis. This kind of logic is previously used by Mishkin and White (2003) and Serwa (2005). The tranquil period cannot be considered to stretch for too long because we do not want any structural breaks during that time. There was quite a sharp fall in the S&P500 index at the end of February, 2008, which stopped at the beginning of March. So, we took March 3rd as the first trading day in March (March 1st and 2nd were at weekend) for our starting date of a tranquil period. This approach also allowed us to have tranquil and crisis period with relatively similar length.

As noted by Billio and Pellizon (2003) and Forbes and Rigobon (2002) correlation based analysis is more suitable than other approaches to shed light on the issues of international diversification, the role of international institutions and bail-out funds, as well as propagation mechanisms.

We test the hypothesis whether the 2008 financial crisis has spilled over contagiously from US to Estonia, Latvia and Lithuania. The logic of the following tests is based on the assumption that contagion occurs when, if a crisis in the US, correlation is stronger because of some structural change in the international economy affecting the links across markets. Relying on this hypothesis and data sample, we consider contagion as significant increase in the correlation coefficient in stock returns between the country of origin of the crisis (the US) and the country of destination (Estonia, Latvia or Lithuania) during the crisis compared to the non-crisis period.

Similarly to many earlier papers (for example Forbes and Rigobon 2002) we consider a model, where stock returns on the country of origin of the crisis are independent variable and influence returns on the country of destination. More specifically, we use the following linear model (see Forbes and Rigobon 2002 and Serwa and Bohl 2005)

$$y_t = \alpha + \beta * x_t + u_t^y \qquad (1)$$
$$x_t = u_t^x \qquad (2),$$

where x_t are stock returns in the crisis market (US) that are exogenous and influence returns on the calm market y_t (Estonia, Latvia or Lithuania);

u_t^x and u_t^y are idiosyncratic shocks to the respective stock markets.

It is assumed that volatility of stock returns on the crisis market changes during crisis times, but the model parameters and the volatility of idiosyncratic shocks in the destination market remain constant.

We estimate the correlation coefficient in both tranquil and crisis times and then control for the significant increase in the correlation coefficient after crisis hits.

The correlation coefficient for the calm period is given by the equation

$$\rho^{non-crisis} = \text{Corr}(x,y) = \frac{\text{Cov}(x,y)}{\sqrt{\text{Var}(x)\text{Var}(y)^{non-crisis}}} = \left[1 + \frac{\text{Var}(u^y)}{\beta^2 \text{Var}(x)^{non-crisis}}\right]^{-\frac{1}{2}} \tag{3}$$

and for the crisis period

$$\rho^{crisis} = \text{Corr}(x,y) = \frac{\text{Cov}(x,y)}{\sqrt{\text{Var}(x)\text{Var}(y)^{crisis}}} = \left[1 + \frac{\text{Var}(u^y)}{\beta^2 \text{Var}(x)^{crisis}}\right]^{-\frac{1}{2}} \tag{4}$$

We agree with Forbes and Rigobon (2002) who show that correlation is conditional on the volatility of stock returns in the crisis market and therefore, the correlation between stock returns in crisis and non-crisis country may rise even when contagion does not occur. Thus, it is not fully correct to test for contagion using simple correlations that to not take into account increased volatility during crises. Therefore we consider that the testing approach with heteroskedasticity adjustment in post-crisis correlations seems to be more reliable.

Thus, estimating correlation coefficients we also adjust for heteroskedasticity by using the Forbes and Rigobon (2002) approach who propose an adjustment so that the correlation coefficient does not depend on the volatility of returns in the crisis market:

$$\rho * \frac{\rho^{crisis}}{\sqrt{1 + \delta[1 - (\rho^{crisis})^2]}} \tag{5}$$

ρ^{crisis} is the correlation coefficient between the crisis and the non-crisis market observed during the crisis period.

The parameter δ represents the relationship between the variances of stock returns from the crisis country during the turmoil period, $\text{Var}^{crisis}(y_t)$ and during the calm period, $\text{Var}^{non-crisis}(y_t)$:

$$\delta = \frac{\text{Var}^{crisis}(y_t)}{\text{Var}^{non-crisis}} - 1 \tag{6}$$

We start with estimating simple correlations and later use the adjustments proposed by Forbes and Rigobon (2002). The correlation coefficients (both not adjusted and adjusted) are transformed through a Fisher transformation, so that they are approximately normally distributed. This transformation is necessary in order to have relevant results from the hypotheses controlling (Dungey and Zhumabekova 2001, Jokipii and Lucey 2006, Lee *et al.* 2007).

3.2. The ARCH-GARCH framework

Although easy to use and providing some other advantages, the correlation coefficients based methods also have several drawbacks. For example, as it is demonstrated by Baur contagion tests that base on correlation coefficient, it can be misleading when correlations are time-varying and volatility is contagious *per se* (Baur 2003).

In order to check for the robustness of the empirical results we also implement the autoregressive conditionally heteroskedastic (ARCH) and generalised ARCH (GARCH) framework of statistical models to explore the possible contagion from the US stock market (S&P 500) to the Baltic States stock markets. The same framework to investigate contagion in emerging markets is used for example by Edwards and Susmel (2001 and 2003).

According to French *et al* (1987) a member of ARCH family, GARCH-M, is a good representation of the daily stock-return behaviour in the US because of its successful capturing of effects of time-varying volatility on a expected return of a stock.

We investigate two main hypotheses. Firstly, we test whether price changes in the US stock market influence prices in the Baltic States stock markets, and secondly, we explore whether changes in price volatility in the US stock market are related to changes in price volatility in the Baltic States stock markets. In order to test these hypotheses we examine daily stock returns in US and Baltic stock markets over the period, March 3, 2008, to March 9, 2009. For the US stock market we use Standard & Poor's Composite Index, for Estonia we use OMXT, for Latvia OMXR and for Lithuania OMXV indices. We focus on average two-day returns to control for the fact that markets in different countries are not open during the same hours (for how to avoid the problem of nonsynchronous trading periods for different markets, see Lin, Engle and Ito 1994). Our sample period includes September 2008 when one of the most severe stock market crashes in history took place. To investigate the contagion effect we have estimated our models over two sub-periods, before and after the Lehman Brothers bankruptcy in September 15, 2008.

We use many extensions of the basic ARCH model that was developed by Engle (1982) and generalized to GARCH model by Bollerslev (1986). Firstly, we allow the conditional mean to be a function of the conditional variance, which was first proposed by Engle, Lilien and Robins (1987). This extension gives us the GARCH(1,1)-M model.

Secondly, we use the extension first given by French, Schwert and Stambaugh (1987), who adjusted the conditional mean return for a first-order moving average. This is done mainly because of nonsynchronous trading in the US and Baltic States which is problematic in the ARCH family of models (see for example Cohen *et al* 1980).

Third, we include a dummy variable into the model, which helps to capture the fact that there are no price movements at weekends. This weekends' influence that gives Mondays somewhat special status is well known in literature (see French 1980, Gibbons and Hess 1981 and others) and is called Monday effects.

And finally, we include stock returns in crisis market as explanatory variable into the non-crisis market's stock returns' equation.

Thus, we implement the MA(1)-GARCH(1, 1)-M model given by the formula:

$$X_t = \alpha + \beta b_t + \gamma D_t + \delta Y_t + \varepsilon u_{t-1} + u_t \qquad (7)$$
$$b_t = a + bb_{t-1} + cu_{t-1^2} + dD_t + fZ_t \qquad (8)$$

where

X_t – stock index return in non-crisis market at time t;

b_t – conditional variance of the R at time t;

D – dummy variable for Monday effect (D takes value of 1 on days following weekends and holidays and is 0 otherwise);

Y_t – stock index return in crisis market at time t, u_t and u_{t-1} are error terms at time t and $t-1$ respectively;

Z_t – squared residual derived from an MA(1)-GARCH(1,1)-M model applied to the returns of US stock market.

This kind of model is first proposed by Hamao, Masulis and Ng (1990).

As we do not have Z_t we first have to estimate the equation

$$Y_t = \alpha + \beta b_t + \delta D_t + \varphi u_{t-1} + u_t \qquad (9)$$
$$b_t = a + bb_{t-1} + cu_{t-1^2} + dD_t \qquad (10)$$

from where we derive needed squared residual.

The empirical results of our study are presented in the next part of the paper.

3.3. Empirical results

In the empirical section of the paper, we first compare the correlation coefficients between stock returns of the US (a crisis country) and Baltic States (Estonia, Latvia and Lithuania) during the non-crisis and crisis period. Secondly, we measure changes in volatility to examine whether conditional means and conditional variances of financial variables are related to each other among countries during the crisis period. Investigation is based on the methodology outlined in the previous section and uses the data and time periods that are also explained in the previous section 3. We use two-day average rolling log stock returns to control for non-synchronous trading hours in the US and Baltic States. The number of observations used is 266. All stock indices used are denominated in US dollars.

Unadjusted correlation coefficients are calculated using formulas 3 and 4 in the previous section. The results are given in the second (pre-crisis correlations) and third row (post-crisis correlations) in the following table 1. The final row in table 1 is obtained by adjusting the unadjusted post-crisis correlations given in the previous row by the adjustment procedure given by the formula 5 (see section 3).

In the empirical section of the paper, we first compare the correlation coefficients between stock returns of the US (a crisis country) and Baltic States (Estonia, Latvia and Lithuania) during the non-crisis and crisis period. Secondly, we measure changes in volatility to examine whether conditional means and conditional variances of financial variables are related to each other among countries during the crisis period. Investigation is based on the methodology outlined in the previous section and uses the data and time periods that are also explained in the previous section 3. We use two-day average rolling log stock returns to control for non-synchronous trading hours in the US and Baltic States. The number of observations used is 266. All stock indices used are denominated in US dollars.

Unadjusted correlation coefficients are calculated using formulas 3 and 4 in the previous section. The results are given in the second (pre-crisis correlations) and third row (post-crisis correlations) in the following table 1. The final row in table 1 is obtained by adjusting the unadjusted post-crisis correlations given in the previous row by the adjustment procedure given by the formula 5 (see section 3).

Table1. Correlation coefficients between US and Baltic stock markets

	US and Estonia	US and Latvia	US and Lithuania
Pre-crisis	0.169	0.112	0.186
Post-crisis, unadjusted	0.435	0.294	0.477
Post-crisis, adjusted	0.286	0.191	0.315

Source: authors' calculations. Sample size is 266 observations.

As seen in table 1, the correlation coefficient for the pre-crisis period (after Fischer transformation) between the US and Estonia is 0.169, between the US and Latvia 0.112 and between US and Lithuania 0.186. The corresponding simple correlations for the crisis period are 0.435, 0.294 and 0.477, and they are statistically significant. It is seen that post-crisis correlations are significantly higher which is confirmed only by the t-test. This finding supports the contagion hypothesis according to which linkages between crisis and non-crisis countries have become stronger after the starting point of a crisis. Thus, there has to have been some changes in the structure of stock market linkages which can be explained by herding behaviour or switches in investors' expectations and attitude.

However, as pointed out in the previous section 3, the higher correlation coefficients in this simple model may be caused by the higher volatility that is present during the crisis times. Because of this bias we adjust crisis times correlations to the higher volatility bias. After doing this (adjusting post-crisis correlations for the presence of heteroskedasticity) the correlations are much lower, 0.286 for Estonia, 0.191 for Latvia and 0.315 for Lithuania but still statistically significant. So it is clearly seen that not adjusting for heteroskedasticity increases the probability to find supporting evidence for the existence of financial contagion. Still, in all three cases the post-crisis correlations are more than 1.5 times higher than pre-crisis correlations and we can deduce that there has been some kind of structural break in the financial shocks' transmission mechanism, although not quite as strong as suggested by the simple unadjusted correlations.

It is expected that the countries´ level of volatility will increase in more turbulent times. It means that conditional and unconditional variances may be changing over time. In order to capture better picture of the contagion it is assumed that there are two regimes in the volatility where one regime associates to lower volatility, tranquil times, and the other to high volatility, so the called turbulent times. So to test for contagion we used as second approach an ARCH or GARCH framework for estimating the variance-covariance transmission mechanism across viewed countries. The used methodology is given by the formulas 7-10 in the previous section 3. Following Table 2 shows the results of the model estimation.

Starting with the pre-crisis period it is seen that statistically significant mean spillover effects (see values of sigma in the Table 2) are observed in Estonian and Lithuanian but not in the Latvian stock market. It means that the conditional mean return in Estonian and Lithuanian stock market exhibits a positive spillover effect from the US stock market – high (low) return in the S&P 500 index is followed by a high (low) return in the OMXT and OMXV, but such relation is not found between S&P 500 and OMXR. It is an interesting finding for which we do not have good theoretical explanation.

Table 2. The results of estimating the MA(1)-GARCH(1, 1)-M model for the spillover effects between US and Baltic States stock markets.

	From US to Estonia		From US to Latvia		From US to Lithuania	
	non-crisis	crisis	non-crisis	crisis	non-crisis	crisis
α	-0.002*	-0.01*	0.002	-0.01*	-0.002	-0.001
β	11.53	16.24*	-32.34	9.27	15.72	-0.99
γ	-0.004	-0.001	-0.002	-0.002	-0.003	-0.002
δ	0.15*	0.20*	0.07	0.14	0.14*	0.20*
ε	0.13	0.06	-0.25*	-0.13	0.09	0.03
a	-0.000	0.000	0.000	0.000	0.000	0.000
b	1.05*	-0.17	0.68*	0.07	0.50*	0.67*
c	-0.004	0.49*	0.08	0.32*	0.38*	0.27*
d	0.000	0.000	0.000	0.000	0.000	0.000*
f	-0.02*	0.02	0.09	0.09	-0.08	-0.001

153

The coefficients are estimated from the MA(1)-GARCH(1, 1)-M model

$$X_t = \alpha + \beta b_t + \gamma D_t + \delta Y_t + \varepsilon u_{t-1} + u_t$$
$$b_t = a + b b_{t-1} + c u_{t-1}{}^2 + d D_t + f Z_t , \text{ where}$$

X_t – stock index return in non-crisis market at time t;

b_t – conditional variance of the R at time t;

D – dummy variable for Monday effect (D takes value of 1 on days following weekends and holidays and is 0 otherwise);

Y_t – stock index return in crisis market at time t, u_t and u_{t-1} are error terms at time t and $t-1$ respectively;

Z_t – squared residual derived from an MA(1)-GARCH(1,1)-M model applied to the returns of US stock market.

Source: authors' calculations.

* statistically significant at 5% level.

Turning attention to the crisis period it is seen that mean spillover effects are now stronger in all three markets. In the crisis period mean spillover effects are statistically significant even between US and Latvian stock markets if 0.1 confidence level is used. This finding is in line with the contagion hypothesis as post-crisis linkages seem to be stronger than those in pre-crisis period.

We also investigate spillover effects in conditional variance (see values of f in Table 3). Unlike conditional mean conditional variance does not exhibit statistically significant positive spillovers in any of the observed markets, nor in the crisis period neither in the non-crisis period. The only statistically significant spillover effect is observed in Estonian stock market in pre-crisis period and it is negative. Thus high volatility in the S&P 500 index does not give any reason to expect that we will see high volatility also in Baltic stock markets. The conditional variance spillover effects are not stronger in the crisis period than in the non-crisis period. This means that no structural breaks in volatility transmission mechanisms are observed and thus no support for contagion hypothesis is found.

Summarizing the findings of the empirical section we can say that the results of the correlation coefficients based and the volatility spillovers based method are somewhat contradictory. Correlations in returns on stock indices between US and Baltic States stock markets are clearly higher during turmoil period compared to tranquil period, which is supporting evidence on the contagion hypothesis. On the other hand the estimation results of the MA(1)-GARCH(1, 1)-M model while showing some increasing spillover effects on conditional mean, did not show any sign neither positive nor increasing during crisis times spillover effects on conditional variance.

4. Conclusions and discussion

The paper examines whether there has been financial contagion from US to the three Baltic States during the 2008 financial crisis by using stock returns data during time period from March 3-rd 2008 until March 9-th 2009. Financial crises and their contagion have been long studied and modelled by economists and several alternative definitions of financial contagion have been used. This paper defines contagion as a structural break in the linear transmission mechanism of financial shocks and applies both correlation coefficients based tests and ARCH-GARCH framework to test for financial contagion.

Correlation coefficients based testing reveals supporting evidence on financial contagion. The unadjusted (for the presence of heteroskedasticity) post-crisis correlation between the US and all three Baltic countries is quite significantly higher than the pre-crisis correlation, which supports the contagion hypothesis and indicates that linkages between the US (crisis country) and Estonia, Latvia and Lithuania (non-crisis countries) have become stronger after September 15-th, 2008 which was agreed upon as the starting date of a crisis. Because of the bias of unadjusted correlation coefficients towards overestimating contagion effects, we adjust crisis times correlations for the presence of heteroskedasticity. Using these adjusted correlations the differences between pre- and post-crisis correlations are much smaller but still more than 1.5 times in favour of post-crisis correlations.

The results of the MA(1)-GARCH(1,1)-M model are mixed. Mean spillover effects from US to Estonia, Latvia and Lithuania are stronger during the crisis period as compared to the tranquil period. During crisis times conditional mean return in all three Baltic stock markets exhibits a positive spillover effect from the US stock market. This is not true for the conditional variance, which does not exhibit statistically significant positive spillovers in any of the observed markets, or in the crisis period either in the non-crisis period. Further, there is no sign for the positive spillovers of conditional variance to strengthen during crisis times. These results also confirm once again that financial contagion is a complex phenomenon and examining it needs further investments into employment and development of study methods.

The contagious transmission of crisis from the US to the Baltic States stock markets (and economy) that the correlation coefficients based testing indicated somewhat undermines the rationale of the merits of international risk diversification and shows the risks that small open economies have to face. However, although in 2009 the Baltic States faced similar problems to Greece's in the recent crisis, they managed to overcome this problem with the help of several retrenches. The rating agency Standard & Poor's has increased all three countries rating outlook bringing out the reason of success in decreasing the budget. Thus, one can judge that the infection was not especially hard for the Baltic countries, as many countries with less open economies are facing even larger problems. Not so great susceptibility to financial contagion of Baltic countries was also indicated by the testing of spillover effects of conditional variance, which revealed that in spite of being extremely open economies the Baltic countries stock markets do not exhibit a positive variance spillover effect from the US stock market and the presence of the 2000 crisis-in the US did not make these spillovers significantly stronger.

Thus, small open economies like Baltic States do not seem to be more susceptible to financial crises than other countries and should probably continue to be as open as possible for both foreign trade and investment, an aspect which has been one of the main reasons for their success story so far. In order to deal with some unavoidable contagion from elsewhere, government interventions to direct knowledge and innovation based development which could enable better mitigation of the negative consequences of crises are probably necessary.

References

Baur, D. (2003). Testing for Contagion – mean and volatility contagion. *Journal of Multinational Financial Management*, Vol. 13, No. 4-5, pp. 405-422.

Bilho, M., Pelizzon, L. (2003), Contagion and Interdependence in Stock Markets: Have they been misdiagnosed?, *Journal of Economics and Business*, Vol. 55, pp. 405 – 426.

Bollerslev, T. (1986), Genaralized autoregressive conditional heteroskedasticity, *Journal of Econometrics*, Vol. 31, pp. 307-327.

Bordo, M. D., Murshid, A.P. (1999), *The International Transmission of Financial Crises before World War II: Was There Contagion?*, Paper prepared for UNU / WIDER conference on Financial Contagion Helsinki, November 19-20, 1999, www.cfr.org/content/thinktank/Depression/Bordo_1.pdf.

Bordo, M. D., Murshid, A.P. (2000), Are financial crises becoming increasingly more contagious? What is the historical evidence on contagion?, *NBER Working Paper Series*, WP 7900.

Cohen, K. Hawaeini, G., Maier, S., Schwartz, R., Whitcomb, D. (1980), Implications of Microstructure Theory for Empirical Research to Stock Price Behaviour, *Journal of Finance*, No. 35, pp. 249-257.

Didier, T., Mauro, P., Schmukler, S. L. (2008), Vanishing financial contagion?, *Journal of Policy Modeling*, Vol. 30, No. 5, pp. 775-791.

Dungey, M., Zhumabekova, D. (2001), Testing for contagion using correlations: some words of caution. *Pacific Basin Working Paper Series*, No. PB01-09, Federal Reserve Bank of San Francisco.

Edwards, S., Susmel, R. (2001), Volatility Dependence and Contagion in Emerging Markets, *Journal of Development Economics*, Vol. 66, pp. 505-532.

Edwards, S., Susmel, R. (2003), Interest-Rate Volatility in Emerging Markets, *The Review of Economics and Statistics*, Vol. 85, pp. 328-348.

Eichengreen, B., Rose A.K., Wyplosz C. (1996), Contagious currency crises: First tests, *The Scandinavian Journal of Economics*, Vol. 98, pp. 463-484.

Engle, R.F. (1982), Autoregressive conditional heteroskedasticity with estimates of the variance of United Kingdom inflation, *Econometrica*, Vol. 50, pp. 987-997.

Engle, R.F., Lilien, D., Robins, R. (1987), Estimating time varying risk premia in the term structure: the ARCH-M model, *Econometrica*, Vol. 55, pp. 391-407.

Estonian Development Fund (2000), *Estonian Development Fund Report 2000*, www.arengufond.ee.

Forbes, K., Rigobon, R.K. (2001), Measuring contagion: Conceptual and empirical issues, in Claessens, S., Forbes K. (eds.), *International financial contagion*, Kluwer Academic Publishers, pp. 43-66.

Forbes, K., Rigobon, R. (2002), No Contagion, Only Interdependence: Measuring Stock Market Co-Movements, *National Bureau of Economic Research Working Paper*, No. 7267.

French, K.R. (1980), Stock returns and the weekend effect, *Journal of Financial Economics*, No. 8, pp. 55-69.

French, K.R., Schwert G.W., Stambaugh, R.F. (1987), Expected Stock Returns and Volatility, *Journal of Financial Economics*, No. 19, pp. 3-30.

Gibbons, M.R., Hess, P. (1981), Day of the week effects and asset returns, *Journal of Business*, No. 54, pp. 579-596.

Haile, F., Pozo, S. (2008), Currency crisis contagion and the identification of transmission channels, *International Review of Economics & Finance*, Vol. 17, No. 4, pp. 572-588.

Hamao, Y., Masulis, R., Ng, V. (1990), Correlations in price changes and volatility across international stock markets, *The Review of Financial Studies*, Vol. 3, No. 2, 281-307.

Jokipii, T., Lucey, B. (2006), Contagion and interdependence: measuring CEE banking sector co-movements, *Bank of Finland Research Discussion Papers*, No. 15, p. 47.

Kuusk, A., Paas, T. (2011), Contagion of financial crises: what does the empirical evidence show, *Baltic Journal of Management*, Vol. 7, No. 3.

Lee, H., Wu, H., Wang, Y. (2007), Contagion effect in financial markets after the South-East Asia Tsunami, *Research in International Business and Finance*, Vol. 21, No. 2, pp. 281-296.

Lin, W., Engle, R., Ito, T. (1994), Do bulls and bears move across borders? Transmission of international stock returns and volatility, *Review of Financial Studies*, Vol. 7, pp. 507-538.

Masson, P. (2004), Contagion: Monsoonal effects, spillovers, and jumps between multiple equilibria, in Agenor, Pierre-Richard, Miller, Marcus, Vines, David, Weber,

Axel (eds.), *The Asian financial crises: Causes, contagion and consequences*, Cambridge University Press, Cambridge.

Mishkin, F., White, E.N. (2003), US stock market crashes and their aftermath: implications for monetary policy, in Hunter, William C., Kaufmann, George G., Pomerleano, Michael (eds.), *Asset price bubbles: the implications for monetary, regulatory and international policies*, The MIT Press, Cambridge, pp. 53-79.

Rigobon, R. (2002), Contagion: How to measure it?, in Edwards, S., Frankel, J. (eds.), *Preventing currency crises in emerging markets*, The University Chicago Press, Chicago, pp. 269–334.

Serwa, D. (2005), *Empirical evidence on financial spillovers and contagion to international stock markets*, http://opus.kobv.de/euv/volltexte/2007/20/pdf/serwa. dobromil.pdf.

Serwa, D., Bohl, M. (2005), Financial contagion vulnerability and resistance: a comparison of European capital markets, *Economic Systems*, Vol. 29, Issue 3, pp. 344-365.

World Bank Group (2009), *Contagion of financial crises website*, http://www1.worldbank.org/economicpolicy/managing%20volatility/contagion/index.ht ml.

Appendix 7.3. Kuusk, A., Paas, T. (2012). A meta-analysis based approach for examining financial contagion with special emphasis on CEE economies. Accepted for publication in *Eastern European Economics*, 50(6), scheduled in November 2012.

A meta-analysis based approach for examining financial contagion with special emphasis on CEE economies[1]

Andres Kuusk[2], Tiiu Paas[3]

Abstract

This paper looks to provide an insight into the realm of financial contagion, and applies a meta-analytical approach to focus on CEE economies. Results show that, on average, asset market correlations have increased, albeit moderately, during turbulent periods compared to more tranquil times. The selected financial crises are found to vary in terms of their contagiousness. Interestingly, the level of development in a given country is not shown to influence the susceptibility to contagion significantly. Our testing of CEE transition economies indicates that, relative to the sample average, they are less susceptible to financial contagion. An interesting finding relating to CEE transition countries is that they seem to have been affected in the most part by crises originating in the US, even though we have also considered crises originating in Russia and the Czech Republic in the sample.

Keywords: financial crises, contagion, meta-analysis, CEE, transition countries

1. Introduction

Financial contagion has become an increasingly popular research topic in recent times. Several crises throughout the 1980's, 90's and in the last decade have spread rapidly to other countries that were sometimes quite different in size, economic structure and even in a different hemisphere. Researchers in the field of economics have borrowed an expression from epidemiology to describe this phenomenon as financial *'contagion'*. According to Rigobon (2002), the issue of *contagion* has been one of the most debated topics in international finance since the Asian crisis. Events over the last year have seen yet another

---

[1] The paper's authors are grateful for the financial support from the Estonian Science Foundation (Grant 7756) and the research project financed by the Estonian Ministry of Science and Education (SF0180037s08).
[2] Andres Kuusk, PhD candidate, Faculty of Economics and Business Administration, University of Tartu, Estonia. Email: hakeem@mtk.ut.ee
[3] Tiiu Paas, Professor of the Faculty of Economics and Business Administration, University of Tartu, Estonia. Email: tiiu.paas@ut.ee

financial crisis 'snowball' around the world and as such, the need to understand this kind of 'contagion' is increasingly important, particularly for policy makers looking to avoid or manage the spread of any possible future crises. The case of transition countries in Central and Eastern Europe (CEE) is particularly interesting in view of their entry into the third stage of the European Economic and Monetary Union. The Maastricht criteria requires that candidate countries should not have devalued their currency in the two years before the adoption of the euro and should also have avoided sharp movements of some other financial variables like inflation and long-term interest rates. In the context of financial turmoil this criteria is not likely to be met.

The aim of this paper is to quantitatively summarise the findings of recent studies on the topic of financial contagion, and relies on the potential of meta-analysis.

If the contagion hypothesis holds, the consequences for our understanding of how financial crises 'snowball' rolls are that we can assume that the irrational behaviour of financial agents plays an important role, and that the benefit of a diversified international portfolio is substantially diminished.

At the juncture of CEE transition economies, our research task is to examine whether recent frequent instabilities in these countries' stock markets have been due to financial contagion or poor policies and fundamentals. Additionally, we investigate whether CEE transition economies have been more or less susceptible to financial contagion than what is deemed as average.

The paper adopts a meta-analysis as its methodology to fulfil the proposed research tasks. As far as the authors are aware no meta-analysis on the subject of financial contagion has been conducted before.

By implementing meta-analysis we rely on the most commonly used approach, according to which financial contagion is defined as an increase in cross-country asset price correlations during times of crisis compared to asset price correlations during times of financial stability. Therefore, our sample includes studies that incorporate both pre-crisis and post-crises asset price correlations between paired countries, namely the country from where a financial crisis originates (the country of origin), and the country into which a financial crisis spills over (the destination country). Suitable studies are obtained from the ISI Web of Knowledge database and from the World Bank Group Contagion of Financial Crisis Website.

The paper consists of five sections. In the next section alternative definitions of financial contagion and recent empirical results are discussed. Section 3 reveals the fundamental steps involved in the implementation of meta-analysis as well as a short overview of data sources. The results of the meta-analysis are presented in section 4. Section 5 concludes the paper.

2. Empirical evidence

In spite of significant theoretical and empirical interest in the topic, economic literature still offers conceptually different definitions of financial contagion. Using the Contagion of Financial Crises Website summary (The World Bank Group 2001), we can distinguish three main definitions of financial contagion:

1) Financial Contagion is the cross-country transmission of shocks or the general cross-country spillover effects of a financial crisis. Unlike the following definitions of financial contagion, this one includes fundamental linkages as a channel of financial contagion.

2) Financial contagion is the transmission of shocks to other countries or the cross-country correlation beyond that which might be credited to common shocks or fundamental linkages among countries. Spillovers based on fundamental linkages are differentiated from financial contagion by a preponderance of the literature. This definition is sometimes referred to as *excess co-movement*, a more-than-expected correlation that remains even after controlling for macroeconomic fundamentals and common shocks. Herding behaviour (whereby individuals in a group act together without planned direction, imitating the acts of other group members who are perceived to be better informed) is typically attributed to the materialization of this kind of more-than-expected co-movement.

3) Financial contagion occurs when cross-country correlations increase during times of crisis compared to correlations during tranquil times. This definition is sometimes referred to as shift-contagion. Forbes and Rigobon (1999) stress that this notion of contagion excludes a constant high degree of co-movement in a crisis period, and views markets as simply interdependent.

As economic literature provides heterogeneous views on financial contagion and its transmission channels it is therefore understandable that the results of empirical studies vary significantly depending on several factors.

We investigated around 75 empirical analyses of financial contagion and found that there are almost no pairs of studies that are identical in their definitions of financial contagion, testing

161

methodology, chosen crises, financial markets and destination countries, which may influence the results of empirical studies. In addition, the problems of omitted variables, feedback dependencies between stock markets, different time zones and arbitrary choices of the crisis window can all affect tests of contagion (see also Billio and Pellizon (2003) and Dungey and Zhumabekova (2001) for an informed study on the subject).

In this paper we focus on earlier papers that have investigated CEE economies. For other countries there are many qualitative reviews that have been written (see for example Dornbusch *et al* 2000, or papers by Roberto Rigobon), which the following overview summarises.

Evidence both confirming and denying the existence of financial contagion has been widely found in recent empirical analyses and there is no clear dominant finding. A superficial view may lead one to take the view that evidence for financial contagion has been found more often than not. On the other hand, this result is mostly obtained when the presence of heteroscedasticity is not taken into account: the papers that control for heteroscedasticity find evidence for financial contagion far less often. Thus, previous empirical studies provide heterogeneous results depending on applied definitions, testing methods, chosen crises and destination countries and financial indices.

The literature investigating financial contagion in the case of transition economies is rather vague and focuses mainly on three CEE economies (Hungary, Poland and the Czech Republic). Wang and Moore (2008) investigate the co-movement between a set of three emerging major CEE markets (Poland, Hungary, and Czech Republic) and the aggregate eurozone market by utilizing the dynamic conditional correlation technique[4]. Between these two collectives, the authors find significant dynamic correlations, and they notice a relatively higher level of links in the aftermath of the crises. The authors' findings reveal that the increase in stock market co-movements can be explained neither by the macroeconomic convergence process nor by monetary convergence with the eurozone. By a process of elimination, the authors hone in on evidence that ascribes the increase in co-movements to extant financial contagion.

Gelos and Sahay (2001) find that correlations in foreign exchange market pressures can be explained by direct trade links, but not by other measured fundamentals. They find no

---

[4] The dynamic conditional correlation measures the contemporaneous conditional correlation between the two series and has been used to provide an indirect measure of the degree of integration between the stock market in the eurozone and the new EU countries.

financial contagion spillovers from either the Czech Republic or Asia to CEE stock markets, but shocks to the Russian stock market Granger caused movements in Czech, Hungarian and Polish stock markets. Weller and Morzuch (2000) argue that during both recent and historic financial crises, the default risk has been lower in CEE transition countries than in other developing (emerging) economies. The authors posit an explanation that there is seemingly less speculative financing and a reduced chance of asset market bubbles in CEE transition countries and, consequently, a diminishing vulnerability to short-term capital flows. Given that default and maturity risks have historically been lower in CEE transition countries than in other emerging economies, it is suspected by Weller and Morzuch (2000) that the risks posed to interest rates and exchange rates are also likely to be lower. Thus, as long as no other problems are encountered by these countries' financial sectors, international investors tend to be less inclined to withdraw their funds from CEE transition countries.

Serwa (2005) uses an extension of the model presented by Forbes and Rigobon (2002) and Corsetti *et al* (2005) to investigate seven financial crises on a sample of some CEE and Western European countries. Serwa (2005) found that financial contagion infrequently or rarely occurred over the course of the investigated financial crises. Jokipii and Lucey (2006) investigate co-movements in the banking sector for Poland, Hungary and the Czech Republic over a period of approximately ten years. They found that financial contagion spreads from the Czech Republic to Hungary.

Based on this literature review, we find that using a qualitative analysis of research studies into historical financial crises is not sufficient to enable researchers to develop working proactive management techniques that would mitigate, if not prevent, a financial crisis from spilling over into other countries.

Accordingly, we propose that a more robust profile of financial contagion may be attained by employing a meta-analysis research method, which we detail in the next section of the paper.

3. The main steps involved in the implementation of meta-analysis and the data sources

Meta-analysis is a research method that amalgamates, quantitatively synthesizes and summarises data from previous empirical analyses on the subject. This procedure uses an established singular measure that is common to all studies to be analysed. This measure is called the 'effect size'. Individual effect sizes are aggregated and after study characteristics are controlled, the resulting overall results can be considered the meta-effect size (we also use the notion of a weighted mean effect size and an effect size mean).

In order to implement meta-analysis, five steps were put in place. The first step was to calculate relevant individual effect sizes and control for their independencies. The next was to compute the meta-effect sizes based on individually calculated effect size weights. The confidence interval was then determined along with the statistical significance of the meta-effect sizes. Penultimately, we tested for homogeneity before finally concluding and interpreting the results.

Before the first of these steps can be put into action, data from all of the studies that are to be analysed must be collected. When searching for appropriate studies to use in our meta-analysis, we used the ISI Web of Knowledge database and the Contagion of Financial Crisis Website from the World Bank Group. From the ISI Web of Knowledge database, studies corresponding to the keywords *financial contagion* are used. As previously discussed we define financial contagion as an increase in cross-country asset price correlations during crisis times relative to asset price correlations during non-crisis times. This is the most common definition of financial contagion in empirical analyses. As noted in section 2 of our paper, this definition excludes a scenario characterized by a constant high degree of co-movement, whereby markets are instead deemed as interdependent. Accordingly, we have only included studies that report on the correlations of both pre-crisis and post-crisis asset prices between countries. These restrictions reduce our data set to 716 data points, of which 394 are independent (by independent we mean that these data points come from different sources or differ in some important characteristics like crisis, destination country or financial index). Our data set has been drawn from 30 constructs (17 studies by 12 authors). In the event that post-crisis correlations are reported in both the long and short term, independency problems are avoided by opting to include only the short-term data, although the problem of independency is discussed in greater detail later on in the paper.

To conduct the first step we have to find appropriate individual effect sizes. The effect size statistic produces a statistical standardization of the study findings so that the resulting numerical values are interpretable in a consistent fashion across all the variables and measures involved (see Lipsey and Wilson 2001). An effect size statistic must be defined that is capable of representing the quantitative findings of the studies in a standardized way that permits meaningful numerical comparison and an analysis to be carried out. There does not seem to be any real alternative to using the difference between pre and post-crisis correlations as an effect size in any given study or construct in trying to achieve this task. Mathematically, our individual effect sizes are computed as:

(1) $ES_i = r_{post_i} - r_{pre_i}$

where ES_i is the individual effect size for study (construct) i and r_{pre_i} and r_{post_i} are pre- and post-crisis correlations respectively for study (construct) i.

After establishing individual effect sizes we have to aggregate them into one meta-effect size. We use the traditional approach of meta-analysis in that we assume that the best estimate for the population effect size is the weighted average of the individual effect sizes.

The weights have to be determined for every individual effect size so that overall value could be found. Hedges (1982, Hedges and Olkin 1985) has demonstrated, that the optimal weights are based on the standard error of the effect size. For Hedges (1982), as a larger standard error corresponds to a less precise ES value, the actual respective weights of the individual ESs should be computed as the inverse of the squared standard error value, known in the meta-analysis lexicon as the inverse variance weight.

Computing weights depends on which type of individual ESs we are dealing with. There are no rules given in the literature as to which is the correct type of effect size if the individual effect sizes to be summarised are changes in correlation coefficients. It is not intuitively clear whether we should deal with these differences as pre-post contrasts or as an association between variables. On the one hand, even if we were not interested in the correlation coefficients themselves, but the way they change between two points in time, it is not clear why these two approaches differ to such an extent that we were unable to use the same computational procedures. As such, it could be taken that we should take these effect sizes to signify correlations. On the other hand, we have data points for both before and after crises, the difference between which we are interested in. The situation is analoguous to the kind when treatment effect is analysed (we can think of crisis starting point as a treatment). Our decision is to use both approaches in parallel. As such, when individual effect sizes are treated as mean differences, we refer to this as Approach 1 and when treating individual effect sizes as correlations we refer to this as Approach 2.

For both the mean differences (gains) and correlation coefficients that are used in the present analysis, the standard error formulations have been worked out and these are available for us. Using approach 2 (taking effect sizes as correlations), in order that we were able to find the

weights by which individual effect sizes could be aggregated into one meta-effect size, we needed to alter the effect sizes to avoid problems in standard error formulations (such problems are discussed in more depth by Rosenthal 1994). A widely accepted modification method to transform correlations is Fischer's Z_r-transformation (see Hedges and Olkin 1985):

$$(2) \qquad ES_{Z_r} = 0.5\ln\left(\frac{1+r}{1-r}\right)$$

where r is the correlation coefficient. In our analysis the difference between post- and pre-crisis correlations is in the placement of r. Once we have obtained the results, in order to interpret them, we transform the Fischer Z-transformed Meta-ES back into standard correlation form by employing the inverse of the Z_r-transformation (Hedges and Olkin 1985):

$$(3) \qquad r = \frac{e^{2ES_{Z_r}} - 1}{e^{2ES_{Z_r}} + 1}$$

After Fischer's z-transformation, the standard error formula for correlation based (Approach 2) effect size mean is the following:

$$(4) \qquad SE_{Z_r} = \frac{1}{\sqrt{n-3}}$$

and inverse variance weights are therefore:

$$(5) \qquad w_{Z_r} = n - 3$$

where n is the sample size of the individual effect size in both equations.

However, we do not have the data necessary to calculate mean weights when treating individual effect sizes as treatment effects (Approach 1). More specifically, we lack information on the correlation between pre-treatment and post-treatment asset prices in each of the individual studies. Therefore, sample size is instead designated as the proxy for weight. Now, when suitable weights are found the overall meta-effect size can be calculated using the following formula:

$$(6) \qquad \overline{d} = \frac{\sum d_i w_i}{\sum w_i}$$

where d_i is the i-th individual effect size and w_i is the weight (inverse variance weight in case of correlation coefficients (Approach 2) and sample size for treatment effects (Approach 1)) of the i-th effect size.

In examining homogeneity, we examined whether or not all of the effect sizes that were averaged into a mean value estimated one common population effect (see Hedges 1983, Rosenthal and Rubin 1982). In a homogeneous distribution, the dispersion of the ESs around their common mean is no greater than the dispersion expected from the sampling error alone.

Homogeneity testing is based on the Q-statistic[5], which is distributed as a chi-square with $k-1$ degrees of freedom, where k is the number of ESs (Hedges and Olkin 1985). The formula for the Q-statistic is:

(7) $$Q = \sum \left[w_i \left(ES_i - \overline{ES} \right)^2 \right]$$

where ES_i is the individual ES for $i = 1$ to k (the number of ESs);

$\overline{ES}$ is the Meta-ES over the k ESs;

and w_i is the individual weight for ES_i.

If Q exceeds the critical value for a chi-square with $k-1$ degrees of freedom, then the null hypothesis of homogeneity is rejected. A statistically significant Q, therefore, indicates a heterogeneous distribution.

Before being able to run a meta-analysis we had to deal with some independency concerns. There are cases for multiple effect sizes within the same studies. This negates the assumption of independence and overestimates the weights of the studies with multiple effect sizes. The traditional way to deal with the situation is to choose only one effect size per study, per construct. However, this approach does not include some of the information contained in the primary studies and we did not want to lose any of the information we had available on different correlation measurement methodologies as possible moderators. It is well known that correlation coefficients adjusted for heteroscedasticity are lower than unadjusted ones, and therefore, the contagion seems to be more likely to occur in cases where there are unadjusted correlation coefficients. Therefore, rather than dropping some of the data points, we diminish the weights of studies with multiple effect sizes per construct by dividing the sample size by the number of effect sizes per construct. (For a discussion of multiple measurements within studies see also Rosenthal 1994)

---

[5] Alternative approach to homogeneity testing, so called 75% rule, is given by Hunter and Schmidt (1990). They partition the observed effect size variability into two components - the portion attributable to subject-level sampling error and the portion attributable to other between-study differences. According to their rule of thumb, the distribution is homogeneous if sampling error accounts for 75% or more of the observed variability.

4. Empirical results

In our empirical analysis we used the methodology described in the previous section. Employing formulas (1)–(6) itemized in section 3, we derived respective estimates of the meta-effect size: 0.053 if we use Approach 1 and 0.072 if we use Approach 2 (these values are given in Table 1). Corresponding standard errors are 0.005 in both cases and for each the associated 95% confidence interval value is well above zero. The results for both approaches indicate that, relative to tranquil periods, asset price correlations are on average observably higher, albeit moderately, during turbulent periods. The Q-statistic (recall formula (7)), however, clearly exceeds the critical value, indicating that the dispersion of the individual ESs around their mean is greater than expected from a sampling error alone, and therefore, the each effect size does not estimate a common population mean.

As we have heterogeneous distribution we continue by searching for moderators to explain the variability in effect sizes. As mentioned above, the methodology for calculating the correlation coefficients is widely accepted to significantly influence the results in financial contagion studies. The logic behind this is that when not adjusting for heteroskedasticity, the post-crisis correlations are higher, and therefore, finding evidence for contagion is more probable. For controlling the measurement of the correlation coefficients as potential moderators, we divided our sample into two sub-samples, differentiating heteroskedasticity adjusted (A) post-crisis correlation coefficients from unadjusted (U) counterparts. For the sample with unadjusted correlation coefficients, the weighted mean effect size is 0.168 using Approach 1 and 0.208 in case of Approach 2 (see Table 1). For the sample with heteroskedasticity adjusted correlation coefficients, the value is 0.030 for both approaches 1 and 2. The difference is more than clear and we can conclude that whether correlation coefficients are heteroskedasticity adjusted or not significantly affects the results of the analysis of financial contagion. By dividing the overall Q into the within and between groups component, it is found that the between groups Q is highly significant, which also indicates that the differences in the measurement of the correlation (heteroskedasticity adjusted or not) accounts for a significant variability in effect sizes.

However, Q-statistic indicates that there is still some heterogeneity left in the distribution; therefore, we also control for other possible moderator variables. Next, we investigate whether different crises have been contagious to differing extents.

For the crisis in Thailand in 1997 using Approach 1, the weighted mean effect size is 0.132. If the effect sizes are treated as correlation coefficients (Approach 2), then the weighted mean effect size is calculated as 0.173. For the crisis in Hong Kong in the same year, the values are respectively 0.100 and 0.098; for the Mexican 1994 crisis, they are 0.141 and 0.160; for the Russian 1998 crisis they are -0.001 and 0.006; for the Brazilian 1999 crisis the values are -0.016 and -0.014. From these figures it is apparent that the Mexican, Thai and Hong Kong crises were contagious, while the Russian and the Brazilian crises were not.

The crises in the US in 1987 and in 2002 were contagious, whereas in Argentina in 2001 and in Turkey in the same year, as well as in India in 2004, the opposite was found to be true – the correlations are on average lower after these crises.

Pre-WWII crises on average were not contagious, as weren't those in the Czech Republic (1997) and in the US (2001). These crises showed some increase in average asset price correlations, but this increase was found to be insignificant.

Given crisis as a grouping variable accounts for a significant variability in effect sizes, although there is still some heterogeneity left inside some of the groups.

Table 1. The results of meta-analysis of financial contagion (whole sample of the study)

Region	Sample size	ESs as treatment effects (Approach 1)			ESs as correlation coefficients (Approach 2)		
		Meta-ES	Standard error (ES)	Q-statistic	Meta-ES	Standard error (ES)	Q-statistic
All	716**	0.053*	0.005	2782.0*	0.072*	0.005	5568.0*
U	159	0.168*	0.007	956.7*	0.208*	0.007	3432.2*
A	545	0.030*	0.007	668.0*	0.030*	0.007	716.1*
Tha 1997	86	0.132*	0.007	853.9*	0.173*	0.007	3367.1*
HK 1997	154	0.100*	0.009	295.6*	0.098*	0.009	323.0*
Rus 1998	46	-0.001	0.027	48.8	0.006	0.027	52.5
Bra 1999	33	-0.016	0.039	17.33	-0.014	0.039	15.4
Prewar	344	0.045	0.026	165.8*	0.059*	0.028*	197.3*
Mex 1994	372	0.141*	0.038	45.7	0.160*	0.045	39.0
US 1987	70	0.185*	0.062	5.8	0.181*	0.071	4.7
Ind 2004	68	-0.091*	0.028	122.0*	-0.116*	0.031	153.5*
Tur 2001	19	-0.194*	0.055	22.2	-0.209*	0.066	19.3
US 2001	82	0.014	0.055	22.4	0.019	0.066	17.8
Arg 2001	33	-0.374*	0.015	126.6*	-0.391*	0.015	156.6*

US 2002	33	0.126*	0.055	12.8	0.133*	0.066	10.3
Cze 1997	45	0.057	0.039	26.2*	0.058	0.041	26.3*
Emerg	344	0.054*	0.006	2254.3*	0.078*	0.006	5116.5*
Devel	372	0.052*	0.009	527.6*	0.051*	0.008	555.8*

* denotes statistically significant results (in 95% confidence interval)

** the meta-sample, numbering 716, exceeds the sum of 159 (U) and 544 (A), since 12 observations in sample 'All' could not be categorised by either U or A

ES - effect size

All - all observations (data points) from the sample with all countries

U – cases with unadjusted (for heteroskedasticity) correlation coefficients

A – cases with adjusted (for heteroskedasticity) correlation coefficients

Tha – Thailand crisis; HK – Hong Kong crisis; Rus – Russian crisis; Bra – Brazilian crisis; Mex – Mexican crisis; US – United States of American crisis; Ind – Indian crisis; Turkish crisis; Arg – Argentinean crisis; Cze – Czech Republican crisis; Prewar – average of 6 pre-World War II crises (Argentine crisis 1890, Baring crisis (UK) 1890, US banking crisis 1893, US stock market crash 1929, Sterling crisis (UK) 1931, devaluation of the US dollar (US) 1933)

Emerg – cases reflect 152 emerging (developing) countries, numbered 31 through 182 per the Human Development Index 2008

Devel – cases reflect 30 developed countries, numbered 1 through 30 per the Human Development Index 2008

Source: authors' calculations

Using only the data where correlation coefficients are adjusted for the presence of heteroskedasticity (see Appendix 1), we found that the results did not change much. The Mexican, Thai and Hong Kong crises are still contagious, although the weighted mean effect sizes are somewhat smaller. Also, the Russian and Brazilian crises are not contagious, and have weighted mean effect sizes that are slightly negative. The only significant change relates to the US 1987 crisis, which is no longer contagious at the 95% confidence interval. However, given that the weighted mean effect size is clearly above zero (0.17) and only slightly below the unadjusted (U) case, it seems that these findings are down to the smaller sample size, rather than the result of any other factor.

We have also looked at the extent to which the destination country is developed so that we could consider whether this will impact on how susceptible a country is to financial contagion. To measure this, we used the Human Development Index (HDI) 2008 to categorise countries as more or less developed. We rated the top 30 countries in the HDI list as developed and all other countries as developing (emerging). This produces quite comparable sample sizes for both groups with 372 and 344 respectively. In the case of less developed

countries, the weighted mean effect size is 0.054 according to Approach 1 (effect sizes taken as treatment effects) and 0.077 according to Approach 2 (effect sizes taken as correlations). In the case of more developed countries, the corresponding values are 0.052 and 0.051 respectively. These results show that when using Approach 1, there is no difference in susceptibility to the spread of crises between developed and developing countries, while according to Approach 2, less developed countries are somewhat more susceptible to the carryover of financial crises. The variability analysis reveals that the level of development of the destination country does not account for a significant variability in effect sizes. From that we may judge that herding behaviour seems more likely to be the transmission force for financial crises than real and stable linkages. This finding is in line with that of Serwa (2005), who found that CEE stock markets are no more vulnerable to contagion than Western European markets. On the other hand, this finding contradicts that of Dungey and Tambakis (2003), who argue that developing countries are more affected by contagion than developed countries.

We also compare developed and developing (emerging) country groups separately for both adjusted (A) and unadjusted (U) cases. The Meta-ES findings are displayed in Appendix 1.

Using Approach 1 for the unadjusted cases, we found meta-effect sizes of 0.12 for developed countries, and 0.19 for developing countries in the absence of any overlapping confidence intervals. Using Approach 2 for the unadjusted cases, the disparity between the meta-effect sizes is even more pronounced, with 0.12 for developed countries and 0.24 for developing countries. These results show that for unadjusted cases, developing countries are more susceptible to financial contagion than their more developed counterparts.

However, for the adjusted (A) cases there are no significant differences between the meta-effect sizes of these two subgroups. Under both Approach 1 and Approach 2 the Meta-ESs are 0.02 for developed countries and 0.04 for developing countries, but the differences in Meta-ES values were not significant at the 95% confidence level.

It is seen in Appendix 1 that there is some heterogeneity left in the distribution of most of the subgroups even when they are based on two moderators. This means that the results must be taken with caution, as all individual effect sizes within each of the groups may not estimate the same population mean. However, we are forced to be reconciled with the heteroskedasticity as we do not have enough studies in the sample to conduct a meta-regression. As a rule a thumb, there should be ten studies per explanatory variable in the meta-regression, which we are clearly short of. Bringing in dummies for all crises in addition

173

to the ones used in the adjusted and unadjusted cases, the development level of the destination country (developed or emerging), and also all cross-effects, would take the number of exogeneous variables to far too great a level for meta-regression to be feasible.

With reference to publication bias, a point of note should be made. Publication bias refers to the fact that studies with significant results are more likely to be published. In the field of financial contagion it is not clear what kind of result – supporting or contradicting the contagion hypothesis – is more interesting. Therefore, we think that controlling for publication bias is not necessary in our study.

We next ran a meta-analysis for the CEE countries (as destination countries) and attempted to compare the results (presented in Table 2) with the results we obtained on the basis of the whole sample, which comprised all 716 observations.

Table 2. The results of meta-analysis of financial contagion for the CEE transition economies

Region	Number of effect sizes	ESs as treatment effects (Approach 1)			ESs as correlation coefficients (Approach 2)		
		Meta-ES	Standard error (ES)	Q-statistic	Meta-ES	Standard error (ES)	Q-statistic
All	89	0.019	0.020	108.7	0.023	0.021	107.1
U	15	0.148*	0.034	32.6*	0.161*	0.034	35.0*
A	74	-0.051	0.025	53.6	-0.057	0.027	46.7
HK 1997	15	-0.004	0.037	14.9	-0.005	0.038	13.7
Rus 1998	19	0.057	0.039	35.4*	0.071	0.041	39.0*
Bra 1999	9	-0.084	0.075	5.3	-0.087	0.081	4.7
Tur 2001	9	-0.187	0.105	5.6	-0.203	0.126	5.1
US 2001	9	0.024	0.105	4.2	0.026	0.126	3.2
Arg 2001	9	-0.052	0.071	2.6	-0.053	0.079	2.3
US 2002	9	0.297*	0.105	2.8	0.308*	0.126	2.6
Cze 1997	10	0.056	0.045	22.2*	0.057	0.046	22.5*

* denotes statistically significant results (in 95% confidence level)

ES - effect size

All - all observations (data points) from the sample with only CEE transition economies

U - cases with unadjusted (for heteroskedasticity) correlation coefficients

A - cases with adjusted (for heteroskedasticity) correlation coefficients

HK – Hong Kong crisis; Rus – Russian crisis; Bra – Brazilian crisis; US – United States of American crisis; Tur – Turkish crisis; Arg – Argentinean crisis; Cze – Czech Republican crisis

Source: authors' calculations

In Table 3 'All' refers to the sample of 89 individual ESs affiliated with CEE transition economies, which includes eight financial crises: the Hong Kong crisis of 1997, the Czech Republic crisis of 1997, the Russian crisis of 1998, the Brazilian crisis of 1999, the Turkish crisis of 2001, the US crisis of 2001, the Argentinean crisis of 2001 and the US crisis of 2002; and four CEE transition countries for which we have data – the Czech Republic, Estonia, Hungary and Poland. The Meta-ES that was calculated for the whole sample of 89 individual ESs is 0.019, according to Approach 1 (ESs taken as treatment effects), and 0.023 according to Approach 2 (ESs taken as correlation coefficients).

We should recall from Table 1 that corresponding meta-effect sizes for the whole sample were 0.053 under Approach 1 and 0.072 under Approach 2. Thus, on average, the rate of contagiousness for destination countries that are CEE transition economies has been lower than average. Also the increases in the correlation coefficients in the sample of CEE transition economies are not statistically significant. This outcome bears some congruence with Serwa and Bohl (2005), who argue that there is no evidence that CEE transition economies are more prone to financial contagion compared with western countries.

If only heteroskedasticity adjusted (A) correlation coefficients are included in the sample of CEE transition economies as destination countries, then the Meta-ESs for CEE transition economies are negative values, -0.051 and -0.057 according to Approach 1 and Approach 2, respectively. Thus, asset price correlations have, on average, decreased during financial crises. Also, compared to the corresponding Meta-ES value for the whole sample, the Meta-ES value for CEE transition countries is lower (meta-effect size was positive in the case of the whole sample).

Comparing different financial crises we see that on average the US crisis of 2002 (accounting scandals) has been the most contagious crisis for CEE transition countries, with a weighted mean effect size 0.30 according to Approach 1 and 0.31 according to Approach 2. These values are both statistically significant. In terms of contagiousness the next are the Russian crisis of 1998 and the Czech crisis of 1997 with meta-effect sizes above 0.05 but statistically

15

insignificant at the significance level of 0.05. Other crises have even less evidence to have been spread significantly to the CEE transition economies.

Compared to the average, CEE transition economies seem to have been affected to the greatest extent by both the Russian crisis of 1998 and the US crisis of 2002, while the Hong Kong 1997 crisis has not spread to CEE transition countries despite being considered contagious while using the whole sample. This finding parallels that of Weller and Morzuch (2000), who demonstrated that although the Asian financial crisis of 1997 spread to Russia and Brazil, the CEE transition economies remained largely unaffected.

If we narrow our focus to consider the results that were obtained by using only heteroskedasticity adjusted (A) data points, (results are not reported in Table 3), then the US 2002 crisis emerges as the sole contagious crisis affecting CEE transition destination countries. The only other crisis during which heteroskedasticity adjusted asset price correlations have increased is that of the US crisis in 2001. For all other financial crises identified within the sample of 89 CEE transition countries, asset price correlations have remained either constant or have decreased during times of crisis.

Our analyses returned an unanticipated finding – CEE transition economies are determined to be more susceptible to financial crises originating in the US as opposed to financial crises originating elsewhere, most notably in Russia and the Czech Republic.

In summing up the results of the applied meta-analysis, we conclude that, on average, asset market correlations have increased during turbulent periods compared to immediately preceding periods of tranquillity. This conclusion gives credence to the relevance of financial contagion as a phenomenon to reckon with in global policymaking circles. This increase, however, is rather moderate and, after controlling for heterogeneity in correlations during turbulent periods, the increase is even smaller, though still statistically significant at the 95% confidence level.

The computational methodology applied to correlations – whether adjusted or unadjusted for heteroskedasticity – and the crisis under observation are found to be significant moderators in explaining heterogeneity in distribution. Among the foremost financial crises experienced during the past two decades, we find the financial crises of Mexico, Thailand and Hong Kong to be contagious, and, conversely, we find the Russian and the Brazilian financial crises not to be contagious. The overall level of development of the destination country does not seem to account for the observed significant variability in effect sizes. CEE transition economies as destination countries compared to the sample of all countries have been on average less susceptible to the spillover of financial crises.

5. Conclusion

Financial contagion is a complex and multidimensional phenomenon with no unequivocally accepted definition or testing methodology. The empirical results on the theme of financial contagion are mixed, and in our view, no unique conclusion can be drawn based on a qualitative analysis of empirical literature. Thus, we propose that using a meta-analysis provides a more profound and adequate picture of financial contagion.

The results of the meta-analysis indicate that on average asset market correlations have increased during turbulent periods, but the increase is rather moderate. Whether correlation coefficients are adjusted for the presence of heteroscedasticity or not is a clear moderating variable in explaining heterogeneity in distribution. In the case of adjusted correlation coefficients, the increase in correlations during turbulent periods is considerably smaller, but still statistically significant.

Further results of our analysis show that the Mexican crisis of 1994, the Thai crisis of 1997 and the crisis in Hong Kong in 1997 were contagious. We also find that the crisis in Russia in 1998, the crisis in Brazil in 1999 and that in Argentina in 2001 were not. We have not investigated the reasons behind this finding, so future investigation is needed in this respect. Yet other findings indicate that the degree to which the destination country can be considered developed does not seem to be a significant contributory factor in determining whether a financial crisis will spread over or not.

With respect to CEE transition economies, the results indicate somewhat surprisingly that, on average, CEE transition economies are less susceptible to financial contagion compared with the average of the whole sample. The Meta-ES for CEE transition countries is statistically insignificant and, after controlling for heteroskedasticity, takes on a negative value. The only crisis in the sample to have had a significant impact on CEE transition countries is the US 2002 accounting scandals. Interestingly, CEE transition economies seem to be more susceptible to financial crises that originate in the US, specifically those of 2001 and 2002, than to financial crises originating elsewhere, most notably Russia and the Czech Republic. The reason behind this may well be the fact that the US has been extremely influential around the world.

One of the most important limitations of the paper is that our meta-analysis is restricted to an analysis based on correlation coefficients only. The vast majority of studies use this methodology, and it is no simple task to conduct the comparable individual effect sizes necessary for the meta-analytic approach using other methodologies. Nonetheless, this might be one of the subjects future research could focus on. Another limitation is associated with the heterogeneity that is left in our samples even after dividing them into several subgroups. Thus, one has to keep in mind that the numerical value of some meta-effect sizes are of questionable validity because all individual effect sizes within the groups may not represent the common population and the groups could be divided even further. Also, studies investigating the US 2008 crisis should be included in the sample in any future meta-analyses on the subject.

References

Alvarez-Plata, P. and Schrooten, M. (2003) Latin America after the Argentine crisis: diminishing financial market integration. [http://www.springerlink.com/content/lbq33rav55ev14j3/].

Baig, T. and Goldfajn, I. (1999). Financial market contagion in the Asian crisis. - *IMF Staff Papers* 46 (1999), pp. 167–195.

Billio, M. and Pelizzon, L. (2003). Contagion and Interdependence in Stock Markets: Have they been misdiagnosed? - Journal of Economics and Business 55, 405 – 426.

Bordo, M. D. and Murshid, A. P. (2000). Are financial crises becoming increasingly more contagious? What is the historical evidence on contagion? NBER Working Paper Series, WP 7900.

Chiang, T.C.; Jeon, M.N. and Li, H. (2007). Dynamic correlation analysis of financial contagion: evidence from Asian markets. - Journal of International Money and Finance. Volume 26, Issue 7, November 2007, pages 1206-1229.

Corsetti, G.; Pericoli, M. and Sbracia, M. (2005). Some contagion, some interdependence: more pitfalls in tests of financial contagion. - Journal of International Money and Finance 8 (2005), 1177–1199.

Dornbusch, R.; Park Y. C. and Claessens S. (2000). Contagion: Understanding how it spreads. - World Bank Research Observer 15 (2000), 177–197.

Dungey, M. and Dambakis, D. (2003). Financial contagion: What do we mean? What do we know? [http://www.g24.org/Dungey-Tambakis2003.pdf].

Dungey, M. and Zhumabekova, D. (2001). Testing for contagion using correlations: some words of caution. - Working Paper No. PB01-09, Pacific Basin Working Paper Series, Federal Reserve Bank of San Francisco.

Forbes, K. and Rigobon, R. (1999). No Contagion, Only Interdependence: Measuring Stock Market Co-Movements. - National Bureau of Economic Research Working Paper No. 7267.

Forbes, K. and Rigobon, R. K. (2002). Measuring contagion: Conceptual and empirical issues. In: S. Claessens and K. Forbes, Editors, International financial contagion, Kluwer Academic Publishers (2001), 43–66.

19

Gelos, R. G. and Sahay, R. (2001). Financial market spillovers in transition economies. - Economics of Transition 9, 53 – 86.

Hedges, L.V. (1982). Fitting categorical models to ESs from a series of experiments. – Journal of Educational Statistics, 7, 119-137.

Hedges, L. V., and Olkin, I. (1985). Statistical methods for meta-analysis. Orlando, FL: Academic Press Inc. Harcourt, Brace, Jovanovich publishers.

Jokipii, T. and Lucey, B. (2006). Contagion and interdependence: measuring CEE banking sector co–movements. – Bank of Finland Research Discussion Papers, No. 15, 47.

Kleimeier, S.; Lehnert, T. and Verschoor, W.F.C. (2008). Measuring financial contagion using time-aligned data: the importance of the speed of transmission of shocks. – Oxford Bulletin of Economics and Statistics. Volume 70, Issue 4, 493-508.

King, M.A. and Wadhwani, S. (1990). Transmission of volatility between stock markets. - Review of Financial Studies 3 (1): 5–33.

Lee, H.; Wu, H. And Wang, Y. (2007). Contagion effect in financial markets after the South-East Asia Tsunami. – Research in International Business and Finance, Volume 21, Issue 2, June 2007, Pages 281-296.

Lipsey, Mark, W. and Wilson, David, B. (2001). Practical meta-analysis. Applied Social Research Methods Series, Volume 49. SAGE Publications.

Rigobon, R. (2002). Contagion: How to measure it? In: S. Edwards and J. Frankel, Editors, Preventing currency crises in emerging markets, The University Chicago Press, Chicago, pp. 269–334.

Rosenthal, R. (1994). Statistically describing and combining studies. – The handbook of research synthesis, Eds. H. Cooper & L. V. Hedges. New York: Russell Sage Foundation, pp. 231-244.

Rosenthal, R. and Rubin, D. B. (1982). A simple, general purpose display of magnitude of experimental effect. - Journal of Educational Psychology, 74, pp. 166-169.

Serwa, D. (2005). Empirical evidence on financial spillovers and contagion to international stock markets. [http://opus.kobv.de/euv/volltexte/2007/20/pdf/serwa.dobromil.pdf].

Serwa, D. and Bohl, M. (2005). Financial Contagion Vulnerability and Resistance: A Comparison of European Capital Markets. – Economic Systems. Vol. 29, Issue 3, September, pp. 344–365.

Wang, P. and Moore, T. (2008). Stock market integration for the transition economies: time-varying conditional correlation approach. – The Manchester School, Volume 76, Issue s1, 116-133.

Wang, K. and Thi T.N. (2006). Does Contagion Effect Exist Between Stock Markets of Thailand and Chinese Economic Area (CEA) during the „Asian Flu"? – *Asian Journal of Management and Humanity Sciences, Vol. 1, No. 1*, pp. 16-36, 2006.

Weller, C. E. and Morzuch B. (2000). International Financial Contagion: Why are Eastern Europe's banks not failing when everybody else's are? – Economics of Transition, Vol. 8 Issue 3, 639-663.

World Bank Group (2001). Contagion of financial crises website. http://www1.worldbank.org/economicpolicy/managing%20volatility/contagion/index.html.

21

Co-Authors' Coordinates

Andres Kuusk
PhD candidate
Department of Economics
University of Tartu
Narva Road 4, Economicum
Tartu 51009, Estonia
Email: hakeem@mtk.ut.ee

Professor Tiiu Paas, Ph.D.
Head of Department of Economics, University of Tartu
Narva Rd. 4, Economicum
Tartu 51009, Estonia
Fax: 3727 376 312
Email: tiiu.paas@ut.ee

Home:
Kotka 11, Tartu 50404, Estonia
Phone/fax 3727 380 553

22

Appendix 1

Results of meta-analysis for subgroups based on two moterators

	Sample size	ESs as treatment effects (Approach 1)			ESs as correlation coefficients (Approach 2)		
		Meta-ES	Standard error (ES)	Q-statistic	Meta-ES	Standard error (ES)	Q-statistic
Emerg and A	237	0.04*	0.009	261	0.04*	0.009	280*
Emerg and U	95	0.19*	0.008	846*	0.24*	0.008	3257*
Devel and A	308	0.02	0.010	404*	0.02	0.011	433*
Devel and U	64	0.12*	0.014	92*	0.12*	0.015	92*
Mex and A	41	0.12*	0.044	30	0.15*	0.050	28
Mex and U	27	0.020*	0.075	15	0.22*	0.103	10
HK and A	116	0.04*	0.012	167*	0.04*	0.012	173*
HK and U	38	0.17*	0.026	78*	0.17*	0.013	93*
US87 and A	9	0.17	0.108	1.7	0.18	0.131	1.2
US87 and U	10	0.19*	0.04	4.0	0.18	0.084	3.4
Ind04 and A	41	-0.10*	0.040	70*	-0.13*	0.044	98
Ind04 and U	10	-0.08*	0.040	52	-0.10*	0.044	55
Cze97 and A	7	0.01	0.056	9.1	0.01	0.058	9.0
Cze97 and U	7	0.10	0.056	16*	0.11	0.058	16*

* denotes statistically significant results (in 95% confidence level)

There are no data points for Brazilian, Turkish, US01, Argentinean and US02 crisis with U (all the data points in case of these crises are calculated using heteroskedasticity adjusted post-crisis correlations).

Appendix 2. Studies and constructs used in the meta-analysis

Author(s)	Year	Within study distinction	No. of effect sizes
Bordo and Murshid	2000	na	106
Forbes and Rigobon	1999	U	63
Forbes and Rigobon	1999	A	63
King and Wadhwani	1995	U	1
Lee, Wu and Wang	2006	U, stocks	23
Lee, Wu and Wang	2006	A, stocks	23
Lee, Wu and Wang	2006	U, interest rates	18
Lee, Wu and Wang	2006	A, interest rates	18
Wang, Thi	2006	Conditional	3
Wang, Thi	2006	Unconditional	3
Kleimeier, Lenhert, Verschoor	2008	Closing prices	28
Kleimeier, Lenhert, Verschoor	2008	Matched intra day prices	28
Baig, Goldfajn	1999	Exchange rates	4
Baig, Goldfajn	1999	Stocks	4
Baig, Goldfajn	1999	Interest rates	4
Baig, Goldfajn	1999	Sovereign spreads	4
Corsetti, Pericoli, Sbracia	2002	Na	17

Serwa	2005	Forbes-Rigobon methodology	76
Serwa	2005	Corsetti-Pericoli-Sbracia methodology	76
Serwa	2005	Residuals based methodology	76
Alvarez-Plata, Schrooten	2003	Stocks	6
Alvarez-Plata, Schrooten	2003	Interest rates	6
Chiang, Jeon, Li	2007	Adjusted	14
Chiang, Jeon, Li	2007	Unadjusted	14
Gelos, Sahay	2001	Stocks, unadjusted	12
Gelos, Sahay	2001	Stocks, adjusted	12
Gelos, Sahay	2001	Exchange rates, U	9
Gelos, Sahay	2001	Exchange rates, A	5

Appendix 7.4. Kuusk, A., Paas, T. (2010). The role of meta-analysis in examining results of empirical studies about financial contagion. Mäeltsemees, S; Reiljan, J. (Eds.). Discussions on Estonian Economic Policy, pp. 176-194, Berlin, Tallinn: Berliner Wissenschafts-Verlag, Mattimar.

THE ROLE OF META-ANALYSIS IN EXAMINING RESULTS OF EMPIRICAL STUDIES ABOUT FINANCIAL CONTGAGION

Andres Kuusk, Tiiu Paas[1]
University of Tartu

Abstract

The paper gives some new insights on the subject of financial contagion using the methodology of meta-analysis. We show that traditional qualitative literature review is not the proper way to summarise empirical findings of financial contagion and we use meta-analytical tools instead. The results of the meta-analysis show that on average asset market correlations have increased during turbulent periods, but the increase is rather moderate. When correlation coefficients are adjusted for the presence of heteroskedasticity, the increase is considerably smaller but still statistically significant. The crises are different in their contagiousness but the level of development of destination country seems not to play significant role whether crises spread over or not.

Keywords: financial crisis, contagion, meta-analysis

JEL Classification: F36, B41, E61, E44

1. Introduction

Financial contagion has become increasingly popular research task in the recent decades. Several crisis in 1980's, 1990's and in the present century were transmitted rapidly to other countries that were sometimes quite different in their size and economic structure as compared to the country of origin and being even located on the other side of the globe. Borrowing the phrase from epidemiology this phenomenon has been called financial *contagion* in the economic literature. According to Rigobon (2002) the issue of *contagion* has been one of the most debated topics in international finance since the Asian crises. The events in last year with yet another financial crisis' 'snowball' rolling over the world show that developing an understanding of financial contagion is clearly indicated for policy makers to manage and avoid future spreading of crises.

Because of that increasing popularity the puzzle of financial contagion has been investigated a lot recently. However, drawing some final conclusions on financial contagion based on empirical evidence is problematic, because of the multidimensionality of the subject. There is still no consensus on neither the definition nor the testing methodology of financial contagion, additionally chosen

[1] The authors of the paper are grateful to the Estonian Science Foundation (research grant No 7756) and for the Estonian Ministry of Science and Education (grant No SF0180037s08) for their financial support. Views expressed in the paper are solely those of the authors and, as such, should not be attributed to other parties.

crises, financial indices and destination countries of spreading of the crises may affect the results. All that leaves qualitative literature review as the research methodology with doubtful value and its' results undermined.

Research methodology that can better deal with this multidimenionality is meta-analysis. Meta-analysis enables us to control for all these study characteristics and come to one quantitative finding. Therefore the aim of the paper is to show that qualitative literature review is ill-designed to summarise recent empirical findings in the subject of financial contagion and to find more adequate results by using quantitative analysis in the form of meta-analysis instead.

The paper consists of four sections. In the next section the methodology of meta-analysis is introduced. The results of qualitative analysis of literature about financial contagiondata and the results of the meta-analysis implemented for examining financial contagion are presented in section three. Finally, a brief conclusion is given in section four.

2. The main features of meta-analysis

Meta-analysis is a research method to synthesise empirical research results from previous studies. De Dominicis *et al.* (2006) have given as the purpose of meta-analysis to review and quantitatively summarise the literature using statistical approach. This very general aim is in the heart of every meta-analysis but there are diffenent approaches and methodologies used in that label and the unique definition of meta-analysis is still not worked out.

The term meta-analysis was first coined by Gene Glass in 1976, although some procedures later known as meta-analytic (for example the concept of effect size) were already present in Karl Pearson's study in 1904. By Glass's definition "Meta-analysis refers to the statistical analysis of a large collection of results from individual studies for the purpose of integrating the findings. It connotes a rigorous alternative to the casual, narrative discussions of research studies which typify our attempt to make sense of the rapidly expanding research literature." (Glass 1976). By Schultze (2004) meta-analysis is a method for systematic literature reviews on a certain substantive question of interest, more specifically on his words: "meta-analysis is a systemetic process of quantitatively combining empirical reports to arrive at a summary and an evaluation of a research findings."

Basu (2003) defines meta-analysis as "synthesis of available literature about a topic. Ideally, synthesis of randomized trials to arrive at a single summary estimate is used." By James Neill's (2006) version "Meta-analysis is a statistical technique for amalgamating, summarising, and reviewing previous quantitative research." The most simple definition we have seen was given by Hunter and Schmidt (1990) who defined meta-analysis as "analysis of analyses".

Abstractly speaking, meta-analysis combines the results of several studies that address a set of related research hypotheses. Usually this is done by identification of a common measure. This common measure is called effect size. Individual effect sizes are aggregated and after study characteristics are controlled the resulting overall results can be considered meta-effect sizes.

Many advantages meta-analysis has over traditional literature review have been pointed out, from which the most important are:
- quantitative estimation and statistical testing of overall effect sizes;
- generalization to the population of studies;
- finding moderator variables to explain heterogeneity in distribution.

The main difference between meta-analysis and traditional literature review is that meta-analysis uses the summary statistics from individual studies as the data points. By accumulating results accross studies, it is possible to get more accurate representation of the population relationship than any of the individual studies can provide.

The main steps of meta-analysis after all relevant studies are congregated, (which we follow in our paper), are the following:
1) calculating relevant individual effect size statistics and controlling for their independency;
2) compute the effect sizes weighted mean for which special weights have to be calculated;
3) determine the confidence interval and statistical significance of the effect size weighted mean;
4) homogeneity testing;
5) conclusions and interpretations.

For conducting the first step the appropriate individual effect size statistics have to be found. What is meant by individual effect size statistic is a quantitative finding from a single study. As those individual effect sizes may be quite different in their nature, different effect size statistics to code different forms of quantitative study findings are worked out. The various effect size statistics are based on the concept of standardization. It means that the effect size statistic has to produce a statistical standardization of the study findings such that the resulting numerical values are interpretable in a consistent fashion across all the variables and measures involved. In our case it means we have to define an effect size statistic capable of representing the quantitative findings of a financial contagion studies in a standardized form that permits meaningful numerical comparison and analysis across the studies. (see Lipsey and Wilson 2001). It is found that good effect size statistics consider both the magnitude and the direction of a relationship (statistical significance which is often in the centre of qualitative literature review is therefore not sufficient statistic). In addition, as brought out by Lipsey and Wilson (2001) the effect size statistics should be defined so that there is relatively little confounding with other issues (such as sample size).

The next step is to aggregate all these individual effect size statistics into one meta-effect size. So one has to derive an overall value from the meta-sample by pooling all the estimates and deriving an overall summary statistic. Usually for finding this overall summary statistic the weighted average of the individual effect sizes computed. That, of course, leads to the question how should the weights be determined. Hedges (1982, Hedges and Olkin 1985) has demonstrated, that the optimal weights are based on the standard error of the effect size. Because a larger standard error corresponds to a less precise effect size value, the actual weights are computed as the inverse of the squared standard error value - called the inverse variance weight in meta-analysis. The standard error formulation has been worked out for the most important types of the individual effect size statistics (including mean differences and correlation coefficients that are used in the present analysis). We discuss these formulations in more detail in the chapter three when computing the weights for our individual effect size statistics.

In the next step there is a question of the homogeneity of the effect size distribution. In other words, whether the various effect sizes that are averaged into a mean value all estimate the same population effect (see Hedges 1982, Rosenthal and Rubin 1982). If the distribution is homogeneous, the dispersion of the effect sizes around their mean is no greater than that expected from sampling error. In other words, in a homogeneous distribution an individual effect size differs from the population mean only by sampling error.

The homogeneity test is based on the Q statistic - a statistical test that rejects the null hypothesis of homogeneity indicates that the variability of the effect sizes is larger than would be expected from sampling error and, therefore, we can't be sure that each effect size estimates a common population mean. If the Q statistic indicates that the distribution is heterogeneous, than there have to be differences among the effect sizes that have some source other than subject-level sampling error. These differences are usually associated with different study characteristics. The Q statistic is distributed as a chi-square with $k-1$ degrees of freedom where k is the number of effect sizes (Hedges and Olkin 1985). The formule for Q is:

(1) $$Q = \sum \left[w_i \left(ES_i - \overline{ES} \right)^2 \right]$$

where ES_i is the individual effect size for $i = 1$ to k (the number of effect sizes), $\overline{ES}$ is the weighted mean effect size over the k effect sizes, and w_i is the individual weight for ES_i. If Q exceeds the critical value for a chi-square with $k-1$ degrees of freedom, then the null hypothesis of homogeneity is rejected. A statistically significant Q, therefore, indicates a heteregeneous distribution.

Alternative approach to homogeneity testing, so called 75% rule, is given by Hunter and Schmidt (1990). They partition the observed effect size variability into two components - the portion attributable to subject-level sampling error and the portion attributable to other between-study differences. According to their rule of thumb, the distribution is homogeneous if sampling error accounts for 75% or more of the observed variability.

All these steps, in that order, with following conclusions and interpretations are implemented in the chapter three, summarising the empirical results in the field of contagion of financial crises.

3. Meta-analysis for summarising empirical results of financial contagion
3.1. Qualitative summary of financial contagion empirical results

We have studied around 75 empirical analyses in the theme of financial contagion, results from which are summarised in Table 1 (see Appendix). Note that not all papers in the table actually test for the presence for financial contagion. So in some cases results in the third column of the table (whether evidence for contagion have been found or not) may be somewhat disputable (see different definitions of financial contagion).

As it can be seen from the table the results obtained on the field of financial contagion are quite hopelessly mixed. Counting *Yes*-es and *No*-s in the table we see that the results that indicate evidence on contagion are twice as frequent as those that suggest the opposite. However, many of the *Yes*-results are undermined by the later papers because of questionable testing methodology (not adjusting for the presence of heteroskedasticity). In many cases the chosen result in favor of *Yes*, *No* or *Mixed* is not clearcut. For example, in correlation coefficients based tests, there are mostly different results – some correlations have increased significantly during crises, some have not changed much and some have even decreased. So summing up the results for one *Yes* or *No* conclusion may not be the perfect way. There are almost no pairs of studies that are identical in all their definition of financial contagion, it's testing methodology and crises and samples under investigation. But all of them may influence the results of the analysis.

The results of the analysis confirm the opinion that empirical studies mainly provide heterogeneous results depending on applied definitions and methods and chosen crises, destination countries and financial indices. The evidence for both for confirming and contradicting financial contagion has been widely found in recent empirical analyses and we found no clue on which clear results is or should be dominating. We are aware that in many cases the results of empirical analyses may be biased and serious additional investments into examining possible consequences of financial crises are still necessary. We conclude that qualitative analysis of published research materials about previous financial crises does not give sufficient information to elaborate proper measures allowing to prevent serious consequences of financial crises. We propose that more adequate picture of financial contagion is possible to obtain by using a meta-analysis, which is exactly what we have done in the following section of the paper.

3.2. Data and technical details

For searching appropriate studies for meta-analysis we use ISI Web of Knowledge database for very recent studies and additionally the Contagion of Financial Crisis Website by World Bank Group for somewhat older ones. From the ISI Web of Knowledge database the studies corresponding to the keywords *financial contagion* are used. We define financial contagion as increase in cross-country correlations during "crisis times" relative to correlations during "tranquil times". Thus we follow the most common definition sometimes called shift-contagion that was first proposed by Forbes and Rigobon (1999) who stated that contagion is a significant increase in cross-market linkages after a shock. This notion of contagion excludes a constant high degree of comovement in a crisis period, in which case markets are just interdependent. Therefore only the studies that report both the pre- and post-crisis asset prices correlations (or their difference) between countries are included into the sample. Because of these restrictions we are left in our data set with 716 effect sizes (394 from these are independent) from 30 constructs (17 independent). If both short and long term post-crisis correlations are reported we use the short term data, as we can not use both because of the independency problems (about independency problems see further).

We follow the classical five steps, presented in chapter two, in our analysis, which for the sake of freshing the memory were the following:
1) calculating relevant individual effect sizes and controlling for their independency;
2) computing the weights and aggregating individual effect size statistics into one meta-effect;
3) determine the confidence interval and statistical significance of the effect size weighted mean;
4) homogeneity testing;
5) conclusions and interpretations.

For conducting the first step we have to find appropriate individual effect sizes. A single research finding on the field of financial contagion is a statistical representation of one empirical relationship between pre- and post-crisis correlation of asset prices. There are no rules given in the literature for which are the correct effect sizes for changes in correlation coefficients. For one thing, it is not intuitively clear whether we should deal the data as pre-post contrasts or association between variables. On the one hand, we have correlation coefficients and even if we are not interested in the correlation coefficients itselves but their changes over two points in time, it is not quite clear why these two approaches differ so much (in terms of the properties of effect sizes) that we could not use the same computational procedures. So, why not just take the effect sizes as correlations and live with that? On the other hand, we have data points for both before and after crises (which we can take as treatment) and we are interested in difference between them, the gain to be precise. Classical pre-post contrasts situation, is not it?

Whichever approach we choose from these two, it seems that the real difference comes into play while calculating the (weighted) mean effect sizes (step 2) and their variances. For calculating individual effect sizes it seems really not to matter. The difference between post- and pre-crisis correlations is by far the most logical individual effect size for a given study (construct). Mathematically, our individual effect sizes are computed as:

(1) $ES_i = r_{post_i} - r_{pre_i}$

where ES_i is the individual effect size for study (construct) i and r_{pre_i} and r_{post_i} are pre- and post-crisis correlations respectively for study (construct) i.

Dealing our effect sizes as correlations we modify the effect sizes a bit, because of the problematic standard error formulation (these problems are more indepth discussed by Rosenthal 1994). Widely accepted method for doing that is transforming the correlations using Fischer's Z_r-transformation (see Hedges and Olkin 1985):

(2) $ES_{Z_r} = 0.5 \ln\left(\dfrac{1+r}{1-r}\right)$

where r is the correlation coefficient. The necessity for calculating standard errors (and therefore need for Fischer's Z_r-transformation) comes into play when calculating weighted mean effect sizes (see further (step 2 and 3)).

Note that not all authors agree in the necessity of Fischer's Z_r-transformation for correlation coefficients as effect sizes. For example Hunter and Schmidt (1990) argue that the transformation gives results upward biased and standard correlations are more precise. However, some other authors claim that standard correlation effect sizes are downward biased and it is not clear which bias is greater and the main problem with standard correlations – problematic computation of standard errors and weights – remains

Later on, for interpreting the results we transform them back into standard correlation form using the inverse of the Z_r-transformation (Hedges and Olkin 1985):

(3) $r = \dfrac{e^{2ES_{Z_r}} - 1}{e^{2ES_{Z_r}} + 1}$

Moving forward to step 2 we need to aggregate all individual effect sizes into one meta-effect size. Before that weights for all individual effect size statistics have to be calculated. We use standard statistical software SPSS and some macros written by David Wilson, that are available via his home page for computational and statistical purposes.

We use standard error based inverse variance weights (re-read chapter two) for calculating correlation coefficients based effect size mean. The standard error formula for correlation based (after Fischer's z-transformation (see earlier)) effect size mean is the following:

(4) $$SE_{Z_r} = \frac{1}{\sqrt{n-3}}$$

and inverse variance weights therefore:

(5) $w_{z_r} = n - 3$

where n is the sample size of the individual effect size in both formulas.

However we do not have data necessary to calculate the effect size mean when treating individual effect sizes as treatment effects. More precisely, we lack information on correlations between pre- and post-treatment asset prices in individual studies. Therefore the sample size is used as weights instead.

The formula for calculating the weighted mean effect size is following:

(6) $$\overline{d} = \frac{\sum d_i w_i}{\sum w_i}$$

where d_i is the i-th individual effect size and w_i is weight (inverse variance weight in case of correlation coefficients and sample size for treatment effects) of the i-th effect size.

3.3. Results and discussion

As preliminary analysis we use all 716 effect sizes we have in the sample as independent data points. This approach is somewhat doubtful because there are some effect sizes within the studies that differ only by the chosen methods of measurement and therefore the independency assumption between different data points is violated. Later on we deal with that problem by choosing the appropriate weights to avoid overestimating the results of those duplicate effect sizes within the studies.

Using the abovementioned formulas (1)-(6) we get the estimate of the population effect size to be 0.054 if we treat the individual effect sizes as treatment effects (we call it Approach 1 in the following) and 0.065 if we treat the individual effect sizes as correlation coefficients (Approach 2 hereafter). Thus on average the asset prices correlations have indeed increased during the turbulent periods but on quite moderate extent. The standard errors are 0.0035 and 0.0036 respectively and the 95% confidence intervals well above zero in both cases.

By calculating Q statistic using abovementioned formula (7) we get it's value to be 3680.5 which is clearly over the critical value of 778 (degrees of freedom = sample size − 1; probability (p-value) = 0.05). So the dispersion of the effect sizes around their mean is greater than that expected from sampling error alone and therefore each effect size does not estimate a common population mean.

As stated above we have some independency problems in the data. There are cases for multiple effect sizes within the same studies. That violates the independency assumption and overestimates the weights of the studies with multiple effect sizes. The classical way to deal the situation is to choose only one effect size per study per construct. However, this approach does not use some information contained in the primary studies and we definitely do not want to lose the information of different correlation measurement methodologies as possible moderators. It is well known that heteroskedasticity adjusted correlation coefficients are lower than unadjusted ones and therefore the contagion seems to be more likely to occur in case of unadjusted correlation coefficients. Therefore rather than dropping some of the data points we diminish the weights of studies with multiple effect sizes per construct by dividing the sample size by the number of effect sizes per construct. (For discussion on multiple measurements within studies see also Rosenthal 1994)

Using this slightly modified sample (results are given in Table 1 below) we get the weighted average effect size to be 0.053 in approach 1 and 0.072 in approach 2 with standard errors 0.0047 and 0.0049 respectively. With 95%-confidence intervals easily above zero we can conclude that asset prices' correlations have increased during turbulent periods.

Table 1. Results of financial contagion meta-analysis

	SS	Mean ES as treatment effects			Mean ES as correlations		
		Mean ES	St. eror	Q stat.	Mean ES	St. error	Q stat.
All	716	0.053*	0.005	2782.0*	0.072*	0.005	5568.0*
U	159	0.168*	0.007	956.7*	0.208*	0.007	3432.2*
A	545	0.030*	0.007	668.0*	0.030*	0.007	716.1*
Tha97	86	0.132*	0.007	853.9*	0.173*	0.007	3367.1*
HK97	154	0.010*	0.009	295.6*	0.098*	0.009	323.0*
Rus98	46	-0.001	0.027	48.8	0.006	0.027	52.5
Bra99	33	-0.016	0.039	17.33	-0.014	0.039	15.4
Prewar	344	0.045	0.026	165.8*	0.059*	0.028*	197.3*
Mex94	372	0.141*	0.038	45.7	0.161*	0.045	39.0
US87	70	0.185*	0.062	5.8	0.181*	0.071	4.7
Ind04	68	-0.091*	0.028	122.0*	-0.116*	0.031	153.5*
Tur01	19	-0.194*	0.055	22.2	-0.209*	0.066	19.3
US01	82	0.014	0.055	22.4	0.019	0.066	17.8
Arg01	33	-0.374*	0.015	126.6*	-0.391*	0.015	156.6*
US02	33	0.126*	0.055	12.8	0.133*	0.066	10.3
Cze97	45	0.057	0.039	26.2*	0.058	0.041	26.3*
Emerg	33	0.054*	0.006	2254.3*	0.078*	0.006	5116.5*
Devel	14	0.052*	0.009	527.6*	0.051*	0.008	555.8*

ES – effect size
SS – sample size
U – cases with unadjusted (for heteroskedasticity) correlation coefficients
A – cases with adjusted (for heteroskedasticity) correlation coefficients
Tha – Thailand crisis, HK – Hong Kong crisis, Rus – Russian crisis, Bra – Brazilian crisis, Mex – Mexican crisis, US – United States of American crisis, Ind – Indian crisis, Tur – Turkish crisis, Arg – Argentinean crisis, Cze – Czech Republican crisis, Prewar – average of 6 pre II World War crises (Argentine crisis 1890, Baring crisis (UK) 1890, US banking crisis 1893, US stock market crash 1929, Sterling crisis (UK) 1931, devaluation of the dollar (US) 1933) Emerg – cases with countries outside first 30 according to Human Development Index 2008 Devel – cases with first 30 countries according to Human Development Index 2008
Source: Author's calculations.

Testing for homogeneity and calculating Q-statistics on that purposes reveals that the distribution is heterogeneous and therefore the individual effect sizes may not estimate the same population effect. Therefore we continue by searching moderators to explain the variabilities in effect sizes. As mentioned above, the correlation coefficients' calculating methodology is widely accepted as significant explaining variable for financial contagion. The logic being that when not adjusting for hetereskedastity, the post-crisis correlations are higher and therefore finding evidence for contagion more probable. For controlling the correlation coefficients measurement as potential moderator we divide our sample into two parts distinguishing heteroskedasticity adjusted (A) and unadjusted (U) correlation coefficients in turbulent periods. For the sample with unadjusted correlation coefficients we get the weighted mean effect size to be 0.168 using approach 1 and 0,208 in case of approach 2. For the sample with heteroskedastity adjusted correlation coefficients the respective values are 0.030 for both approaches 1 and 2. The difference is more than clear and we can conclude that the fact whether correlation coefficients are heteroskedastity adjusted or not significantly affects the results of financial contagion analyses. By dividing the overall Q into the within and between groups component, it is found that the between groups Q is highly significant which also indicates that the differences in correlation measurement (heteroskedastity adjusted or not) accounts for significant variability in effect sizes.

Still, there is some heterogeneity left in the distribution. Therefore we also control for other possible moderator variables. We are interested in, for example, if different crises have been different in the extent of contagiousness. For the Thailand 1997 crisis the treatment effects based (Approach 1) weighted mean effect size is 0.132 and 0.173 if effect sizes are treated as correlation coefficients (Approach 2). For the Hong Kong 1997 crisis the same values are 0.100 and 0.098; for the Mexican 1994 crisis 0.141 and 0.160; for the Russian 1998 crisis -0.001 and 0.006; for the Brazilian 1999 crisis -0.016 and -0.014 respectively. From these numbers it is clearly seen that the Mexican, the Thailand and the Hong Kong crisis are contagious while the Russian and the Brazilian crisis are not.

From other crises the US 1987 and the US 2002 crises are contagious; for the Argentinean crisis 2001, the Turkish crisis 2001 and the Indian crisis 2004 the opposite is true – asset prices correlations have decreased during turbulent periods;

pre-World War II crises on average are not contagious, as well as the Czech crisis 1997 and the US crisis 2001 with some but insignificant increase in average asset prices correlations. Again the given crisis as grouping variable accounts for significant variability in effect sizes, but there are still some heterogeneity left inside groups.

Using only data where correlation coefficients are adjusted for the presence of heteroskedasticity (not reported on the Table 1 below, but available on request) the results do not change much. The Mexican, the Thailand and the Hong Kong Kong crises are still contagious, although the weighted mean effect sizes are somewhat smaller. Also, Russian and Brazilian crises are not contagious with weighted mean effect sizes slightly negative. The only change is related with the US 1987 crisis, which is not contagious any more in the 95% confidence interval. However, with the weighted mean effect size clearly above zero (0.17) and only slightly below the unadjusted (U) case, the reason seems to be mainly because of small sample size.

We also investigate whether the level of development of the destination country makes it more or less susceptible for the spread of the crisis. The need for that differentiation is suggested for example by Hartmann *et al.* (2001) who find only very weak evidence of contagion on the sample of G5 countries and speculated that it may be different for emerging economies. We use Human Development Index (HDI) 2008 values for dividing countries as more or less developed ones. We call first 30 countries according to HDI as developed and all other countries as developing. Thus we have quite comparable sample sizes for both groups with 372 and 344 respectively. For the sample with less developed countries, the weighted mean effect size is 0.054 according to Aapproach 1 (effect sizes as treatment effects) and 0.077 according to Approach 2 (effect sizes as correlations). For the sample with more developed countries the corresponding values are 0.052 and 0.051 respectively. So according to the Approach 1 there is no difference in susceptibility for the spreading of crises between developed and developing countries, while according to the Approach 2 less developed countries are somewhat more susceptible for the carryover of the financial crises. The variability analysis reveals that the level of development of destination country does not account for significant variability in effect sizes. From that we may judge that herding behaviour seems to be more likely transmission force for financial crises than real and stable linkages. This finding is in line with Serwa (2005) who found that The Central and Eastern European stock markets are not more vulnerable to contagion than Western European markets. On the other hand the finding is in contradiction with Dungey and Tambakis (2003) who argue that developing countries are more affected by contagion than developed countries.

However, we also compare these two groups separately for adjusted (A) and unadjusted (U) cases (not reported in Table 2). The findings reveal that in the case U the less developed countries are indeed more susceptible to contagion of financial crises according to both approaches 1 and 2. Using Approach 1 the weighted mean effect sizes are 0.19 for developing and 0.12 for developed countries with not overlapping confidence intervals and in case of Approach 2 the differences are even greater: 0.24 and 0.12 respectively. In the case A the according numbers are 0.04 for developing and 0.02 for developed countries (according to both approaches 1 and 2) but the differences are not significant at the 95% confidence level.

Summing up the results of the section we can conclude that on average asset market correlations have increased during turbulent periods, which gives some evidence to the support of financial contagion conception. Nevertheless, the increase is quite moderate and after controlling for heterogeneity in turbulent periods' correlations it's even smaller (although still statistically significant in 95% confidence level). Both the correlations' calculating methodology (heteroskedasticity adjusted or not) and the crisis under observation are significant moderators to explain heterogeneity in distribution. From the most important financial crises during past one and half decade the Mexican, the Thailand and the Hong Kong crisis are contagious while the Russian and the Brazilian crisis are not. The level of development of destination country on overall does not account for significant variability in effect sizes. Still, less developed countries are on average somewhat more susceptive to the financial crises contagion compared to the well developed countries.

4. Conclusion

Meta-analysis is a research method to synthesise empirical research results of several individual studies that address a shared research hypotheses. Meta-analysis is especially called for if the multidimensionality of the research topic makes traditional literature review as summarising analysis a doubtful and risky business. One of those topics is the contagion of financial crises.

Financial contagion is extremely complex and multidimensional phenomena with no uniquely accepted definition or testing methodology. Because of the rapid transmission of initial country-specific shocks to economies from which some were very different in both their size and structure compared to the country of origin, the 'financial contagion' puzzle has become one of the most newsworthy research task for economists during the last decades. The crises spreaded over the world like snowballs becoming bigger and bigger during the course and even countries with apparently sound fundamentals were not left unaffected. The events in last year with yet another 'snowball' rolling over the world show that developing an understanding in the subject of financial contagion is clearly indicated for policy makers to manage and avoid future spreading's of crises. The empirical results on the topic of financial contagion are mixed and in our view no unique conclusion can be made only based on the qualitative analysis of empirical literature. Thus, we propose that more profound and adequate picture of financial contagion is possible to obtain by using a meta-analysis.

The most important advantages meta-analysis has over traditional literature review are the following:
- quantitative estimation and statistical testing of overall effect sizes;
- generalization to the population of studies;

- finding moderator variables to explain heterogeneity in distribution.

The key element in meta-analysis is so-called effect size, which is a common measure from individual studies and permits meaningful numerical comparison and analysis across the studdies. Individual effect sizes are aggregated using special weights that determine the relative importance of each of them and after study characteristics are controlled for the resulting overall results can be considered meta-effect sizes.

The main steps of meta-analysis, which is also followed in our paper, are the following:
1) calculating relevant individual effect size statistics and controlling for their independency;
2) compute the effect sizes weighted mean for which special weights have to be calculated;
3) determine the confidence interval and statistical significance of the effect size weighted mean;
4) homogeneity testing;
5) conclusions and interpretations.

The results of our meta-analysis indicate that on average asset market correlations have increased during turbulent periods, but the increase is rather moderate. Still, we find some evidence of financial contagion even after the turbulent periods' correlations are adjusted for the presence of heteroskedasticity. The results of our analysis show that the Mexican 1994, the Thailand 1997 and the Hong Kong 1997 crisis were contagious while the Russian 1998, the Brazilian 1999 and the Argentinean 2001 crisis were not. The level of development of the destination country seems not matter much for the financial crisis to spread over or not. Still, the meta-effect sizes are on average slightly higher in the case of less developed countries as compared to the well developed ones.

One of the main limitations of the paper is that our meta-analysis is restricted to correlation coefficients based analyses only. Studies using this methodology are the vast majority and it is not that simple to conduct comparable individual effect sizes necessary for the meta-analytic approach from the studies using other methodologies. Nonetheless this might be one of the subjects future research could focus on.

References

1. **Basu, A.** (2003). *How to conduct a meta-analysis.*
   http://www.pitt.edu/~super1/lecture/lec1171.
2. **De Dominicis, L., de Groot, H., Florax, R.** (2006). *Growth and inequality: a meta-analysis.* http://www.tinbergen.nl/discussionpapers/06064.pdf.
3. **Dungey, M., Dambakis, D.** (2003). *Financial contagion: What do we mean? What do we know?* http://www.g24.org/Dungey-Tambakis2003.pdf.

4. **Forbes, K., Rigobon, R.** (1999). "No Contagion, Only Interdependence: Measuring Stock Market Co-Movements." *National Bureau of Economic Research Working Paper No. 7267.*
5. **Glass, G. V.** (1976). Primary, secondary and metaanalysis research. – *Educational Researcher*, 5, p. 3-8.
6. **Hartmann, P., Straetmans, S., de Vries, C. G.** (2001). Asset Market Linkages in Crisis Periods. – *Tinbergen Institute Discussion Paper*, TI 2001-071/2.
7. **Hedges, L.V.** (1982). Fitting categorical models to effect sizes from a series of experiments. – *Journal of Educational Statistics*, 7, pp. 119-137.
8. **Hedges, L. V., Olkin, I.** (1985). *Statistical methods for meta-analysis.* Orlando, FL: Academic Press, viidatud: Lipsey, M. W., Wilson, D. B. 2001. Practical meta-analysis. Applied Social Research Methods Series, Volume 49, SAGE Publications.
9. **Hunter, J. E., Schmidt, F. L.** (1990). *Methods of meta-analysis: Correcting error and bias in research findings.* Newbury Park, CA: Sage.
10. **Lipsey, M. W., Wilson, D. B.** (2001). *Practical meta-analysis. Applied Social Research Methods Series*, Volume 49. SAGE Publications.
11. **Neill, J.** (2006). *Meta-analysis research methodology.* http://wilderdom.com/research/meta-analysis.html.
12. **Pearson, K.** (1904). *Mathematical contributions to the theory of evolution.* http://visualiseur.bnf.fr/Visualiseur?Destination=Gallica&O=NUMM-55992.
13. **Rigobon, R.** (2002). Contagion: How to measure it? In: S. Edwards and J. Frankel, Editors, *Preventing currency crises in emerging markets*, The University Chicago Press, Chicago, pp. 269-334.
14. **Rosenthal, R.** (1994). Statistically describing and combining studies. – *The handbook of research synthesis*, Eds. H. Cooper & L. V. Hedges. New York: Russell Sage Foundation, pp. 231-244.
15. **Rosenthal, R., Rubin, D. B.** (1982). A simple, general purpose display of magnitude of experimental effect. – *Journal of Educational Psychology*, 74, pp. 166-169.
16. **Serwa, D.** (2005). *Empirical evidence on financial spillovers and contagion to international stock markets.* http://opus.kobv.de/euv/volltexte/2007/20/pdf/serwa.dobromil.pdf.
17. **Schultze, R.** (2004). *Meta-Analysis. A Comparison of Approaches.* Hogrefe & Huber Publishers, 242 p.

Authors	Year	Contagion	Method	Sample	Market
Hartmann, Straetmans, de Vries	2001	Weak	extreme value analysis	G5 countries	Asset prices
Forbes, Rigobon	1999	No	Increase in correlation, adjusted	28 countries, 1987 US stock market crash, 1994 Mexican peso collapse, 1997 East Asian crisis	Stocks
Lomakin, Paiz	1999	No	Probit analysis	various countries	Bonds
Rigobon	1999	No (Yes less 10%)	Directly identified model; shift-contagion	Mexican, Asian, Russian crises	Stocks
Rigobon	2002	No	HS based identification method	Argentina, Mexico 1994-1999	Brady bonds
Craig, Dravid and Richardson	1995	No	CDR approach	US and Japanese stocks	Stocks
King, Wadhwani	1995	Yes	Correlation coefficient based tests	US, UK and Japan after 1987 US crash	Stocks, bonds
Lee, Kim	1993	Yes	Correlation coefficient based tests	12 major markets after US 1987 crash	Stocks
Calvo, Reinhart	1996	Yes	Correlation coefficient based tests	1994 Mexican peso crisis. Asian and Latin American emerging markets	bonds and equities
Baig and Goldfajn	1999	Mixed	Correlation coefficient based tests, adjusted	emerging markets during the 1997-98 East Asian crisis	Stocks, exchange rates, interest rates
Chou, Ng, Pi	1994	Yes	Var-covar transm mechanism (ARCH/GARCH)	1987 U.S. stock market crash	Stocks
Hamao, Masulis, Ng	1990	Yes	Var-covar transm mechanism (ARCH/GARCH)	1987 U.S. stock market crash	Stocks
Edwards	1998	No	Var-covar transm mechanism (ARCH/GARCH)	Mexican peso crisis. Mexico to Chile	Bonds
Edwards	1998	Yes	Var-covar transm mechanism (ARCH/GARCH)	Mexican peso crisis. Mexico to Argentina	Bonds
Longin and Solnik	1995	Yes	Co-integration based tests	seven OECD countries from 1960 to 1990	Stocks
Baig and Goldfajn	1999	Yes	Increase in correlation	1997-98 East Asian crisis	Sovereign spreads

Authors	Year	Contagion	Method	Sample	Market
Forbes	1999	Yes	Directly measure changes	Asian and Russian crises, individual companies around the world	Stocks
Eichengreen, Rose and Wyplosz	1996	Yes	Probit model	ERM countries in 1992-3	currencies
Kaminsky and Reinhart	1998	Yes	Probit model	Mexican 1995 and Asian 1997	Assets
Gravelle, Kichian, Morley	2003	No	Shift-contagion	4 emerging-market countries 1991-2001	Brady bonds
Gravelle, Kichian, Morley	2003	Yes	Shift-contagion	7 developed countries 1985-2001	Currencies
Kali, Reyes	2005	Yes	Network approach	Tequila Crisis Mexican 1994), the Asian Flu, and the Russian Virus	Stocks
Kali, Reyes	2005	No	Network approach	Venezuelan and Argentine crises	Stocks
Iwatsubo, Inagaki	2006	Yes	CDR approach	22 Asian firma and 7 indexes, Asian crises	Stocks
Didier, Mauro, Shmukler	2008	Yes	Theoretical analysis		
Sander, Kleimeier	2003	Yes	Increase in correl using Granger-causality methodology	Asian crisis, 1996-2000	Bonds
Arestis, Caporale, Cipollini, Spagnolo	2005	Yes/Mixed	Shift contagion	1997 Asian crisis; from Thailand, Indonesia, Korea, Malaysia to Japan, UK, Germany, France	Assets
Bordo, Murshid	2000	No/Weak	Correlation coefficient based tests	Different historical and current crises	Bonds, interest rates
Wolf	1996	Weak	Granger-causality	21 sectors of 24 developing countries, 1976-1995	Equity
Cerra, Saxena	2002	Yes	Probit model	Indonesian currency crisis	stocks, currency
Moussalli	2007	Yes	Directly measure changes	Asian, Russian, Brazilian crisis; Asian, East-European, Latin-American countries	Stocks, currencies
Woo, Carleton, Rosario	2000	Yes	Logit model	Asian crisis; 6 Asian countries 1990-1998	Currency
Woo	2000	Yes	Qualitative analysis	Asian crisis; from Thailand to 4 Asian countries	Bonds

Authors	Year	Contagion	Method	Sample	Market
Tornell	1999	No	Directly measure changes	Mexican 1995 and Asian 1997	Currency
Corsetti, Pesenti, Roubini	1998	No	Directly measure changes	Asian crisis; 24 developing countries	Currency
Kelejian, Tavlas, Hondroyiannis	2006	Yes	Directly measure changes	6 crisis; 25 developing countries	Currency
Corsetti, Pericoli, Sbracia	2005	Yes	Increase in correlation, adjusted	Hong Kong stock market crisis 1997	Stocks
Favero, Giavazzi	1999	Yes	VAR model	7 European countries; ERM crisis, 1988-1992	Interest rates
Serwa	2005	Weak	Increase in correlation	7 crises, 1997-2002; 17 Western Europe and CEE countries	stocks
Serwa	2005	Yes	VAR model	Asian crisis 1997	capital markets
Serwa	2005	No	Markov switching framework	HSI and Nikkei 225; 1997 Asian crisis	stocks
Serwa	2005	Weak/No	transition matrices	US, UK , Japan, Germany	stocks
Forbes, Rigobon	2000	No	Shift-contagion	1990s	bonds, stocks
Hon, Strauss, Yong	2004	Yes	Increase in correlation, adjusted	2001 terrorist attack, 25 economies, OECD and Asia	stocks
Lee, Wu, Wang	2007	No	Increase in correlation, adjusted	earthquake in South-East Asia on Dec 26, 2004, 26 international stock indexes	stocks
Lee, Wu, Wang	2007	Yes	Increase in correlation, adjusted	earthquake in South-East Asia on Dec 26, 2004, 26 international exchange rates	exchange market
Wang, Thi	2006	Yes	Increase in dynamic conditional correlation coef	Asian crisis 1997, Thailand, China, Hong Kong, Taiwan	stocks
Kleimeier, Lenhert, Verschoor	2008	Yes	Increase in correlation	Asian crisis, Thailand + 14 countries	stocks
Candelon, Hecq, Verschoor	2005	No	serial correlation common feature	Mexican 1994, Asian 1997	stocks
Arestis, Caporale, Cipollini	2003	No/Weak	shift contagion, adjusted	Asian 1997; from 4 Asian countries to 5 developed countries	stocks

Authors	Year	Contagion	Method	Sample	Market
Fazio	2007	Weak	Probit analysis	1990-1999, 14 emerging market economies	currency
Bayoumi, Fazio, Kumar	2007	Yes	correlations and distance relationships	15 countries, 1991-2001	stocks, exchange rates
Bayoumi, Fazio, Kumar	2003	Yes	correlations and distance relationships	16 countries, 1991-2001 (Tequila, Asian, Russia, Argentine)	stock
Alvarez-Plata, Schrooten	2003	No	correlations	7 Latin-American countries, 2001-02 Argentinean crisis	stocks, interest rates
Wang, Moore	2008	Yes	dynamic conditional correlation	4 CEE countries, 1994-2006	stocks
Kallberg, Pasquariello	2008	Yes	excess comovement, adj	82 US industry indexes, 1976-2001	stocks
Chiang, Jeon, Li	2007	Yes	dynamic conditional correlation	9 Asian countries, 1990-2003	stocks
McAleer, Nam	2005	Yes	increase in co-movement (FR)	6 Asian countries, Asian crisis 1997	exchange rates
Haile, Pozo	2008	Yes	panel probit model	37 advanced and emerging market economies, quarterly data 1960-1998	currency
Sola, Spagnolo, Spagnolo	2002	Yes	Markov switching framework	Asian crisis 1997; from Thailand to South-Korea	stocks
Sola, Spagnolo, Spagnolo	2002	No	Markov switching framework	Asian crisis 1997; from South-Korea to Brazil	stocks
Baur	2003	Yes	regression analysis	Asian crisis, 11 Asian markets	stocks
Alba, Bhattacharya, Claessens, Ghosh, Hernandez	1998	Unclear	Qualitative analysis	Asian crisis	stocks, exchange rates
Frankel, Schmukler	1996	Yes	Correlation coefficient based tests	Mexican 1994, to Asia and Latin-America	Country fund prices
Valdes	1997	Yes	Correlation coefficient based tests	Mexican 1994, from Mexico to Latin-America	secondary market debt prices and credit ratings
Agenor, Aizenman, Hoffmaister	1999	Yes	Correlation coefficient based tests	Mexican 1994, from Mexico to Argentina	Interest rates
Boyer, Gibson, Loretan	1999	No	Increase in correlation, adjusted	Germany, Japan, USA; 1991-1998	Exchange rates

Authors	Year	Contagion	Method	Sample	Market
Loretan, English	2000	No	Increase in correlation, adjusted		3 pairs of asset returns
Gelos, Sahay	2001	No	Increase in correlation, adjusted	from the Czech Republic, Asia, and Russia to CEE	Stocks, exchange rates, sovereign spreads
De Gregorio, Valdes	1999	Not tested	conditional probability	1982 debt crisis, Mexican 1994, 1997 Asian	Exchange rates, credit ratings
Caramazza, Ricci, Salgado	2004	Yes	conditional probability	Mexican 1994, Asian 1997, Russian 1998; 41 countries	currency
Glick, Rose	1999	Not tested	conditional probability	5 crises and 161 countries	Currency
Park, Song	1998	Yes	conditional probability	Asian crisis, 8 Asian countries	Exchange rates, stocks, interests
Longin, Solnik	2001	Yes	GARCH framework	US, UK, France, Germany, Japan; 1959-1996	Stocks

SUMMARY IN ESTONIAN - KOKKUVÕTE

Finantskriiside nakkuslikkus: meta-analüütiline lähenemine
rõhuasetusega Kesk- ja Ida-Euroopa riikidele

1. Töö aktuaalsus ja olulisus

Finantskriiside ülekandumine teistesse riikidesse on majandusteadlaste hulgas oluliseks uurimisobjektiks tõusnud eelkõige viimase kahe aastakümne jooksul. Põhjuse selleks andis möödunud sajandi viimase kümnendi finantskriiside kiire levimine üle maailma riikidesse, mis olid tugevad nii makromajanduslike näitajate kui rakendatava finantspoliitika osas ega pruukinud omada sarnast majanduse struktuuri kriisi lähteriigiga võrreldes.

Sellist nähtust on epidemioloogiast tuleneva laenu analoogial hakatud nimetama *nakkuslikkuseks* (ka lumepalliefekt) ning antud teema on viimastel aastatel rahvusvahelises rahanduses olnud üheks peamiseks uurimisobjektiks. 2008. aasta finantskriis koos sellele järgneva majandussurutisega on selgeks näiteks, et finantskriiside nakkuslikkus (edaspidi *finantsnakkus*) on endiselt teravalt päevakorral ning selle vastu võitlemiseks on vaja teda põhjalikult analüüsida ja tundma õppida. Kriis alles kestab, aga juba on ilmunud kümmekond teadusartiklit antud kriisi nakkuslikkuse uurimisest, mis tõestab ilmekalt, et teema aktuaalsus ja olulisus on võib-olla kõrgem kui kunagi varem.

Finantsnakkuslikkuse teema uurimine on oluline mitme aspekti osas. Kõige otsesemalt ilmneb antud teema tähtsus rahvusvahelisest investeerimisportfelli diversifitseerimisest tulenevate kasutegurite kontekstis. Vastavalt üldlevinud teoreetilisele seisukohale võimaldab rahvusvaheline diversifitseerimine investeerimisportfelli riskantsust oluliselt vähendada, kuid see teooria peab paika ainult juhul, kui kriis ei taba paljusid riike üheaegselt või ajas lähestikku. Finantsnakkuse esinemise korral saavad aga ühes riigis alguse saanud kriisist kiiresti kannatada ka paljud teised riigid, kaasa arvatud need, mille langemist nakkuse ohvriks pole millegagi võimalik põhjendada ega seega ka ette ennustada. See aga õõnestab oluliselt kõnealuse teooria aluspinda. Finantsnakkuslikkuse esinemise hüpoteesi toetuseks tõendite leidmine võimaldab järeldada, et finantskriiside lumepallina riigist riiki ülekandumisel ei ole määrava tähtsusega mitte riikide makromajanduslikud fundamentaalnäitajad, vaid finantsagentide ühiskondlikus mõttes irratsionaalsest käitumisest tulenev ootuste isetäitumine ning investeerimisportfelli diversifitseerimisest tulenevad kasud on teooria põhjal eeldatust oluliselt väiksemad.

Lisaks diversifitseerimise teooriale on finantsnakkuslikkuse uurimisel oluline panus ka näiteks optimaalse finantsarhitektuuri alastes küsimustes ning kohalikesse turgudesse investeerimise riski hindamisel. Riigi ja valitsuse tasandil on oluline teada, mida saab teha, et vältida kriisi ülekandumist riiki ning kas ja kuidas on võimalik vähendada riigi vastuvõtlikkust kriiside ülekandumisele.

Rõhuasetus Kesk- ja Ida-Euroopa (KIE) riikidele kui peamiselt väikese avatud majandusega ja postsotsialistliku rajasõltuvusega riikide grupile on oluline eelkõige leidmaks, kas need riigid on keskmisest rohkem finantsnakkuslikkusele vastuvõtlikud, mis tähendaks spetsiifiliste poliitikameetmete vajadust. Teoreetilistest lähtekohtadest võib välja tuua kaks peamist põhjust, miks Kesk- ja Ida-Euroopa riigid võiksid olla keskmisest erineva finantsnakkuslikkusele vastuvõtlikkuse tasemega, seejuures on need põhjused vastupidiste mõjudega. Ühest küljest on antud riikide rühmale omane olnud kohati äärmuslik majandusvabadus ja majanduse avatus, mida võib pidada väga olulisteks põhjusteks, et transformatsiooniprotsess turumajandusele üleminekuks kujunes paljude Kesk- ja Ida-Euroopa riikide jaoks kiireks ning edukaks, kuid mis võib muuta riigi vastuvõtlikumaks finantskriiside ülekandumise suhtes. Senises empiirilises kirjanduses pole majanduse avatuse mõju nakkuslikkusele vastuvõtlikkuse määrale uuritud kuni Didier *et al* (2012) artiklini, milles tuvastati mõningane finantsnakkust soodustav mõju suurema finantsvabaduse puhul mitte aga suurema kaubanduse avatuse puhul. Teisest küljest on Kesk- ja Ida-Euroopa riigid paistnud silma sellega, et neisse on tehtud keskmisest oluliselt vähem spekulatiivse eesmärgiga investeeringuid, mis omakorda peaks neid kriiside lumepalli eest paremini kaitstuna hoidma. Seega võimaldab KIE riikide finantsnakkuslikkuse üldise keskmisega võrdlemine selgitada, kumb neist kahest ülaltoodud aspektist on domineerivam ning kas poliitikategijatel võiks finantsnakkusele vastuvõtlikkuse vähendamiseks olla kasulik majandusvabadust piirata.

Lisaks teema aktuaalsusele ja olulisusele ilmneb doktoritöö vajalikkus ka asjaolus, et vaatamata uuringute paljususele, on finantsnakkuse pusles endiselt enamus tükke kokku panemata. Individuaaluuringute tulemused on tihti üksteisele vasturääkivad ning varasemate tulemuste agregeerimisel on seni piirdutud vaid traditsiooniliste kirjandusülevaadetega, mis aga olulist selgust pole toonud. Seega on vajadus kvantitatiivse agregeeriva analüüsi jaoks ilmselge, mida doktoritöös on tehtud meta-analüüsi metoodikat kasutades. Sellest tulenevalt on doktoritööl oluline panus nii praktilises kui teoreetilises vaatavinklis. Praktilise külje pealt on lõpuks ometi olemas respekteeritava usaldusväärsusega tõestusmaterjal finantsnakkuse eksisteerimise või mitteeksisteerimise kohta, teoreetikud on aga varustatud teadmisega, kuhu suunas peaksid edasi liikuma tulevased individuaaluuringud, et edasised meta-analüüsid nende tulemusi sisenditena paremini kasutada saaksid.

2. Töö eesmärk ja uurimisülesanded

Oluline on mõista, et kriiside riikidevaheline ülekandumine ei ole veel finantsnakkus. Kriiside levimine on ilmselge ja seda testida pole erilist mõtet. Doktoritöö rõhuasetus on pigem sellel, kas riikidel on võimalik ennast võimalike tulevaste finantskriiside eest kaitsta ning investoritel potentsiaalseid kriisi levimise sihtriike ette ennustada. Siinkohal ongi oluline finantsnakkuse eristamine lihtsalt kriiside riikidevahelisest ülekandumisest. Kui ülekandumise taga on ainult nö objektiivsed tegurid nagu tugevad kaubanduslikud sidemed riikide vahel või nõrgad makromajanduse fundamentaalnäitajad[28], ei ole vastavalt doktoritöös kasutatavale definitsioonile tegu veel finantsnakkusega, vaid lihtsalt tugeva vastastikuse sõltuvusega (*interdependence*) riikide vahel. Finantsnakkuslikkuse eksisteerimisest saab rääkida alles siis, kui kriiside ülekandumise taga on lisaks nimetatud objektiivsetele faktoritele ka käegakatsumatud tegurid nagu investorite käitumisega seonduv.

Lähtuvalt eelnevast on doktoritöö eesmärk leida vastus küsimusele, kas finantskriiside riikidevahelist ülekandumist on võimendanud finantsnakkuslikkus või on see põhjustatud ainult stabiilsetest ühenduskanalitest kriisi- ja sihtriigi vahel. Kui kriiside ülekandumine toimub ainult läbi stabiilsete fundamentaalkanalite (nagu kaubanduslikud ja finantskanalid), peaks ohus olema eelkõige nõrkade fundamentaalnäitajatega riigid ning head makromajanduslikud fundamentaalnäitajad võiks võimaldada kaitset kriisi leviku eest. Kui aga kriiside levimise taga on lisaks stabiilsetele ühenduskanalitele ka finantsagentide kollektiivses mõttes irratsionaalne käitumine, avaldugu see karjakäitumise, finantspaanika või millegi muuna, siis võivad tõsiselt kannatada saada ka tugevate fundamentaalnäitajatega riigid. Vastavalt sellele, kumb nimetatud alternatiividest kinnitust leiab, on võimalik teha järeldusi riigitasandi poliitikasoovituste ning rahvusvaheliste investeerimisstrateegiate kohta.

Uurimiseesmärgi saavutamiseks on püstitatud järgmised uurimisülesanded:

1) selgitada ja sünteesida šokkide ja kriiside ülekandumist selgitavaid teooriaid;

2) anda teoreetiline ülevaade finantsnakkuslikkuse alternatiivsetest definitsioonidest ja ülekandumise kanalitest;

3) anda varasemate uurimuste põhjal ülevaade peamistest finantsnakkuslikkuse testimismeetoditest ja senistest tulemustest;

4) töötada välja sobiv kvantitatiivne mõõdik varasemate empiiriliste tulemuste adekvaatseks võrdlemiseks ja agregeerimiseks ning läbi viia kvantitatiivne analüüs meta-analüüsi raamistikku ja metoodikat kasutades;

---

[28] Fundamentaalnäitajate hulka kuuluvad väga erinevad näitajad, näiteks välisvõla suhe SKP-sse, täitmata laenude osakaal, lühiajalise võla suhe rahvusvahelistesse reservidesse, pankade krediidireitingud, jooksevkonto osakaal SKP-sse, rahvusvahelised reservid jne.

5) teostada eraldi analüüs 2008. aasta USA finantskriisi nakkuslikkuse kohta, kuna doktoritöö baasartiklite valmimise ajaks ei olnud selle kriisi kohta empiirilisi uuringuid, mida meta-analüüsi kaasata. Nende uurimisülesannete lahendamine peaks võimaldama saavutada uurimiseesmärgi täitmist.

3. Töö ülesehitus

Doktoritöö tugineb neljale avaldatud artiklile, mis on muutmata kujul ära toodud eelnevates lisades (vt Appendix 7). Kuna aga finantsnakkuslikkuse teema on äärmiselt aktuaalne ning uued publikatsioonid koos varasemate seisukohtade edasiarendustega ilmuvad pidevalt, siis täienduste ja edasiarenduste sisse viimise eesmärgil on doktoritöö formaalselt monograafia kujul. Lisaks oluliste uute aspektide kajastamisele võimaldab see ka täiustada mõningaid baasartiklites kasutatud metoodikaid. Kõigis baasartiklites on doktoritöö autoril olnud juhtiv ja vastutav roll nii teoreetilise alusraamistiku loomisel, andmete kogumisel ja analüüsil kui ka tulemuste tõlgendamisel ja nende baasil järelduste tegemisel. Uurimused 1, 2 ja 4 käsitlevad antud uurimisobjekti erinevaid tahke ning kasutavad erinevaid metoodikaid. Uurimus 3 on edasiarendus Uurimusest 4.

Doktoritöö koosneb neljast peatükist, kuid nad ei ole seotud konkreetse artikliga, vaid peatükkide ja artiklite sisu on omavahel läbi põimunud. Baasartiklite metoodika ja analüüsi objekt ning artiklitele vastavad peatükid ja alapunktid doktoritöös on ära toodud järgnevas Tabelis 1.

Tabel 1. Ülevaade doktoritöö baasartiklite metoodikast, analüüsi objektist ja vastavatest peatükkidest ning alapunktidest doktoritöös.

Uurimus	Uurimuse metoodika	Uuritav nakkuslikkuse suund	Vastavad osad doktoritöös
Uurimus 1	Kvalitatiivne kirjanduse analüüs	Üldine	1.1. 2.1.-2.6. ja 2.8
Uurimus 2	Korrelatsioonikoefitsientide võrdlus ja GARCH raamistik	USA-st Balti riikidesse	1.1., 3.2. ja 4.2.
Uurimus 3	Meta-analüüs	KIE majandused sihtriigina	1.1, 3.1. ja 4.1.
Uurimus 4	Meta-analüüs	Üldine	1.1, 3.1.1. ja 4.1.

Allikas: autori koostatud.

Töö esimene peatükk käsitleb finantsnakkuslikkuse teoreetilist raamistikku, alternatiivseid definitsioone ja ülekandumise kanaleid. Peatüki esimeses osas tutvustatakse finantsnakkuslikkuse olulisust ja alternatiivseid definitsioone. Peatüki teises osas on toodud ülevaade šokkide ülekandumist selgitavatest teoreetilistest käsitlustest, klassifitseerituna dissertatsiooni eesmärgile vastavalt finantsnakkuslikkusele viitavateks ja mitteviitavateks teooriateks. Peatüki esimeses osas on kasutatud kõiki nelja artiklit, peamiselt aga Uurimust 1. Peatüki teine osa on spetsiaalne täiendus doktoritöö tarbeks.

Teine peatükk on pühendatud seniste empiiriliste tulemuste kirjanduse ülevaatele. Peatükk algab selliste teoreetiliste aspektide välja toomisega, mis loogilistest kaalutlustest lähtudes võiksid põhjustada empiiriliste analüüside tulemustes olulist varieerumist. Seejärel esitatakse ülevaade empiirilistest tulemustest klassifitseerituna testimismetodoloogiate alusel nelja gruppi: riikidevahelistel korrelatsioonikoefitsientidel põhinevad meetodid, tingimuslikel tõenäosustel baseeruvad meetodid (eelkõige logit- ja probit-mudelid), volatiilsuse muutustel põhinevad meetodid (ARCH-GARCH raamistik) ning muud enimkasutatud meetodid. Seejärel on eraldi välja toodud KIE riike käsitlevate empiiriliste uuringute tulemused. Kõik need osad põhinevad Uurimusel 1. Peatüki eelviimane alapunkt käsitleb värskeid empiirilisi uurimusi, mis analüüsivad USA 2008. aasta kriisi nakkuslikkust. Need uuringud on ilmunud pärast baasartiklite valmimist ning seega on tegu täiendusega puhtalt doktoritööks. Peatükk lõpeb kokkuvõtva kvalitatiivse analüüsiga seniste empiiriliste uuringute tulemuste kohta ning soovitusega liikuda edasi kvantitatiivse analüüsi juurde. See kokku võttev analüüs põhineb samuti peamiselt Uurimusel 1.

Doktoritöö kolmas peatükk käsitleb empiirilises osas kasutatud andmeid ja uurimismeetodeid. Esmalt tutvustatakse meta-analüüsi ideed ja meetodeid ning vastavas analüüsis kasutatud andmestikku. Välja on toodud meta-analüüsi idee ning eelised võrreldes traditsioonilise kvalitatiivse kirjanduse ülevaatega, kogu protseduuri etapid ja põhiliste komponentide - nagu individuaaltulemus, meta-tulemus ja homogeensuse testimine – olemus. See osa põhineb Uurimustel 3 ja 4. Peatüki teises pooles selgitatakse metoodikat, mida on kasutatud 2008. aasta USA finantskriisi nakkuslikkuse uurimisel. Esiteks tutvustatakse korrelatsioonikoefitsientidel põhinevat metoodikat ja kasutatud andmeid ning seejärel tehakse analoogne protseduur läbi ARCH-GARCH raamistikku kuuluva MA (1) - GARCH (1, 1) – M mudeli ja selle hindamiseks kasutatud andmete osas. Siin tuginetakse Uurimusele 2.

Töö neljandas peatükis tutvustatakse empiirilise analüüsi tulemusi. Analoogiliselt kolmanda peatükiga on esmalt välja toodud olulisemad tulemused ja järeldused, mis ilmnesid meta-analüüsi metoodika rakendamisel ning lõpuks esitatakse tulemused 2008. aasta USA finantskriisi Balti riikidesse ülekandumise kohta. Viimatinimetatud tulemused ja järeldused on jällegi eraldi välja toodud korrelatsioonikoefitsientide muutude uurimise ja MA (1) - GARCH (1, 1) – M mudeli puhul ning lõpuks on neid tulemusi omavahel võrreldud ja sünteesitud. Nagu kolmandaski peatükis põhineb meta-analüüsi puudutav osa Uurimuste 3 ja 4 tulemustel ning 2008. aasta finantskriisi puudutav analüüs Uurimus 2 tulemustel.

Doktoritöö lõpeb kokkuvõtva osaga, kus on rõhutatud peamisi asjaolusid ja tulemusi kõigi töö osade kohta. Sellele tuginedes on esitatud mõningad majanduspoliitika soovitused, mis võiksid aidata ennetada või vähendada finantsnakkuslikkusega kaasnevaid negatiivseid tagajärgi. Samuti on välja toodud dissertatsiooni olulisemad piirangud ja edasise uurimise suunad antud valdkonnas.

4. Teoreetiline ja empiiriline taust

Vaatamata intensiivsele uurimisele ja empiiriliste analüüside rohkusele, pole endiselt saavutatud üksmeelt finantsnakkuse täpse definitsiooni ega levimiskanalite kohta. Tarvilik tingimus finantsnakkuse esinemise jaoks on kindlasti finantskriiside ja krahhide ülekandumine kriisi lähteriigist muudesse riikidesse, kuid erimeelsused tekivad selle tingimuse piisavuse osas. Kõige laiema definitsiooni pooldajad leiavad, et nimetatud tingimus on tõesti piisav, teised väidavad, et vajalik on ka kontrollimine riikide fundamentaalnäitajate (majanduse suurus ja struktuur, rakendatav poliitika jms) suhtes ning kolmandate arvates saab nakkuslikkusest rääkida sootuks alles siis, kui riikide vahelised ühenduskanalid on pärast kriisi ilmnemist (võrreldes nö rahuliku ajaga) oluliselt tugevnenud.

Finantsnakkuse defineerimisel on kasulik aluseks võtta just kriiside levimise kanaleid. Kõige üldisemalt saab kriiside ülekandumise kanalid jagada fundamentaalseteks ehk stabiilseteks ühenduslülideks ja investorite käitumisest tulenevateks ebastabiilseteks ühenduskanaliteks. Olulisimateks fundamentaalseteks ühenduslülideks peetakse:

* finantskanalid (*financial linkages*) – riigid on omavahel seotud läbi rahvusvahelise finantssüsteemi;
* kaubanduslikud seosed (*real linkages*) – riigid on seotud läbi rahvusvahelise kaubanduse, kas olles kaubanduspartnerid või konkureerides samal välisturul;
* poliitilised ühenduskanalid (*political links*) – riikidevahelised poliitilised suhted.

Paljud autorid on jõudnud seisukohale, et fundamentaalsed ühenduslülid ei suuda täielikult selgitada erinevate finantsnäitajate riikidevahelisi koosliikumisi ning muutusi selliste seoste tugevuses. See pöörab tähelepanu investorite käitumisega seotud irratsionaalsetele aspektidele, eriti nn *herding*-kontseptsioonile ehk karjakäitumisele. *Herding-*

kontseptsioonis on keskselt kohal informatsiooni asümmeetrilisus, mis põhjustab informatsiooni hankimise kulukuse tõttu väheminformeeritud investorite poolse (eeldatavalt) paremini informeeritud agentide tegevuse jälgimise ja matkimise. Kui selline matkiv käitumine muutub massiliseks, võib kogu turg liikuda kiirelt ühes ja samas suunas. Taolise massilise pikast positsioonist loobumise katalüsaatoriks olnud eeldatavalt hästi informeeritud investorite poolne raha välja võtmine ei pruukinud aga olla põhjustatud mitte olemasolevast siseinformatsioonist, vaid puhtalt vajadusest kohandada mujal ilmnenud kriisi põhjustatud investeerimisportfelli balansist välja langemist. Karjakäitumise ilmnemisel on riikide aktsia- või valuutaturu rünnaku alla sattumine täiesti etteennustamatu ja probleemid võivad tekkida ka väga heade fundamentaalnäitajatega riikides.

Viimasel kümnendil, alates K. Forbes'i ja R.Rigoboni töödest (2000, 2001 ja 2002) on valdavaks muutunud seisukoht, et kriiside ülekandumisel fundamentaalsete levimiskanalite kaudu ei ole tegemist finants-nakkuslikkuse vaid lihtsalt vastastikuse sõltuvusega (*interdependence*) riikide vahel. See omakorda seab kahtluse alla kõige laiema tingimusteta finants-nakkuse definitsiooni ning käesoleval sajandil käsitletaksegi finantsnakkusena peaaegu eranditult kitsamaid variante. Nagu eespool mainitud, on niisugust eristamist järgitud ka antud doktoritöös ning empiirilise analüüsi juures igasugust kriiside ülekandumist finantsnakkuseks ei loeta.

Nagu mainitud, on finantsnakkuse kontseptsiooni viimastel kümnenditel empiiriliselt väga palju uuritud. Seejuures on saadud väga erinevaid tulemusi, mis on arvestades käsitletava probleemi mitmedimensionaalsust ka teatud mõttes loogiline. Erinevad ju empiirilised uurimused lisaks kasutatavale finantsnakkuslikkuse mõistele ka mõõtmismetoodika, vaadeldavate kriiside ja finantsturgude ning mitmete muudegi tehniliste aspektide osas. Heaks näiteks on siinkohal Serwa (2005) uurimus, kes kasutas nelja erinevat testimismetoodikat ja nelja erinevat valimit ning erinevad olid ka tulemused.

Tulemuste üldistamiseks on käesolevas doktoritöös läbi uuritud üle 75 finants-nakkuslikkuse empiirilise analüüsi, mille tulemused on kokkuvõtvalt esitatud lisades 1-4. Pelgalt loendades võib järeldada, et finantsnakkuse esinemist toetavaid tulemusi (*Jah*-tulemus) on ligi kaks korda rohkem kui mittetoetavaid (*Ei*-tulemus). Suur osa *Jah*-tulemustest on aga saadud korrelatsioonikoefitsientide muutusel põhinevate testidega, kus tulemusi pole heteroskedastiivsuse esinemise suhtes kontrollitud ega kohandatud. Viimase kümnendi uurimused on aga selgelt näidanud sellise kohandamise vajalikkust. Selliseid kahtlase väärtusega tulemusi mittearvestades on *Jah*- ning *Ei*-tulemused ligikaudu tasakaalus, samuti ei ole mitmete uuringute puhul ühtne järeldus *Jah* või *Ei* kasuks päriselt õigustatud, kuna ühe uuringu raames võib esineda nii finantsnakkuslikkust toetavaid kui ka mittetoetavaid tulemusi.

Peamiseks probleemiks traditsioonilise kirjanduse ülevaate põhjal konkreetsete üldistavate järelduste tegemisel on aga siiski juba mainitud uurimisprobleemi mitmetahulisus. Uuringusse kaasatud kolmveerandsajast empiirilisest analüüsist on vaid väga üksikud, mis kasutavad nii sama finantsnakkuslikkuse definitsiooni, sama testimismetoodikat, samu kriise kui ka sama uuritavat finantsturgu. Kõik need valikud võivad aga mõjutada saadud tulemusi.

Kõigest sellest järeldub, et pelgalt kvalitatiivse empiiriliste tulemuste analüüsiga finantsnakkus kohta konkreetseid järeldusi teha on äärmiselt problemaatiline kui mitte võimatu. Seetõttu oleks järgmiseks loogiliseks sammuks edasi kvantitatiivse agregeeriva analüüsi rakendamine adekvaatsetele tulemustele jõudmiseks.

5. Metoodika, andmed ja tulemused
5.1. Meta-analüüsi metoodika, andmed ja tulemused

Meta-analüüsi jaoks vajaliku andmestiku kogumiseks on kaasatud uuringud Maailmapanga (*World Bank Group*) *Financial Crisis Website* leheküljelt ning *Thomson Reuters* (varem *ISI*) *Web of Knowledge* andmebaasist vastavalt märksõnadele *financial contagion*. Sellisel viisil leitud uuringuid, kus finantsnakkuslikkuse eksisteerimist kvantitatiivselt testiti, leidus üle 70 (viimastel aastatel lisandunud uuringud pole meta-analüüsi kaasatud, kuid ülevaade neist on töös toodud alapunktis 2.7.).

Kuna varasemalt finantsnakkuse teemal meta-analüüsi läbi viidud ei ole, siis tuli autoril välja pakkuda omapoolne kontseptsioon sobivaks kvantitatiivseks mõõdikuks, mis oleks üle uuringute võrreldav, ühtselt interpreteeritav ja agregeeritav. Kuna finantsnakkuse hüpoteesi testimistulemuse statistiline olulisus (kas finantsnakkuslikkus leidis kinnitust või mitte) ei ole sellise mõõdikuna sobiv[29], siis kõiki uuringuid kaasavat mõõdikut leida polnud paraku võimalik. Valituks osutus kriisi-ning sihtriigi finantsvahendite (aktsiad, väärtpaberid, intressimäärad või vahetuskursid) hinnamuutuse korrelatsioonide vahe kriisi aegsel ja kriisi eelsel perioodil. Antud valiku otstarbekust kinnitab asjaolu, et see on otseselt seotud kitsaima finantsnakkuse definitsiooniga, mille kohaselt esinevad finantsnakkuse korral olulised struktuursed muutused riikidevahelistes ühenduskanalites ning mille testimiseks kasutatakse

---

[29] Lihtne on näidata, et täpselt seesama kvantitatiivne tulemus võib olla ühes uuringus statistiliselt oluline ning teises ebaoluline.

peamiselt just korrelatsioonide erinevuse suurust kriisi aegsel ja kriisi eelsel perioodil. Paraku aga tähendas selline valiku langetamine, et valimisse on kaasatud ainult need uuringud, kus on ära toodud nii kriisi eelse kui ka kriisi aegse perioodi finantsvahendite hindade korrelatsioonid (või nende vahe). Sel viisil on saadud 28 uuringut ja 716 individuaaltulemust, mis pärinevad 17-st publikatsioonist. Juhul kui uuringus on esitatud nii lühiajalise kui pikaajalise kriisijärgse perioodi korrelatsioon, on sõltumatuse probleemi tõttu uuringusse kaasatud vaid lühiajalise perioodi näitaja.

Traditsiooniliselt on meta-analüüsi eesmärk ühe konkreetse numbrilise tulemuseni jõudmine. Antud töös on aga leitud kaks meta-tulemust: ühel juhul on alusmõõdikuks võetud korrelatsioonikoefitsientide muutu käsitletud kui mõjuefekti (*kontseptsioon 1*) ning teisel juhul kui korrelatsiooni (*kontseptsioon 2*). Kahe alternatiivse lähenemise kasutamise tingis asjaolu, et meta-analüüsi käsitlevas kirjanduses pole sellist alusmõõdikut (individuaaltulemust) käsitletud ning töö autori arvates pole ka intuitiivselt selge, millise neist valima peaks[30] (valik on oluline, kuna meta-analüüsi agregeerimismetoodika on nende lähenemiste puhul erinev). Seetõttu ongi paralleelselt toodud tulemused mõlema kontseptsiooni korral.

Meta-analüüsi tulemused on kokkuvõtlikult esitatud alljärgneval Joonisel 1 (lihtsuse huvides on esitatud vaid kontseptsiooni 1 meta-tulemused). *Kontseptsiooni 1* kasutades on meta-tulemuseks (kaalutud keskmiseks korrelatsioonikoefitsientide muuduks) 0,053 standardhälbega 0,0047 ja *kontseptsiooni 2* kohaselt 0,072 standardhälbega 0,0049. Mõlemal juhul jäävad 95% usalduspiirid selgelt üle nulli ning võib järeldada, et keskmiselt on kriisiperioodidel korrelatsioonid tugevnenud.

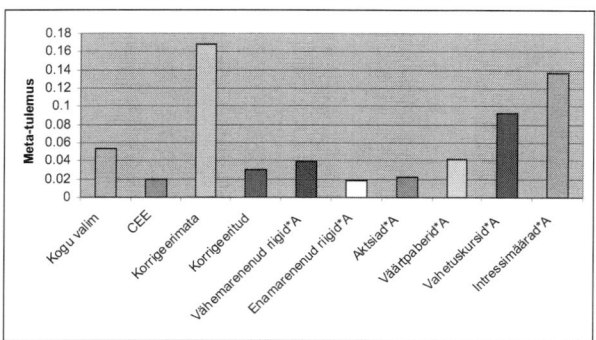

Joonis 1. Meta-analüüsi põhitulemused finantsnakkuslikkuse uurimisel. Korrigeerimata – meta-tulemus leitud heteroskedastiivsuse suhtes korrigeerimata kriisiperioodi korrelatsioone kasutades.

---

[30] Ühest küljest võiks korrelatsioonide vahe olla samade omadustega kui korrelatsioon ise, teisest küljest on tegu tüüpilise mõjuefektiga, kus kriisi võib vaadelda kui mõjurit.

Korrigeeritud - meta-tulemus leitud heteroskedastiivsuse suhtes korrigeeritud kriisiperioodi korrelatsioone kasutades.
A=korrigeeritud.
Allikas: Autori koostatud

Kontrollides jaotuse homogeensust Q-statistiku[31] abil selgub aga, et jaotus on heterogeenne ning seega ei pruugi kõik individuaaltulemused esindada ühte ja sama üldkogumit. Seetõttu on vajalik jätkata analüüsi otsimaks võimalikke varieeruvust põhjustavaid moderaatormuutujaid (*moderator variables*).

Esmalt on võimaliku moderaatorina kontrollitud heteroskedastiivsuse suhtes kohandamist või mittekohandamist kriisijärgsete korrelatsioonide arvutamisel. Selleks on valim jagatud kaheks vastavalt sellele, kas heteroskedastiivsuse suhtes kohandamist on teostatud (juht A) või mitte (juht U). Selgub, et kaalutud meta-tulemus on juhul A tunduvalt väiksem, olles 0,030 nii *kontseptsiooni 1* kui 2 korral, samas kui juhul U on vastavad tulemused 0,168 ja 0,208. Sellest järeldub selgelt, et tegu on olulise moderaator-muutujaga, mida kinnitab samuti gruppide vahelise Q-statistiku statistiline olulisus.

Kuna aga jaotuses jäi endiselt alles heterogeensust, on moderaator-muutujana kontrollitud ka erinevaid kriise. Selgub, et viimaste kümnendite suurematest kriisidest olid 1994. aasta Mehhiko kriis ja 1997. aasta Aasia kriis selgelt rohkem nakkuslikud kui 1998. aasta Vene, 1999. aasta Brasiilia ning 2001. aasta Argentiina kriisid. Samuti olid nakkuslikud USA 1987. ja 2002. aasta kriisid, mitte aga Türgi 2001, India 2004, Tšehhi 1997 ega USA 2001 kriisid.

Kolmanda võimaliku moderaatorina on kontrollitud sihtriigi arengutaset, jagades valimi arenenud ja vähemarenenud riikide rühmaks vastavalt 2008. aasta inimarengu indeksile. Arenenud riikidena on siinkohal defineeritud nimetatud indeksi järgi 30 esimest riiki, mis on valitud eesmärgiga hoida valimi mahud mõlemas grupis umbkaudu võrdsed (vastavalt 372 ja 344). Selgub, et ülekandemehhanismid arenenud riikidesse on kriisiperioodidel tugevnenud keskmiselt mõnevõrra väiksemal määral kui vähem arenenud riikidesse, kuid see erinevus on väga väike ja statistiliselt ebaoluline. Seega sihtriigi arengutase võimaliku moderaatorina kinnitust ei leidnud ning võib järeldada, et riigi hea arengutase ei paku küllaldast kaitset kriiside nakkusliku leviku eest.

Viimaks on analüüsitud, kas tulemusi mõjutab vaatlusalune turg – vastavalt aktsiad, väärtpaberid (*bonds*), intressimäärad või vahetuskursid. Tulemused näitavad, et intressimäärade ja vahetuskursside uurimise korral on metatulemus kõrgem kui aktsiate või väärtpaberite korral. Statistilises

---

[31] Q-statistik on leitud valemiga $Q = \sum \left| w_i \left(ES_i - \overline{ES} \right)^2 \right|$, kus ES_i on i-s individuaaltulemus, $\overline{ES}$ on meta-tulemus ja w_i on i-nda individuaaltulemuse kaal (erineb kontseptsioonide 1 ja 2 puhul).

mõttes oluline erinevus gruppide vahel ilmneb intressimäärade ja aktsiate võrdlemisel. Siiski on ka aktsiate puhul metatulemuse väärtus statistiliselt oluliselt positiivne[32].

Uurides eraldi Kesk- ja Ida-Euroopa majandusi sihtriikidena, on valimis 89 individuaaltulemust kaheksa kriisi ja nelja riigi (Tšehhi Vabariik, Eesti, Poola, Ungari) kohta. Mõlema kontseptsiooni (individuaaltulemused kui korrelatsioonid ja kui mõjuefektid) puhul on metatulemuseks 0,02. Kõrvutades seda kogu valimi tulemustega – 0,05 *kontseptsioon 1* ja 0,07 *kontseptsioon 2* korral – on näha, et KIE riikide meta-tulemus on üldkeskmisega võrreldes madalam. Statistiliselt olulist erinevust nende meta-tulemuste vahel siiski ei ole, kuid saab tõdeda, et vähemalt keskmisest rohkem finantsnakkuslikkusele vastuvõtlikud Kesk- ja Ida-Euroopa riigid ei ole. Samale tulemusele on varem jõudnud näiteks Serwa ja Bohl (2005) ja Serwa (2005), kellel ei õnnestunud leida tõendeid selle kohta, et Kesk- ja Ida-Euroopa riigid oleksid *finantsnakkuse* poolt kergemini haavatavad kui lääneriigid. Veelgi selgemalt tuleb see tulemus esile, kui valimisse kaasata vaid uuringud, kus kriisi aegsed korrelatsioonikoefitsiendid on heteroskedastiivsuse suhtes kohandatud. Mõlema kontseptsiooni korral on KIE valimis meta-efekt nüüd negatiivne (ehkki mitte statistiliselt olulisel määral) ning statistiliselt oluliselt madalam kogu valimi põhjal leitud üldkeskmisest. Ühe põhjusena oodatust väiksemale finantsnakkusele vastuvõtlikkusele Kesk- ja Ida-Euroopa riikides võib tuua suhteliselt väiksema spekulatiivsel eesmärgil tehtud investeeringute osakaalu ning väiksema tõenäosuse mullide tekkeks teiste arengumaadega (ja ka arenenud riikidega) võrreldes.

Huvitavaks tulemuseks on veel, et kõige tugevamini on Kesk-ja Ida-Euroopa riikidesse nakkuslikult üle kandunud kriisid, mis on alguse saanud USA-st. See võib olla üheks seletuseks praeguse, 2008. aastal USA-st alguse saanud, kriisi väga rasketele tagajärgedele Balti ning teiste Kesk- ja Ida-Euroopa riikide jaoks. USA kriiside nakkuslikkuse põhjuseks võib olla selle riigi keskne koht nii maailma majanduses kui poliitikas, mille tõttu on sealsed kriisid alati meedia huviorbiidis jõudes nii ka enamike investorite teadvusesse.

5.2. Metoodika, andmed ja tulemused 2008. aasta USA finantskriisi nakkuslikkuse uurimisel

Doktoritöö baasartiklite, sealhulgas meta-analüüsi rakendavate, valmimise ajaks ei olnud kasutada ühtegi empiirilist uuringut 2008. aasta USA finantskriisi nakkuslikkuse uurimiseks, mistõttu polnud võimalik seda kriisi lisada läbi viidud meta-analüüsi. Seetõttu on nimetatud kriisi nakkuslikkuse uurimiseks läbi viidud eraldi analüüs.

---

[32] Kui ülejäänud meta-analüüsi puudutavad osad põhinevad Uurimustel 3 ja 4, siis viimatinimetatud analüüs baasartiklites ei kajastu ning on täiendus doktoritöö tarbeks.

Ühest küljest andmete kättesaadavuse ning teisalt töös kasutatava KIE riikidele suunatud rõhuasetuse tõttu on uurimise alla võetud kriisi ülekandumine USA-st Balti riikidesse: Eestisse, Lätisse ja Leedusse. Andmetena on kasutatud riikide aktsiaindeksite (vastavalt OMXT Eesti, OMXR Läti, OMXV Leedu ja S&P500 USA jaoks) juurdekasve perioodil 3. märts 2008 kuni 9. märts 2009. Ajavahemikku nimetatud perioodi alguspunktist kuni Lehman Brothers'i pankrotini 15. septembril 2008 on käsitletud kui kriisi eelset perioodi ning järgnevat ajavahemikku 15. septembrist kuni 9. märtsini aastal 2009 kui kriisi perioodi. Mitte kokkulangevate kauplemistundide tõttu USA ja Balti riikide aktsiaturgudel on kasutatud kahe päeva libisevat keskmist[33] näitajat.

Sarnaselt meta-analüüsile on ka selles osas finantsnakkuse definitsioonina kasutatud kõige kitsamat alternatiivi ehk struktuurset muutust šokkide ülekandemehhanismis, mida mõõdetakse kui tugevnenud seost riikide aktsiahindade vahel kriisiperioodil võrreldes kriisieelse perioodiga. Testimiseks kasutatakse alternatiivselt nii riikidevahelisel korrelatsioonikoefitsientidel baseeruvat kui ka volatiilsuse muutustel põhinevat metoodikat.

Korrelatsioonikoefitsientidel baseeruva metoodika idee on leida USA ja Balti riikide indeksaktsia hindade muutuste korrelatsioonid kriisieelsel perioodil ning testida, kas see korrelatsioon on kriisiperioodil oluliselt suurem. Kui kõrgem korrelatsioon kriisiperioodil leiab kinnitust, siis loetakse seda finantsnakkuse hüpoteesi toetavaks tulemuseks. Kuna antud metoodika puhul on problemaatiline korrelatsioonikoefitsientide võrdlemine erineva volatiilsuse tõttu kriisi eelsel ja kriisi perioodil (kriisi perioodil on volatiilsus kõrgem), siis on lisaks tavalisele korrelatsioonikoefitsiendile kasutatud kriisiperioodi jaoks ka volatiilsuse erinevust arvesse võtvat kohandatud korrelatsioonikordajat. See kohandamismehhanism, mille pakkusid esmalt välja Forbes ja Rigobon (2001 ja 2002) on antud valemiga $\rho^* = \dfrac{\rho}{\sqrt{1 + \delta\left[1 - (\rho)^2\right]}}$, kus ρ on tavaline kohandamata korrelatsioonikoefitsient kriisiperioodil. Kohandamistegur δ on leitav valemiga $\delta = \dfrac{Var^{crisis}(y_t)}{Var^{non-crisis}(y_t)} - 1$, kus $Var_{crisis}(y_t)$ ja $Var_{non-crisis}(y_t)$ on S&P500 indeksi dispersioonid vastavalt kriisiperioodil ja kriisieelsed perioodil.

Analüüsi tulemused on kokkuvõtlikult ära toodud alljärgneval joonisel 2. Tulemused näitavad, et kohandamata kriisiperioodi korrelatsioonikordajad (korrelatsioon S&P500-ga) on statistiliselt oluliselt kõrgemad kriisieelse perioodi väärtusest kolmest Balti riigist kahe, Eesti ja Leedu jaoks, mis on vastavuses finantsnakkuse hüpoteesiga. Kui aga kriisi aegsed korrelatsioonid on heteroskedastiivsuse suhtes kohandatud, siis on

---

[33] Käesoleva ja eelmise päeva aritmeetiline keskmine.

218

korrelatsioonide muutused USA ja kõigi kolme Balti riigi aktsiaturu vahel küll punkthinnangult positiivsed aga statistiliselt ebaolulised. Siiski tuleb märkida, et ka kohandatud kriisijärgsed korrelatsioonid on kaks (Läti puhul) või kolm korda (Eesti ja Leedu puhul) kõrgemad kriisi eelsest väärtusest. Kuna aga suhtelised erinevused rakendatud t-testi tulemustes ei kajastu ning absoluutsed erinevused ulatuvad kõigest 0,06-st (Läti) 0,18-ni (Leedu), siis see selgitabki korrelatsioonide muutude statistilist ebaolulisust.

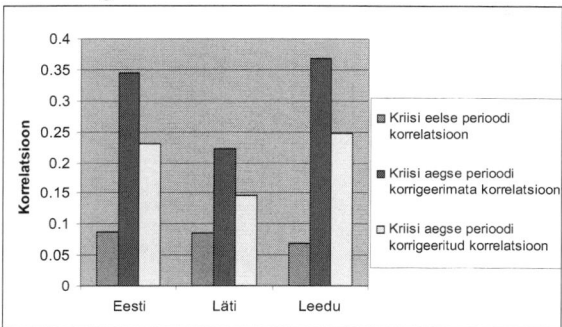

Joonis 2. Korrelatsioonikoefitsientide väärtused S&P 500 ning Balti riikide aktsiaindeksite (OMXT, OMXR ja OMXV) hinnamuutuste vahel 2008. aasta USA finantskriisile eelneval perioodil ning kriisi ajal.
Allikas: autori koostatud.

Lisaks korrelatsioonikoefitsientide uurimisele, on 2008. aasta kriisi ülekandumist USA-st Balti riikidesse parema robustsuse eesmärgil analüüsitud ka ARCH-GARCH raamistikku kuuluva MA (1) - GARCH (1, 1) – M mudeliga. See mudel on hinnatud järgmise regressiionivõrrandiga:

$X_t = \alpha + \beta b_t + \gamma D_t + \delta Y_t + \varepsilon u_{t-1} + u_t$

$b_t = a + bb_{t-1} + cu_{t-1}^2 + dD_t + fZ_t$,

kus

X_t – aktsiaindeksi muut mitte-kriisi riigis (Eesti, Läti või Leedu) perioodil t;

b_t – X_t tingimuslik dispersioon perioodil t;

D – fiktiivne muutuja, nn *esmaspäeva efekt* (D omandab väärtuse 1 nädalavahetustele ja pühadele järgnevatel päevadel ja on võrdne nulliga muudel päevadel);

Y_t – indeksaktsia muut kriisiriigis (USA) perioodil t,

u_t ja u_{t-1} – vealiikmed vastavalt perioodil t ja $t-1$;

Z_t – jääkliikme ruut USA aktsiaindeksi jaoks rakendatud MA(1)-GARCH(1,1)-M mudeli kohta.

Kuna Z_t pole teada, siis on selle ruutjuur esmalt hinnatud regressiooonivõrrandiga S&P 500 jaoks:

$Y_t = \alpha + \beta b_t + \delta D_t + \phi u_{t-1} + u_t$

$$b_t = a + bb_{t-1} + cu_{t-1}^2 + dD_t$$

ja seejärel vajalik muutuja arvutatud valemiga $Z_t = u_t^2$.

Tulemused näitavad, et nii kriisi eelsel kui järgsel perioodil on statistiliselt oluline keskväärtuse ülekandeefekt (positiivne δ väärtus) Eesti ja Leedu mitte aga Läti aktsiaturul. See tähendab, et positiivsele (negatiivsele) muutusele S&P 500 indeksi väärtuses järgneb positiivne (negatiivne) muutus OMXT ja OMXV indeksis mitte aga OMXR indeksis. Teoreetilist selgitust antud tulemusele on aga pakkuda paraku keeruline. Ülekandeefekt on kõigi kolme Balti riigi puhul tugevam kriisijärgsel perioodil, mis toetab finantsnakkuse hüpoteesi. Siiski on vahe ülekandeefekti tugevuses võrreldes kriisi eelse perioodiga suhteliselt väike. Volatiilsuse ülekandeefekti USA ja Balti riikide aktsiaturgude vahel aga ei ilmnenud ning samuti polnud mingit indikatsiooni sellest, et nimetatud efekt võiks kriisi perioodil olla tugevam.

2008. aasta kriisi analüüsi tulemusi kokku võtvalt võib tõdeda, et ilmnes mõningaid viiteid nakkuslikkuse esinemise kohta, kuid selle mõju on suhteliselt nõrk. Nakkuse hüpoteesi kinnitasid kriisi perioodi tugevamad korrelatsioonid ning S&P 500 indeksi ees oleva parameetri suurem väärtus MA(1)-GARCH(1,1)-M mudelis eelneva rahumeelse perioodiga võrreldes. Absoluutsuurustes olid mõlemad nimetatud efektid aga nõrgad ning kohandatud näitajate põhjal leitud korrelatsioonide erinevused statistiliselt ebaolulised Seega on tulemused üldjoontes sarnased meta-analüüsi kasutades leituga.

6. Põhitulemused ja järeldused

Teoreetilist kirjandust silmas pidades on üheks olulisemaks doktoritöö tulemustest tulenevaks järelduseks selgusele jõudmine, et finantsnakkus kuulub selliste mitmemõõtmeliste uurimisprobleemide hulka, millele isegi kvalitatiivse kirjanduse ülevaatega, seda enam individuaaluuringutega, on keeruline selgeid ja adekvaatseid tulemusi ning järeldusi leida. Aastakümneid on tegeletud järjest täiuslikumate testimismeetodite välja töötamisega, kuid ikka ja jälle kerkivad kõigil neil esile omad puudused. Töö autori ettepanek antud kontekstis on loobuda pingsaist parima statistilise olulisuse testi otsinguist ja keskenduda hoopis konkreetse kvantitatiivse mõõdiku leidmisele, mis oleks üle uuringute ühtselt interpreteeritav ja agregeeritav ning ühismõõdustaks sellega erinevate uuringute tulemused. See revolutsiooniline seisukoht tähendab täiesti uut põhirõhku teemakohaste kvantitatiivsete uurimismeetodite valikul, kuid ei viita kuidagi statistilise olulisuse testimisest loobumise vajadusele. Selliste testide tulemused jääksid oluliseks täiendavaks väljundiks võrdlust ja agregeerimist võimaldava kvantitatiivse mõõdiku kõrval, kuid mitte enam põhiliseks analüüsitulemuseks. Sobiva ühismõõdustaja leidmine on äärmiselt oluline tuleviku meta-analüüse silmas pidades, kuna siis saaks kvantitatiivsesse agregeerimisraamistikku kaasata juba oluliselt rohkem uuringuid, kui see antud doktoritöös võimalik oli.

Panus teoreetilisse kirjandusse on ka ühe võimaliku üle uurimuste interpreteeritava ja summeeritava mõõdiku - vahe kriisi aegse ja kriisi eelse perioodi finantsvahendite hindade muutuste riikidevahelise korrelatsioonikoefitsiendi väärtuses – välja pakkumine. Samuti on välja toodud kaks alternatiivset lähenemist antud mõõdiku kasutamisel meta-analüüsi sisendina ning näidatud, et tulemused nende lähenemiste korral erinevad väga vähe. Seega on loodud esmane raamistik, mida tulevased meta-analüüsid antud teemal aluseks võtta saavad.

Kui juba varem oli korrelatsioonikoefitsientidel baseeruva metoodika alases teoreetilises kirjanduses näidatud kriisiaegse korrelatsiooni heteroskedastiivsuse suhtes kohandamise mõju nakkuse avastamise tõenäosusele, siis antud töös läbi viidud meta-analüüs kinnitas korrigeeritud ja korrigeerimata korrelatsioonikoefitsientidel põhinevate tulemuste statistiliselt olulist erinevust. Samuti selgus, et nakkuslikkuse testides on oluline ka vaadeldava finantsturu valik ning näiteks intressimäärade korrelatsioonide uurimisel on nakkuslikkuse avastamine tõenäolisem kui aktsiahindade korral. Finantsturu mõju analüüsi tulemustele pole samuti varem uuritud, ehkki on leitud, et järeldused võivad erinevate turgude korral olla erinevad. Seega peaks edaspidine teoreetiline ja ülevaatekirjandus olulist rõhku panema kasutatud metoodikale ning vaadeldud finantsturule, kuna erinevate valikute korral ei pruugi analüüside tulemused olla omavahel adekvaatselt võrreldavad.

Püstitatud uurimiseesmärgiga kõige otsesemalt seonduv põhitulemus on tõendite leidmine finantsnakkuse eksisteerimise kohta, mis tõsi küll, osutus üpris nõrgaks. Nõrkade nakkusefektide esinemisele viitasid nii meta-analüüs kui korrelatsioonikoefitsientide ja volatiilsuse muutustel põhinev 2008. aasta finantskriisi analüüs. Seejuures selgus, et kõrgemalt arenenud riigid ei ole nakkuse ülekandumise eest kaitstud paremini kui vähemarenenud majandused. Need tulemused viitavad asjaolule, et kriiside riigist riiki levimist ei saa selgitada ainult tugevate riikidevaheliste ühenduskanalite ega halbade makromajanduslike fundamentaalnäitajatega, vaid tuleb otsida põhjuseid investorite käitumuslikest aspektidest. Äärmiselt oluliseks muutuvad kriisi tingimustes *herding*-kontseptsioonist ja muudest kollektiivses mõttes irratsionaalse käitumise aspektidest tulenevad iseenese täitumisele viivad ootused. Niisugustes tingimustes tuleb traditsioonilistesse investeerimisportfelli riskantsuse vähendamisele suunatud teooriatesse suhtuda ülima ettevaatlikkusega, kuna nende õigsus on äärmiselt küsitav. Need teooriad ülehindavad oluliselt investeerimisportfelli rahvusvahelise diversifitseerimisega saavutatavat riskiastme vähenemist, kuna eeldavad investorite ratsionaalset käitumist riski tingimustes. Seega tuleks nimetatud teooriaid edasi arendada käsitledes eraldi nö rahumeelseid ja kriisi perioode, kuna diversifitseerimise riski vähendav mõju on kriisi perioodidel märkimisväärselt väiksem.

Väga olulisi järeldusi pakub antud tulemus ka sobiva finantsarhitektuuri kontekstis. Kuna finantskriiside levimise lumepalli eest ei ole kaitstud ka mitte tugevaimad riigid, peaks majanduspoliittika kujundajad senisest oluliselt rohkem rõhku panema kriisiga kaasnevate negatiivsete tagajärgede ennetavale minimeerimisele. Profülaktiline tegevus on selle eesmärgi saavutamiseks vajalik, kuna puhtalt tagajärgedega võitlemiseks ei pruugi kriisist räsitud riigil olla piisavalt vahendeid. Seega peaks riigid juba headel aegadel mõtlema selle peale, et majanduskasv ei kesta pidevalt ning varuma finantsvahendeid reservi, et oleks mida nakkuse ohvriks langedes kasutada ja niiviisi kriisiga kaasnevaid negatiivseid tagajärgi pehmendada.

Läbi viidud meta-analüüsist selgus, et erinevate kriiside nakkuslikkuse aste võib olla vägagi erinev. Antud töös seda aspekti põhjalikumalt ei uuritud, kuid see võiks olla oluline uurimisobjekt tulevasi uuringuid silmas pidades. On ju poliitikakujundajatel äärmiselt oluline teada, millistel kriisidel on suurem tõenäosus muutuda nakkuslikuks ja millistel väiksem. Seega viitab antud doktoritöö selgelt vastavateemalise analüüsi vajalikkusele, mis seniajani praktiliselt puudub.

Veel ühe olulise tulemusena selgus, et Kesk- ja Ida-Euroopa riigid, sealhulgas Balti riigid, kui väikesed ja avatud majandused ei ole vastavalt analüüsi tulemustele keskmisest enam finantsnakkusele vastuvõtlikud. See leid võimaldab pehmendada korduvalt välja käidud seisukohta, mille kohaselt väga suur majanduse avatus muudab riigid kriisi situatsioonis oluliselt rohkem haavatavaks. See haavatavus võib olla suurem kriiside levimisel stabiilsete fundamentaalkanalite kaudu, kuid nakkuslikkuse ohtu majanduse avatus ei suurenda. Seega võib Balti riikidele soovitada jätkuvalt suurt majanduse avatust, mis on neile viimastel kahel kümnendil palju edu toonud.

Huvitavaks tulemuseks on asjaolu, et CEE riikide jaoks on kõige nakkavamad USA-st alguse saanud kriisid. See võib põhjustatud olla USA väga olulisest rollist maailmamajanduses ja -poliitikas, mistõttu väga suur hulk investoreid investeerib oma raha sellesse riiki ning sealsed kriisid on alati meedia huviorbiidis. Seega on investorid USA kriisi korral hästi informeeritud investeerimisportfelli kohandamise vajadusest ning välja võetava raha hulk on suhteliselt suurem võrreldes kriisidega mujal. Ühtlasi viitab antud leid asjaolule, et suur osa investoritest, kes paigutavad oma raha Kesk- ja Ida-Euroopa turgudele investeerivad ka USA-sse. Mujalt (kui USA) alguse saanud kriisidesse mitte nakatumine ei tähenda muidugi veel, et need kriisid Kesk- ja Ida-Euroopa riikidele negatiivselt ei mõjuks. Mõju avaldub lihtsalt pigem läbi riikidevaheliste stabiilsete fundamentaalkanalite kui finantsnakkuse kaudu.

7. Piirangud ja soovitused edasisteks uuringuteks

Käesoleva doktoritöö üheks olulisemaks piiranguks on meta-analüüsi piiritlemine vaid korrelatsioonikoefitsientidel põhinevate uuringutega. Muid testimismeetodeid kasutatavate uuringute kaasamise peamiseks probleemiks on raskused võrreldavate individuaaltulemuste kogumisega. Nende raskuste ületamisel oleks see kindlasti antud teema puhul oluliseks ja vajalikuks edasiarenduseks. Siinkohal on sobilik meelde tuletada ühte töö kvalitatiivsest kirjanduse ülevaatest tulenevat põhiseisukohta. Nimelt järgnevate meta-analüüside täiustamise eesmärgil on hädavajalik, et individuaaluuringute autorid oma tulemuste esitamisel juba arvestaksid võimaliku tulevase meta-analüüsi perspektiivi. Vastasel juhul on paratamatu, et paljud uuringud ühismõõdustamise probleemi tõttu meta-analüüsist välja jäävad.

Teine oluline meta-analüüsi puudutav piirang on seotud asjaoluga, et individuaaltulemused on kohati heterogeensed ka kõige väiksema agregeerituse tasandiga gruppides. See tähendab, et konkreetsetesse numbrilistesse meta-tulemustesse tuleks suhtuda teatava ettevaatlikkusega, kuna kõik individuaaltulemused antud grupis ei pruugi esindada ühte ja sama populatsiooni, mistõttu peaks teoreetiliselt gruppe veelgi väiksemateks osadeks jagama (reaalselt pole see paraku liiga väikese valimi mahu tõttu enam teostatav). Veel üks oluline edasiarenduse võimalus seoses meta-analüüsiga on 2008. aasta USA finantskriisi tulemuste lisamine analüüsi sisendiks.

Doktoritöö viimase osa juures, mis uurib 2008. aasta USA kriisi Balti riikidesse ülekandumise nakkuslikkust, on oluliseks piiranguks analüüsi piiritlemine vaid kahe põhilise metoodikaga: korrelatsioonide ja volatiilsuse erinevusel baseeruva lähenemisega. Võimaliku edasiarendusena oleks kasulik rakendada ka muid metoodilisi lähenemisi, mis võimaldaks kindlustada tulemustele paremat robustsust.

CURRICULUM VITAE

Name: Andres Kuusk
Date and place
of birth: Kuressaare, 05.07.1981
Nationality: Estonian
Present position: Assistant, Faculty of Economics and Business Administration, Institute of Economics, Chair of Economic modelling
E-mail: akuusk@ut.ee

Education:

2006-2011 Doctoral studies (PhD), Economics and Business Administration, University of Tartu, Estonia
2004–2006 Master of Science in Economics (MA), University of Tartu, Estonia
2000–2004 Bachelor Degree, University of Tartu, Faculty of Economics and Business Administration
1997–2000 Co-educational Gymnasium of Saaremaa

Foreign languages: English, Russian, Italian, German

Employment:

2011–... University of Tartu, Faculty of Economics and Business Administration, Institute of Economics, Chair of Economic modelling; Assistant (0.50)
2011–... OÜ Cumulus Consulting, analyst
2008–2011 Tartu University, Faculty of Economics and Business Administration, Institute of Economics, Teaching Assistant
2005 Tartu University, Narva College, Teaching Assistant
2003 Estonian Ministry of Education and Research, trainee

Main research interests:

Financial contagion, spatial econometrics, income inequality, decision theory, game theory

Academic work:

1) Editing and reviewing

2009–...   Supervision of student thesis (successfully defended)
· BA level (1 student)
Reviewing
· MA level (2)
· BA level (11)

3) Teaching
1998–2011 Composing and conducting courses, lectures and seminars on
the topics:
Decision theory (MA level)
Game theory (MA level)
Oeconometrics (BA and MA level)
Statistics (BA level)

CURRICULUM VITAE IN ESTONIAN

Nimi: **ANDRES KUUSK**
Sünnikoht ja-aeg: Kuressaare, 05.07.1981
Kodakondsus: Eesti
Amet: Majanduse modelleerimise assistent, rahvamajanduse instituut, majandusteaduskond, Tartu Ülikool
E-post: akuusk@ut.ee
Haridus:
2006–2011 doktorant, TÜ majandusteaduskond
2004–2006 magistrant, TÜ majandusteaduskond
2000–2004 BA, majandusteadus, Tartu Ülikool
1998–2000 Saaremaa Ühisgümnaasium

Võõrkeeled: inglise keel, vene keel, itaalia keel, saksa keel

Teenistuskäik:
2011–... Majanduse modelleerimise assistent (0,5), rahvamajanduse instituut, majandusteaduskond, Tartu Ülikool
2011–... Projektipõhine analüütik, OÜ Cumulus Consulting
2008-2011 Õppeülesandee täitja Tartu Ülikooli majandusteaduskonnas
2005 Õppeülesande täitja Tartu Ülikooli Narva Kolledžis
2003 Praktikant Haridus- ja Teadusministeeriumis

Peamised uurimisvaldkonnad:
Finantskriiside nakkuslikkus, ruumiökonomeetria, tulutasemete ebavõrdsus, otsustusteooria, mänguteooria

Akadeemiline tegevus:
1) Toimetamine ja retsenseerimine

2009–... Kaitsmiseni jõudnud üliõpilaste juhendamine
  • BA tase (1 üliõpilane)
  Retsenseerimnine
  • MA tase (2 tööd)
  • BA tase (11 tööd)

3) Õppetöö
1998–2011 Kursuste, loengute ja seminaride ettevalmistamine ja läbi-viimine teemadel:
  Otsustusteooria (magistri tasemel)

Mänguteooria (magistri tasemel)
Ökonomeetria (bakalaureuse ja magistri tasemel)
Statistika (bakalaureuse tasemel)

Printed in Great Britain
by Amazon.co.uk, Ltd.,
Marston Gate.